Photo by Pip Smith

DICK SMITH is the entrepreneurial businessman who founded Dick Smith Electronics, *Australian Geographic* and Dick Smith Foods. A Companion of the Order of Australia, an Australian of the Year and one of the National Trust's Living Treasures, he is an aviator who has flown five times around the world, including the first solo helicopter circumnavigation, and across Australia and the Tasman Sea by balloon.

——— Solo World helicopter flight Jetranger VH-DIK – 1982–1983

——— Solo flight to the North Pole Jetranger VH-DIK – 1987

——— Around the World, Pole to Pole Twin Otter VH-SHW – 1988–1989

- - - Across Australia by Balloon VH-DSE – 1993

DICK SMITH'S ADVENTURES

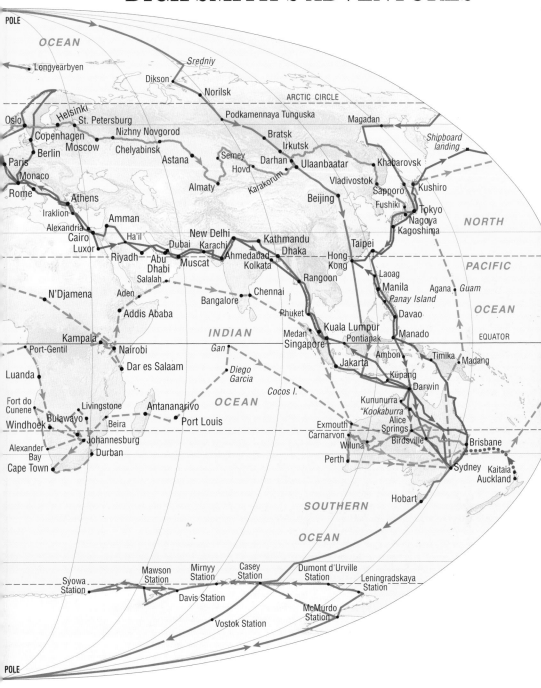

Around the World by helicopter S-76 VH-SHW – 1994–1995
Twice around the World in Cessna VH-SHW – 1999–2003
Trans-Tasman balloon flight VH-DSE – 2000
Around the World by Earthroamer, Ford F550 – 2006–2008

'I have known Dick Smith for such a long time and he truly is a "one-off"! This marvellous tale of his fascinating life adds colour and insight to what most Australians know of him as a leader, businessman, philanthropist and great Aussie stirrer. To this all I can add only one phrase: he is a true patriot.'

—General the Honourable Sir Peter Cosgrove
AK AC (Mil) CVO MC (Ret'd)

'A compelling yarn of an extraordinary Australian life—one that he was lucky not to lose on about ten occasions by my count!'

—Peter FitzSimons AM

'Businessman, adventurer, philanthropist . . . Dick Smith is a true Australian legend.'

—Greg Mortimer OAM

My
Adventurous
Life

DICK
SMITH

My Adventurous Life

ALLEN&UNWIN
SYDNEY · MELBOURNE · AUCKLAND · LONDON

Allen & Unwin
83 Alexander Street
Crows Nest NSW 2065
Australia
Phone: (61 2) 8425 0100
Email: info@allenandunwin.com
Web: www.allenandunwin.com

 A catalogue record for this
book is available from the
National Library of Australia

NATIONAL
LIBRARY
OF AUSTRALIA

ISBN 978 1 76106 805 8

Map by Will Pringle
Set in 12.75/17.5 pt Adobe Garamond Pro by Midland Typesetters, Australia
Printed and bound in Australia by Griffin Press, part of Ovato

10 9 8 7 6 5 4 3 2 1

CONTENTS

To view the documentaries and read the publications
that cover many of my adventures, please go to
www.dicksmithadventure.com.au

For my grandchildren

Prologue

It was the longest, most awful night we had ever experienced—and as the hours ticked by we realised that what we'd first suspected was undeniably true—goods worth tens of thousands of dollars had been stolen from us. Even so, we still didn't want to believe it. We went through all the invoices again, checking them against stock that wasn't there. There had to be some explanation for the deficiency—but finally we had to admit that there was only one: we'd been robbed—and what made it worse, it had been done by a person we trusted.

It was my own fault. I'd given in to the temptation to diversify the two-way radio business I'd started three years earlier to include selling electronic components. I should've remained with something I knew. But I was over-confident—and this was to teach me a lesson I'd never forget.

I was twenty-seven years old. My wife, Pip, and I had worked fantastically hard to get the business going. The company had just seemed to grow by itself. I'd had no real ambitions beyond employing two or three people, and earning maybe $200 a week by the time I was in my early thirties. We'd given ourselves two years to get the business off the ground; if it failed, we would've tried something else.

But now, with this crisis, it looked as if we were about to lose everything.

We had a baby on the way, we were trying to save enough money to buy a house—and now, suddenly, we had debts we didn't believe we could ever repay. It was the blackest day of our lives. We'd found ourselves in a tunnel that we couldn't see any way out of.

CHAPTER 1

Whatever will
happen to Dick?

My first memories are of living in Dudley Avenue, Roseville, a northern suburb of Sydney. Just next door, a small creek wound through a vacant block of land covered in gum trees and thick scrub. From as young as four, I would disappear into the bush. One day I discovered the entrance to a stormwater drain that emptied into Middle Harbour. As I crawled upstream in the darkness, the pipe got smaller and smaller, until it was barely big enough to squeeze through, but this did not stop me. After making my way about half a kilometre up the drain, I ended up under someone's backyard. Peering out of the pipe, I spotted a woman having a cup of tea in her garden. 'Hello,' I said.

The poor woman shrieked and dropped her cup. I quickly retreated, and they never found out who was there.

I always loved drain crawling as a kid. When my mother heard about these forays, she became quite worried and wrote to Council to have bars put on the drain; she never discovered that I could still squeeze my way in. Later, when I saw how anxious she was over my disappearances, I tried to reassure her by saying, 'Don't worry, I'll always turn up.' Decades later, when I was on my solo flight around the world, she would remember my words and quote them when the media asked her if she was concerned for my safety.

I loved that block of bushland. Sometimes I would sit quietly without moving, just watching nature all around me. I never felt lonely or threatened. Often when I came back home, Mum would see that I had a clasped hand and would gradually pry it open, asking, 'What do you have there?' She would have been dreading it was a deadly funnel-web or even a red-back spider; but even then I had common sense and it would be a beautiful little lizard or a frog.

Although I didn't notice it at the time, there must have been sadness in our household. I was born on 18 March 1944, at the height of World War II, and already my family had endured two war deaths. My mother's brother, Harold, was killed during the siege of Tobruk. He was my grandfather's only son after five daughters and his death nearly destroyed my grandpa. Two years later, my aunty Rainbow's husband was killed on the HMAS *Hobart* when it was hit by a Japanese torpedo.

My dad was in the army, and a month before I was born he was transferred to Townsville for training, before being

4

sent to New Guinea. He was fighting in Bougainville when the Americans dropped the atomic bomb on Hiroshima on 6 August 1945, but he didn't get home until December.

My mum told me a wonderful story of how he rang from Roseville railway station before walking the fifteen minutes to our house. As he approached in his uniform, my mum, Joan was standing at the top of the front steps with my sister Barbara and me. I was eighteen months old and took one look at him, then started screaming and ran down the hall and hid in our old dining room, which was stacked with furniture and difficult to access. It was more than half an hour before I could be enticed out to meet this strange man.

Within months, Dad was discharged from the army and returned to his job as a salesman at Murdoch's department store, but not for long. He later told me that he wasn't happy at the job. To sell blankets, he was coached to hold the blanket up and stoop down behind it to make it look longer than it was. He didn't think this was ethical, and Dad was a very honest person—even though our family took pride in being descended from not one but five convicts, including one from the First Fleet.

After he left Murdoch's, he found a job as a travelling book salesman for Leuteneggers Book Distributors. Mum was a house-wife, but she earned a few extra pounds doing casual work for my grandfather, who lived opposite us. My grandpa, Harold Cazneaux, was a commercial photographer, and quite famous. Today his best works are held in the National Library.

Grandpa Caz's house was divided into living quarters on one side and his photographic business on the other. In the attic, my mother would retouch photos. In one of the bedrooms that had been turned into a darkroom, I would often stand beside Grandpa as he placed photographic paper into the developer tray and watch as enlargements would magically appear. I was fascinated by the process.

From the darkroom, a passageway led to a small studio attached to the east side of the house. Here the elite of Australian society would come to have their wedding photos taken, often wandering out among the fruit trees and gardens in the backyard, where I loved to play. There was even a hidden tap to turn on a fountain.

But, of all the rooms in my grandpa's house, the one that had the greatest impact on my life was my uncle Harold's room. I must not have been more than five, and bored, when my grandma said, 'Would you like to look in Harold's room?' She led me to a semi-detached room at the back of the house, which had been locked up and left since they got the terrible news that Harold had been killed. Even his bed had been left made up.

My grandma opened the door and I stepped into the room to be greeted by the most amazing sight. The walls were covered in panels that held meters and transformers, resistors and capacitors, batteries, valves, everything you could think of. Harold was a wireless technician. Naturally, he'd gone off to war as a signaller, a soldier responsible for battlefield communications.

From that day on, I was sometimes allowed to take bits and pieces from Harold's room and experiment with them myself. This was my first interest in radio and then electronics. That interest would, in time, inspire a career that would save me, just when I thought I was about to become a complete failure.

———

In May 1949, two months after I turned five, my mother took me to my first day of kindergarten, at Roseville Public School. According to my mother, after one glance at the class of forty kids I disappeared. She couldn't find me anywhere. An hour later, when she got home, there I was, playing in the cubbyhouse.

'What happened to you?' she asked.

'Oh, I didn't like "cool", so I came home over the back fences,' I answered.

Over the next few weeks, she gradually enticed me to go to 'cool' (I had a speech defect and couldn't say anything that started with the letter 's'). I think my problem with school was the large number of students. To me, just two or three people was a crowd; I loved being by myself or with just one other person. I've always been like that.

At school I was a bit of a misfit or, as my mother explained to her friends, 'Dick marches to the beat of a different drum.' Often I would bring something strange to class. Once I found a tortoise in Machine Creek at the bottom of Archbold Road, so I took it in and it got away. We found it three days later under the school piano. Another time I brought in a blue-tongue lizard, much to everyone's astonishment, because back then many people thought lizards were dangerous. Of course, in Australia they are not.

When I moved up to first class, we had a new teacher and on our first day she asked each of us to stand and say our name. This was a bit of a shock to me, and when it was my turn, I said, 'Dick Fish,' and everyone laughed. I then said, 'Dick Miff' and put on a little act—I think I pulled a face and danced a quick jig. I don't know why I did that, but the teacher thought I was being smart and kept asking me my name. I didn't have enough sense to tell her that I couldn't say it.

The class roared with delight, so she sent me to the principal, who rang my mother. 'Oh, Dick has a speech defect and he can't say "s",' she explained.

These days I would be sent to a speech therapist, but not back then. Instead, I simply returned to the classroom and everything carried on as usual. The other kids were mostly kind to me, but I was certainly treated differently and not just because of my speech. Some called me 'Ching Chong Chinaman' because of my narrowed eyes.

When I mentioned this to my mum, she said, 'You tell them the Chinese had the first civilisation in the world, so you would be very proud to be Chinese.' Of course, this didn't help. But when I saw other kids being bullied, it made me more convinced than ever that I should try to be kind to people. Eventually, when I was about ten, I somehow cured my speech problem, but I never really liked school.

————

In July 1949, we moved to East Roseville, later renamed Roseville Chase. My father had used his share of an inheritance (£180) to buy our quarter-acre block of land. He was then able to take out a War Service Loan for £500 and have a small brick house built on the block. He was paying off the loan and we could just manage to live on the balance of what he earned.

Our life at East Roseville was wonderful. Although houses were gradually being built around us, there were no sealed roads or kerbs and fortunately there were still lots of trees to climb. Our street was next to bushland and when I got home from school the only rules were to change my clothes and be home by dark. Nearly every afternoon, I would disappear, usually by myself, and set off through the bush. I loved that natural world, with its towering trees, ferns and sandstone cliffs.

I slowly built up my knowledge of lizards and how to collect them. I kept them in a lizard pit that my dad built for me—not a pit in the ground, but four fibro walls (and yes, we cut fibro up with a handsaw, with the asbestos dust going everywhere). Later I started breeding lizards, learning that the blue-tongue had live young, whereas the beautiful bearded dragon, one of my favourite lizards, laid eggs. All fascinating stuff for a young boy, at a time when no permit was required for keeping lizards.

To earn pocket money, I had to do chores. Every night, my sister Barbara and I did the washing-up. In the kitchen, we had the classic three china ducks on the wall, and we often fought about the ducks' names: I said they were 'Mummy Duck, Daddy Duck and Dickie Duck', and Barbara said, 'Mummy Duck, Daddy Duck and Penny Duck.' We once ended up throwing the ducks at each other and breaking them, and Mum had to secretly glue them together with Tarzan's Grip so Dad wouldn't find out and punish us.

Clearly, Dad was the disciplinarian and Mum was the kind one who covered up for us. Sometimes if there was something difficult to wash up, like a roasting pan, she would hide it in the oven and do it herself the next day.

In those days, nearly everything was delivered, but if we needed anything else, Mum would walk to the local shops. In fact, she lived her whole life without ever learning to drive.

We were a very close family. As we ate our evening meal, we sometimes listened to the radio, either the news or my favourite serial—aviation hero *Hop Harrigan*. We also listened to Jack Davey and *The Argonauts*. Besides listening to the radio, we discussed many things as a family.

My dad was a gentle man. He loved native parrots and used to breed them; we always had one in the house. He spent his weekends growing Australian native trees from seed. When they had grown into small seedlings, he'd give them to the neighbours to plant. This is one of the reasons there are thousands of beautiful trees in Roseville Chase.

I suppose we were working class, as there was hardly any money around. I remember in the bookshelf at home all we had were two books plus four volumes of the *Australian Encyclopaedia* that my dad had been given. We never had the full set because we couldn't afford them. I did not know at the time that one day I would be the publisher of the *Australian Encyclopaedia.*

At the same time, I think Dad and Mum thought we were middle class. They used to shop at David Jones, and Dad was a top sportsman. At school he had been a New South Wales tennis champion. In contrast, I was a complete fumble-fingers. In the early days at Roseville Public School, I was given a chance to play on the cricket team, but they soon made it clear they didn't want me. I quickly discovered that I was completely hopeless at sport.

I knew all the kids in our street. We formed our own little club and on weekends would take off into the bush after breakfast and not return until late in the day. More often than not, though, my walking and adventuring was done completely by myself, given I loved being on my own so much.

None of us had any money or expensive toys, so we made our own billycarts. We'd get old wheels from a pram and attach them to an IXL jam box and push it around the suburb. Over time, as the dirt roads were gradually sealed with bitumen this made our billycarts go more easily.

When I was about eight, I told Dad that I wanted a bike. He said, 'You will have to earn half of the money.' By then I'd saved up my pocket money from chores, carefully putting it away in my little Commonwealth Bank moneybox. I thought I'd saved a huge amount of money, but when we opened it up, it wasn't much. Even when Dad put in the other half, there was only enough for a second-hand Malvern Star; I had secretly wanted a new Speedwell, like most of my mates, but it wasn't to be.

In fact, the Malvern Star proved to be great, because it broke down a lot. One day when I was riding, there was a terrible noise and its three-speed gearbox just tore apart. I wheeled my bike home, where Dad had a workshop with plenty of tools, and I took the gearbox completely apart, managed to fix it and put it back together again. When I hopped back on my bike and rode it, I suddenly realised that I was really good at practical things like mechanics, which was a huge relief.

By then I knew that I was hopeless at school. The only subject I was any good at was social studies. My sister Barbara was academic and really good at all subjects. My parents used to say to each other, 'Whatever will happen to Dick?' They were quite worried, but didn't know what to do. It worried me too. I couldn't learn my times tables.

I was never tested, so I had no idea what my defect was. I just thought I was dumb.

had a big effect on me when I said it: 'On my honour, I promise that I will do my best—To do my duty to God and the Queen, to help other people at all times and to obey the Scout law.'

Just as important, the Scouting movement taught me what I call today 'responsible risk-taking', which was to save my life in the future. It also taught me leadership, which helped me do so well in business. There is no doubt in my mind that the Scouting movement is the best youth leadership training organisation in the world.

And though I owe a lot to Scouts, this doesn't include my first camping trip. For that I'm indebted to my cousin, Bob, who was ten years older than me. In 1953, Bob and I hired a boat from Smith's Boatshed (they were called 'Smithy's Submarines' because they leaked so much) near Roseville Bridge and we rowed up Middle Harbour to the bridge near St Ives. We camped in a small cave and I loved it. I'm sure that my early exposure to such beautiful bushland and nature had a huge effect. I worry about kids today, especially those who are forced to live like termites in high-rise buildings, and I'm forever grateful that I was a free-range kid.

But it wasn't just the outdoors that was about to change my life. Thanks to visits to my late uncle Harold's room at my grand-parents, and my fascination with the radio parts I borrowed, I decided to build my first crystal set. Soon I was busy building more radios and experimenting with other things.

I found an article in *Hobbies Illustrated* about how to make a hectograph. Before copying machines were common, teachers used this process to duplicate lessons. First they would write a message on a sheet of paper with special ink, then lay the sheet of paper on a waxed surface—called the hectograph—press the paper into the wax and then remove it, then make up to fifty copies by putting other sheets on the wax.

I decided to build one, and after buying the glycerine from the chemist and mixing it with gelatine to make the 'wax', I followed the instructions to boil it on our kitchen stove. Unfortunately, it caught alight—just a tiny flame—so I grabbed the saucepan, put it into the sink and turned the cold water tap on full. I thought that was the best way to put out the fire.

I couldn't believe what happened. There was a tremendous explosion and flame shot up, right across the room. It singed my eyebrows and completely blackened the ceiling. Luckily it went out quickly.

When Mum and Dad came home, they were shocked to see what had happened, but I didn't get into trouble. I wasn't even made to pay for the repainting of the ceiling—Dad did that. They understood that I was trying to be inventive. Wow, I was certainly fortunate. I could have easily burned down the kitchen or the whole house.

———

As I progressed from crystal sets to one- and two-valve radios, I needed money to buy components. So I taught myself some conjuring tricks and earned a bit of money as a magician at kids' parties.

From the age of nine, I had a job either after school or on the weekend. I started working for the local chemist, delivering prescriptions by bike, and also worked for the hardware store. I was a paperboy for the newsagency, and this included standing out on busy Babbage Road on a Saturday afternoon to sell papers. Talk about risky—cars would suddenly come off the bitumen and skid to a stop beside me on the dirt.

Everything I earned went towards buying radio parts. I'd give Dad a list, and he'd go to Price's Radio in Angel Place in the city and come back with what I needed. I had no idea I would turn this into a career, but already I had the makings of an entrepreneur.

Not long before this, I had started selling white mice. I had bought two of them for ten and sixpence each at the railway pet shop and started breeding them. Before long, I had about fifty. My parents didn't think I was looking after them properly, so my father said, 'I'll give you until tomorrow afternoon to get them down to twenty-five.'

The next day, my Mum looked out and saw all these little boys coming in through the gate, then going out again with cardboard boxes. She later said, 'I found Dick was selling the mice. He'd put a note up at school, "White Mice, 10 shilling 6 pence at the railway pet shop. At Dick Smith's, 3 shillings each".' I was about eight at the time.

In October 1954, a four-page catalogue for Price's Radio components appeared in *Radio & Hobbies* magazine. It became my bible, and I used it to buy all my parts. These were the days of valve equipment—transistors weren't available yet—and valves needed a high-voltage 'B' battery for power. According to an old cash sale docket from the following February, the 'B' battery cost 18 shillings (over $40 today), a staggering amount for an eleven year old to be spending.

One of my early Christmas presents was a soldering iron. Up until then, I'd built my radios on a piece of timber with little wood screws to hold the parts. Years later when I introduced *Dick Smith's Fun Way into Electronics* books and kits at Dick Smith Electronics, the kits were based on the same idea of a piece of wood with self-tapping screws. Tens of thousands of the books were sold and the kits made, and even today space engineers with PhDs come up to me and say, 'Dick, I got into electronics through your *Fun Way* kits.' They look at me in awe. If they only knew how hopeless I was back when I was eleven.

———

In 1954, in fifth class, my report shows that I was forty-fifth out of forty-seven in the class and I had been absent ten days over the six-month period. My class teacher, whom I liked, wrote the report and he really put pressure on me. When he tried to teach me to spell the word 'parallel', I couldn't get it right. In my report, he wrote, 'Dick's tables, spelling and social studies are very weak. Home prac of these would help him.'

How was I that dumb? I didn't understand why, because I tried very hard. It was very depressing, and that's why I escaped more and more to the bush, or to my room, where I worked on radio parts by myself.

When I was in sixth class, I hoped to go to North Sydney Technical High School. I clearly loved mechanical things and wanted to do a technical course. The problem was, North Sydney Tech was selective and my pass at the end of sixth class was certainly not going to get me there. My sixth class teacher suggested to my mum that I repeat the year—and I did. Interestingly, on the second time around I did even worse but, for some reason, they let me in to North Sydney Tech. I'm glad they did, because it was a wonderful school.

In 1956, the year I repeated sixth class, I was twelve years old and the world around me was changing. On 16 September, I went with my Uncle Dud to Benjamin's Building Centre, a retail store on Victoria Street, Chatswood, where we looked through the window to watch Bruce Gyngell greet Sydney with the words, 'Good evening, and welcome to television.' It was incredible to watch, as we'd only had radio up until then, and I realised that a major change in communications was underway.

In November, I went to the national fitness camp, Broken Bay Sport and Recreation near Patonga, sixty minutes north of Sydney. There I annoyed the teachers a bit when I caught a red-bellied black snake and a yellow-faced whip snake. They wouldn't let me take them home in my suitcase, which was really disappointing. By then I was keeping snakes at home, which was fascinating, but did cause a few problems.

For instance, I kept my green tree snake in a little glass cabinet in my bedroom. One day I got home from school and Mum said, 'Dick, quick, your green tree snake has escaped because you left the top off the cabinet, and your father's got an important person coming for dinner tonight.'

We searched high and low until I found that the snake had slipped under the enclosed bath in the bathroom and was peering out through the ventilator. I sat in the dry bath for half an hour, looking over the side until the snake stuck its head out far enough to grab it, then I gradually eased it out and put it back in its cabinet.

In January 1957, I attended my first day at North Sydney Technical High School. The school motto was 'Carpe Diem', meaning 'seize the day', and I certainly did just that. What a wonderful school. It had incredible comradery, and even though I was hopeless at studying, for the first three years I couldn't think of a better place to be until I was fifteen and could then leave school for good.

But that year also marked the start of a darker time. In October, I remember running around to Malga Avenue, one of the roads running through Roseville Chase, and looking up to see Russia's *Sputnik* satellite traversing the night sky.

It was in the days of the Cold War and, as a young person, I was quite frightened that one day a nuclear bomb would go off in Sydney. Sometimes I would walk down into our backyard, look south over the back fence towards the city, and visualise a huge red flame rolling towards me and incinerating everyone in Roseville Chase. We were about 10 kilometres north of the central business district. I wasn't obsessed by it, but many of my friends thought there could be a nuclear war, that Sydney would be targeted, and we'd all be wiped out.

Fortunately, my fears were never realised. Instead, the Russian *Sputnik* heralded the advent of satellites that would usher in the Global Positioning System (GPS), which so helped me during my last two flights around the world.

But the Cold War wasn't the only thing that was to mark 1957 as one of the most disturbing times in my life. It was also the year my father suffered a breakdown.

―――

Early in the year, my dad announced that he was going to leave his job as a manager with Leuteneggers Book Distributors and start his own printing business. He'd been working part-time for Art Lovers Gallery, a company that published Albert Namatjira prints, which he sold to shops.

At the time, Art Lovers Gallery was having difficulty finding high quality printing for its reproductions, so Dad came up with the idea of putting in some of his own money and borrowing some from friends to raise the £5000 needed to buy a small German printing press and set up his own business.

I was incredibly excited and I remember bragging to my school friends how Dad was opening his own printing business,

Colourmaster Press. Dad was confident that it would be successful. As a family, we were all part of it and thought it was the most wonderful thing.

Dad hired an expert printer, Bruce Austin, and they started the business at the end of 1957. For reasons I've never really understood, the enterprise was a failure from the start. Much later on, my mother would often blame the Menzies credit squeeze for this misfortune, but in reality that national economic setback did not officially begin until November 1960.

My dad and Bruce hardly got any work and, to stop the ongoing losses, the business was forced to close down after six weeks. Dad had lost half the initial working capital and the stress of the catastrophe caused him to have a complete mental breakdown.

I went from feeling the excitement of my dad opening his own business to dealing with my dad taking to his bed. He wouldn't get up, and was like that for over four months. My parents were in dire financial straits as both Barbara and I were at school and there was no income to even make our mortgage payments or buy food.

My mother, who had never had a job outside our home, immediately went out and found work in a Sydney hat factory. Each week day, she would leave for work before I went to school and return home well after me. She didn't like doing this but, because dad was sick in bed, what else could she do?

At the time, my diary (for some reason I've always kept diaries) shows that I was trying to figure out how we could live for less money. I learned that the lamb we were buying was twice the price of hogget chops, so we switched from lamb to hogget.

Eventually my dad got out of bed, sought psychiatric help and found a job, but his breakdown had a major effect on his life and ours. To his credit, over the next ten years, he paid back every cent that was borrowed from friends. Later I learned that they had told him, 'Look, Herb, we don't want the money back,' but he insisted on making good his losses. He was that type of person. In his whole life, the only swear words I ever heard from him were 'bally' and 'darn'.

Eventually Dad was given a job at Halstead Press selling Christmas cards, but he was affected by his business failure. A few years later, when he was fifty-six, he moved with Mum to Dunbogan on the Mid North Coast, where he took over an oyster lease. Unfortunately, after five years raising the oysters to prime condition, a huge flood came down and the fresh water killed them—and his business. By then he had taken over as caretaker of my small farm at Rossglen, just south of Port Macquarie, where he was planting trees and enjoying life. And mum was following her dream to be a printmaker and was selling her work at nearby Thrumster Village.

————

During my family's difficult times, I found escape and enjoyment on bushwalks with the Scouts. I loved the Blue Mountains, especially the Wild Dog Mountains, not just for their raw beauty, but because I felt an affinity with Aboriginal Australians who called this area home. Sometimes when my friends and I took a break beneath a sandstone overhang, I imagined what it would have been like to live there. It didn't feel strange to be in the bush; I felt like it was where I belonged.

In February 1958, I joined the North Sydney Technical High School Cadets. It was my second year at North Sydney Tech and I have no idea why I joined, but I did quite well. I was an accurate shooter and won one of the prizes. However, I didn't like that we had to stab a chaff-filled bag with our bayonets and imagine it was the enemy. Some of my school-mates absolutely adored this, saying, 'Take that, Hun' or 'Take that, Jap' as they stabbed away, but I was horrified. I couldn't imagine actually stabbing someone—maybe I could if I was trying to defend myself.

I did like the discipline, the marching and keeping our uniforms in tiptop condition. The highlight of the year was the Army Cadet Camp at Singleton, where we went for field training. I left Cadets after one year, but I'm glad I had that military experience. More than anything else, it taught me to respect those who go overseas and fight for our country's freedom.

Meanwhile, inside the classroom, my first three years at North Sydney Tech were turning into a disaster. I was good at metalwork, woodwork and technical drawing, but not much else. Take French, for instance. After three years of study, I got 7 per cent in the intermediate certificate. Talk about frustrating.

The feet of young men

Every school day, Reg Burdon, my teacher and the deputy headmaster, required us to learn ten French words. I would come home and try to learn them. By bedtime, Dad, Mum and Barbara would know them, but not me. Over three years, I only learned one word—*la pomme* is the apple.

To this day I have no idea why things like this just won't stay in my brain. Maybe I should never have tried to learn a language, but it was compulsory at the time. It made me feel bad that I was so hopeless. I really believed that there was something mentally wrong with me.

Amazingly, many years later, when I was featured on Channel Nine's *This Is Your Life*, who should appear from behind the doors but Reg Burdon. He said what a wonderful student I had been and how he always thought I would do well. I was sure that either Reg had me mistaken for someone else, or he was a really good actor.

While I was at North Sydney Tech, some of my friends were becoming involved with religion, which is how I ended up going to the Billy Graham Crusade. I was amazed to see so many thousands walk forward to give their lives to Christ. And though I loved the singing and theatre, Billy Graham had no effect on me at all. But, then, I'd never really been religious.

According to my mum, when I was about six I came home from scripture class and said, 'Mum, the teacher said there is a God, who is on everyone's shoulder—but there are hundreds of people in the world, so that's impossible.'

My mum and dad weren't particularly religious, but she replied, 'Look, you've just got to have faith, we can't understand everything.' That never worked for me, though. I either had to understand something or I simply didn't accept it. Even today I consider myself an agnostic; that is, I don't know if there is a God or not. There seem to be so many incredible religions in the world that I'm not sure how you could pick one and say all the others are wrong. But I do believe in Karma: do good things and good things will happen to you!

During Easter 1959, I went on a four-day bushwalk in the Wild Dog Mountains, south of Katoomba, with our Scout master. It was my first long bushwalk and I was told to wear big boots. I ended up with bad blisters after the second day and by the time we got back to Katoomba on Monday night, I thought, 'I will never do another bushwalk in my life.' A week or two later, I found myself thinking that maybe it wasn't so bad and that I wouldn't mind doing it again. From then on, bushwalking would play a major role in my life. But I never wore big boots again.

In November that year, the day arrived when I could legally leave school. I was fifteen years old, had completed my intermediate certificate and just wanted to get out. I loved my school friends and the school itself, but I could see a great new world was opening up for me.

By then I'd advanced from building crystal radio sets to designing and building what I called a noughts and crosses machine. It really was an early computer. I used second-hand parts from a telephone exchange to build it. It would play noughts and crosses against anyone and no one could beat it. This was a great boost to me, because while I was no good at rote learning and theory, I was fine at practical things. The fact that my mind was capable of working out how to build this complex machine gave me confidence as I left school. Now I just had to find a job.

CHAPTER 3

The power of love

In January 1960, I began my first full-time job, at Godfrey Electrical Industries. Godfrey's had a factory for high-voltage electrical switching gear on Eastern Valley Way, Roseville, just a couple of kilometres from home. As an apprentice, I was given process work—my supervisor seemed to have no idea about my knowledge of radios and electronics.

My first two weeks, I operated a press that bent out springs for switches. Bang, bang, bang, bang, all day, every day. Besides the mind-numbing monotony, the factory had a steel roof, no air-conditioning, and Sydney was in the midst of record temperatures. It was almost impossible to work.

After three weeks, I realised that I disliked the job even more than school—if that was possible. I went home to Mum and

Dad and said, 'Look, I think I'd like to go back and complete my leaving certificate.' My mum thought it was a good idea but Dad instantly said, 'You made up your mind to leave, you can't chop and change and it's now too late to go back to school, so you'll miss a whole a year.'

My lovely mother rang Mr Hornibrook, the headmaster at North Sydney Tech. She must have given him a great story, because he said, 'Look, send Dick along.' I knew Mr Hornibrook well because I had fixed the school's public address amplifier the year before, so I was a bit of a hero. He wrote out a note for Reg Burdon, my teacher, that said something like, 'Because Dick Smith was of such wonderful assistance to the school, I've decided he should be accepted for his last two years.'

Wow, what a wonderful break! Suddenly I was back at North Sydney Tech studying for my leaving certificate. And something else happened that would have the most extraordinary effect on my life—I had a girlfriend, Carolyn.

I should mention that I've always liked pretty girls. In fact, that was the problem. Being hopeless at sport, not good-looking and a bit weird, there was simply no way I was going to end up with one of them.

My first 'girlfriend' was Jenny. She was an absolute beauty and I would see her at Roseville Baths. Fifty years later, with media help, I searched for and eventually found her, but she said she couldn't even remember a 'Dick Smith'. Of course she couldn't; I never actually spoke to her, just dreamed from afar.

The power of love

My second girlfriend was Lesley. During my second year at North Sydney Tech, we would meet for a chat after school on a street corner in East Roseville. I was clearly in love, but after five weeks, Lesley stopped turning up.

The following year, I joined St Andrew's Fellowship at the Roseville Anglican Church. I admit, I did this to meet girls, because in those days, there were no girls in Scouts and I went to an all-boys school. In early April, I attended a fellowship camp in Deer Park, in Sydney's south, where I found myself holding hands with Carolyn. She was my age but a year ahead at North Sydney Girls High. She was lovely, and far more mature than me, and from the start I was convinced our relationship was doomed to failure. Instead, we ended up seeing each other outside fellowship.

Then, one Sunday night, we were on her verandah, kissing goodnight, when she said, 'I love you.' Wow, a pretty girl who was in love with me—extraordinary! It only took me a few days to decide I was in love with her, too. From then on, we did absolutely everything we could together. Fortunately, we caught the same train from Roseville to our schools in North Sydney. We would often stand in the guard's compartment facing each other with our shoes interlocked.

Most importantly, she was the first person who said to me, 'You're not dumb, Dick. You're actually quite smart.' That gave me confidence, and no doubt in trying to prove her right, I put more work into my studies and suddenly began to excel at school. In October 1961, I found that in the trial leaving certificate I came in third for my year.

Nearly every weekend, I was going out with the Scouts. I'd begun rock climbing, canyoning and canoeing. We had the most wonderful Scout masters, who all volunteered their time. One was Ken Ewen, a successful businessman who owned a family building company with thirty staff, yet devoted his spare time to teaching us leadership—at no charge.

These men had returned from World War II, where many would have been exposed to the most terrible risks. Yet those who took the greatest risks were seen as heroes. Perhaps that's why they judged risk so differently from the way it is assessed today.

For instance, to get to the Scout camp in the Blue Mountains, thirty of us would pile into the back of Ken's truck, all yelling and shouting, packed in with tent poles and patrol boxes. There was not a seatbelt in sight. Yes, we were being exposed to risks, but as a result we were discovering the spirit of adventure.

In those days, many young people hitchhiked, and I became an expert at it. With Carolyn living 3 kilometres away, I would hitchhike back and forth from her place. On Sunday nights, we would go to fellowship, then return to her house for coffee. My parents had a rule that I had to be home by 10 p.m., so I would leave her about 9.30 p.m. and hitch. I'd usually get picked up by the second or third car and be home a few minutes before 10 p.m.

By then I was well into my mid-teens, yet I always obeyed my parents. Although I considered my dad to be quite strict, there was never any physical punishment. If I did something wrong, like cutting a branch of a tree to make a tree house, for instance, I would be told to write out 'I must not cut a limb off a tree' two hundred times, or I wouldn't be allowed to go away for the day or weekend. Over time, I learned that if I cleaned up his workshop, he might change his mind.

It was lucky that my mother balanced this by being a complete softie, often covering up something that I had done wrong. Lots of mothers are like that—just wonderful.

Because like all the Cazneaux daughters she was a very artistic person, after her father died in 1953, Mum had taken printmaking classes in Chatswood. She also went to adult education classes run by the Workers' Educational Association, studying topics like history, literature, art and poetry.

In November 1961, I was seventeen years old and starting the general maths component of my leaving certificate at North Sydney Tech. Carolyn was going to Sydney University, but nearly every Friday night I would either take her to the pictures or, to save money, we would walk to my aunty Rainbow's house to watch television—usually *77 Sunset Strip*. At the time, neither of our parents had a television set, so we had to cadge one where we could.

When the results of my leaving certificate were posted in January 1962, I learned that I'd passed with two As and four Bs, which allowed me to matriculate to any Australian university. What an achievement for someone who started out as such a hopeless student. How did this happen? Maybe it was that

I matured late, but I'd like to think that Carolyn's belief in me gave me the confidence to do well.

———

I immediately enrolled in Electrical Engineering at both the University of Sydney and the University of New South Wales. Carolyn was at Sydney Uni, so I went to an Orientation Week lecture to see what it was like. As I walked into the Wallace Theatre, I was stunned to discover that there were over six hundred people there, probably everyone who was enrolled in Engineering and Science. The huge crowd really frightened me, as I was still only comfortable in small groups. A little voice inside kept saying, 'Dick, this is not for you. You're not going to succeed here, you're going to fail.' And I listened.

Instead, I managed to get a job at Weston Electronics, a small manufacturing company that made two-way radios for taxis and the Royal Flying Doctor Service. It took me over an hour each way by motor scooter to get from East Roseville across the Sydney Harbour Bridge to Sydenham. I was given a half-day off each week to gain my Electronics & Communications Certificate at Gore Hill Tech.

Mostly I sat on the rear bench of the factory, winding coils (an essential part of a radio's tuning circuit) for the LM18 bushfire radio. Sometimes, though, a taxi would park out the back and one of the rear bench boys would have to install a Weston two-way radio.

On my first go, I fixed the two-way radio under the dashboard, then attached the aerial onto the roof, in under two hours. The foreman supervising me was horrified.

'There's one thing you should learn,' he growled, 'and that's never do an installation in less than three hours.'

I stared at him in amazement. 'Why?'

'Because if you do,' he replied, 'you'll always be expected to do it in two hours. That's not good, because some installations are more difficult and it means you'll have to work hard all the time.' This seemed crazy to me, but I was learning how the typical 'system' worked in Australia. I ignored what he said and continued to do the installations as quickly as possible.

One day, when I'd been at Weston's for six months, I applied for a job at a small two-way radio manufacturing company, Findlay Communications. I got the job at $35 per week.

This would completely change my life. Not just because the new job was close to home, which was important, but it would lead me to meet a most extraordinary person, who—after my wife, Pip—would have the greatest effect on my life.

While I was changing jobs, I was still very active in the Scout movement. In March 1962, I passed my Queen's Scout badge. Many people think the Queen's Scout is the highest award in Scouting, but that's the Baden Powell Award. Although I would go on to receive one of these as well, I really valued my Queen's Scout Award.

It came with a letter from Malcolm Maitland, the state commissioner, that read, 'I trust as a Queen Scout, you will keep in mind the important responsibilities, which are now yours, particularly as you wear a badge, which indicates your willingness to use your Scouting knowledge in the Queen's Service and the service of the community.' It meant a lot to me and I've tried to live by it ever since.

At the time, I must have been as fit as ever. With Dave Larkin, a fellow Rover Scout, I walked from Kanangra Walls to Katoomba in the Blue Mountains, traversing the spectacular Mt Cloudmaker and Wild Dog Mountains. What was normally a four-day walk took us just two. Back then, there were many people out bushwalking, but now when I walk in the same area, I hardly see another person, even though Sydney's population has more than doubled.

My first job at Findlay Communications was putting together the Findlay 8A11 taxi two-way radio. As well as pop-riveting valve sockets onto a chassis, I soldered and wired all the parts in place and then tested it. Maurie Findlay, the owner of the business, rented a small office and production space at Gilco Engineering, owned by his friend Jack Gilham.

I worked at a big steel bench on the Gilco factory floor. It was noisy, with the steel fabrication and welding of switchboards, transformers for fluorescent and neon lights, and switching gear for the high-voltage power transmission industry. I shared the space with the girls who made the transformers—and who listened to 2SM so loudly you could hear it above all the racket. Toni Fisher's song 'West of the Wall', about love separated by the Berlin Wall, was popular at the time. A few years later,

I would be coming through that very wall with the person who was to so influence my life.

———

Outside of work, I had a new interest—amateur radio. I had already passed the government exam for a limited certificate, but to get the full certificate I had to learn morse code. Try as I might, I simply couldn't do it. It was just like French; it wouldn't stay in my brain. Without a full amateur radio licence, I couldn't communicate long distances around the world, but I could use a very high frequency (VHF) radio to communicate with 'hams' (as we called amateur radio operators) around Sydney.

Maurie knew that I was trying to get my full licence and that I wanted to talk to anyone who could help me. He told me that one of the investors in his business, a wealthy anaesthetist named Dr Tony Balthasar, was a ham radio enthusiast. Maurie gave me Tony's number and I phoned him, only to be met with a guarded response. I wasn't sure if my call was welcome or not, but it didn't stop me from asking if I could come over and look at his ham radio equipment.

Tony lived on his own in a penthouse in Buckhurst, an historic building in Sydney's eastern suburb of Point Piper. His parents had passed away, but he still retained his Estonian housekeeper, Lena, who had been his nanny when he was a child.

I'd never mixed with Eastern Suburbs people and imagined that Tony would have been born with a 'silver spoon in his mouth'. In his case, I was right. His father was the Belgian consul and a major wool buyer. Tony had gone to school at exclusive Cranbrook. He was an only child and his mother was incredibly strict. She didn't want him using public transportation, so he would arrive at school each day in a chauffeur-driven Rolls Royce.

He'd actually joined the Cubs and advanced to Scouts, but when it was time to go away to camp, he wasn't allowed. His mother didn't want him mixing with 'rude mechanicals', meaning the typical boys in the Scout movement. He later told me that although he'd taken out several women while at university, his mother made it clear she didn't approve of them.

The first time I met Tony, he was an eccentric forty-six year old (he wore a monocle and would sometimes answer in French) and I was eighteen, but there was an instant rapport. Tony was quiet, even withdrawn, with a passion for ham radio and a wide range of interests. Besides being an anaesthetist, he was a wool classer, surfer, scuba diver and TV serviceman. He had his Marconi School of Wireless certificate displayed proudly on the wall.

As I got to know Tony, I could see that he was lonely, so one day I invited him to our Rover Scout meeting to show slides of his recent visit to Europe. I remember saying to him, 'Tony, if you come to the Rover crew meeting, you mustn't wear your monocle and please don't speak French.'

The power of love

'Why, Dick?' Tony asked.

'Well,' I said as diplomatically as I could, 'people will think you are a nutter!'

Tony later told me I was the first person who actually 'said it how it is'. I suppose I thought I had nothing to lose. I even talked him into taking some of our Rovers skiing at Perisher. We went in his 1963 Mark II Jaguar, doing a hundred miles an hour on the way!

Over time, I suggested that he get more involved in Scouting, join our Rover crew and train to become our assistant leader. At first he said he didn't have the confidence, but eventually he agreed. It was the start of a relationship with the Scouting movement that Tony would maintain for the rest of his life.

———

As for me, I was eighteen and—with my new job at Findlay Communications, a full-time girlfriend, my friendship with Tony and involvement in the Scouts—life was looking good. Maybe I wasn't going to be a failure after all.

And then one day the phone rang. It was Carolyn.

'Dick,' she said, 'I don't love you anymore.'

I couldn't believe what I was hearing. We had been together for nearly three years and I thought things had been going really well.'

As Carolyn hung up, I felt sick to my stomach. I was very much in love with her and was now completely heartbroken.

The break-up devastated me. I never went back to Tech. I simply couldn't study. I have never managed to get any qualifications to this day. I nearly left my job, but instead pitched myself into it, along with Scouts and the outdoors. Later that year, the twenty-two Rover Scouts in my crew voted me in as the Rover mate (even though I'd never been a sixer in Cubs or a patrol leader). Frank Jamieson was our Rover Scout leader and Tony Balthasar our assistant Rover leader. I also trained and became an assistant cub master.

Besides our outdoor adventures, we had a great social campaign, including helping older people and raising money for charity. We didn't just believe in the Scout promise of 'Help other people at all times', we practised it.

As 1964 began, I joined Tony and two other friends in Tasmania to walk the Overland Track, from Cradle Mountain to Lake St Clair. Wow, what a magnificent place. Some say the bush has healing powers, and they might be right. Gradually I got over my heartache. I also started rock climbing in earnest, on The Three Sisters and Narrow Neck at Katoomba. Those vertical walls would stand me in good stead for my first great adventure—an expedition to Ball's Pyramid.

CHAPTER 4

Planning my first expedition

It was 24 May 1964. I'd just dropped into the Roseville Chase Newsagency to see what new magazines had come in, when the latest issue of *PIX* caught my eye. I picked up the magazine and began flicking through.

Splashed across pages 30 and 31 was a photo of a fantastic sea spire and the headline: *A Grim Challenge to Man—Two Australians Try to Conquer a Rugged Mountain Peak off Lord Howe Island.*

'Like a great, jagged, decayed tooth, Ball's Pyramid rises 1843 feet out of the turbulent sea 11 miles south of Lord Howe Island,' I read. 'Even before any attempt to scale the near vertical peak with its hazardous overhangs begins, there are dangers, seen and unseen.'

The story was about a failed attempt by Rick Higgins and David Roots to climb Ball's Pyramid. It stated, 'Both men intend to make another assault on the rock next year,' and Rick was quoted explaining: 'It's impossible to reach the top in one day. We are convinced the only way to reach the top is to take our own boat out from Sydney and spend a week on the Pyramid.' I quickly recognised Rick from his photo, because he was in another Rover crew, First Roseville, and I knew him from there.

It was the first I'd heard of Ball's Pyramid and the more I read, the more excited I became. By the time I reached the counter to pay for the magazine, one thought had stuck firmly in my head—'One day, I'm going to try and climb that!'

After I bought the magazine, I walked home dreaming about this potential adventure. I kept thinking, 'How can I get enough money to charter a boat to sail to Ball's Pyramid?' Very quickly I thought, 'I know! Tony Balthasar!'

I knew Tony had lots of money and didn't really know how to spend it—at least that's what I thought. I didn't understand wealthy people—why wouldn't they spend their money on adventures? I would if I had any! Maybe I could convince him that this would be something worthwhile to sponsor.

The next time I saw Tony, I did everything I could to enthuse him to sponsor the expedition: 'Tony, look, it would only cost about two thousand pounds and you can't take it with you. Would you come up with the money?' I asked. Within minutes, I had talked him into it.

42

Planning my first expedition

We decided to call it a Rover Scout expedition, even though I knew full well, as I think Tony did too, that there were no Rovers at East Roseville capable of climbing the Pyramid. I was probably the most experienced climber; even so, I was still more of a second, rather than a lead, climber.

Fortunately, when I told Rick Higgins that Tony Balthasar would come up with the money to fund a new expedition, he agreed to be the expedition leader. We soon met and began planning the expedition. I found Rick to be a very good organiser and delegator, and he quickly organised the team. From the East Roseville crew, there would be my close friend Dave Larkin, me and, of course, Tony Balthasar as 'expedition doctor'. Rick also brought some talented climbers on board. Among the first of these was Dave Roots, Rick's partner on his previous attempt on the Pyramid.

Up until now I hadn't even mentioned to Frank Jamieson, our Rover Scout leader, nor to Ken Ewen, our group Scout master, that I had convinced Tony to fund a 'Rover Scout expedition' to Ball's Pyramid. When I finally told Frank, it wasn't to gain his permission, but to share my enthusiasm that Tony had agreed to foot the bill. Not for a moment did he say, 'Hold on, Dick, we should get approval from the Scouting head office.' Today I doubt such an expedition would be allowed, due to the high risks involved. How fantastically free those days were, when risk-taking was encouraged, and not restricted in so many ways.

Then, on 9 November, just two weeks before we were planning to sail for the Pyramid, I woke with an extreme pain in my groin. I immediately rang Tony and he said, 'Quick—get to the local doctor.' Within an hour, I was in the doctor's rooms, where he diagnosed an inguinal hernia.

I spent the next two days in hospital having it repaired, with Tony as the anaesthetist. The first thing I asked Tony when I woke up was, 'Will I still be able to climb on Ball's Pyramid?'

Tony replied, 'Let's see how you go—but I think it's doubtful.'

On the same day as my operation, Prime Minister Robert Menzies introduced conscription for the Vietnam War. By sheer luck, I missed out because I was just over the age limit. Otherwise I would have been in the ballot and possibly off fighting in Vietnam instead of, as time would reveal, setting up my own business. It was the start of a lucky streak that would continue throughout my life.

Before we left, I discussed my post-operative condition with Tony and he agreed that I should be safe enough going by boat, but he added, 'Dick, I think it would be very unwise for you to climb on the Pyramid.' His words weighed heavily on my mind as we sailed out through the Heads.

———

On 25 November 1964, our expedition left Sydney in the 50-foot ketch *Tai Hoa*. When I look back, I realise this was a very risky adventure. Ball's Pyramid has no beaches or sheltered anchorages. Landing required us to jump into the ocean and swim to the rock face. When we got there, huge waves were battering the proposed landing area, a rock shelf covered in slime. But we all managed to get ashore. I knew that there was no way I could climb the Pyramid, because I still had pain from the operation, but I did at least have the chance to land and lead a new way to a suitable camping cave.

Unfortunately, the climbing party quickly encountered great difficulties, with many overhangs and stretches of smooth rock offering only minute hand and foot holds. At night, they were tormented by hungry centipedes that didn't take kindly to visitors.

Finally, at daylight on the fourth day, the lead climbers could appreciate the heart-stopping precariousness of their situation. There was a sheer drop of some 1300 feet (400 metres) on three sides, while the route ahead appeared to be a ridge line, with one crumbling rock tower after another, followed by a huge overhang. Although the summit was estimated to be less than 200 metres higher, the difficult terrain and a wind gusting to 80 kilometres per hour put paid to any chance of reaching the top that day and Rick felt the risk of continuing was becoming too great: he made the call that they should turn back.

———

While the climbers were descending Ball's Pyramid, Tony and I, who were waiting for them on Lord Howe Island, set off early that morning to climb Intermediate Hill. As we approached the top, Tony asked me to stop for a second, as he had something to say.

'Dick,' he began, 'you have changed my life. When we first met, I was quite lonely and couldn't have believed that my life could become so fulfilled. I love being involved in Scouts, and being a major part of this expedition is the best thing I've ever done. I wish to do something for you. I'd like to pay for you to go to university.'

For a minute I couldn't answer; I just stood thinking about my friend's offer.

'Tony,' I replied at last, 'that's incredibly generous, but I would be hopeless!'

'No, Dick,' he replied. 'You have the ability. You'd make a really good engineer. Please think about it.'

I did, for a few seconds.

'That's a wonderful offer,' I said, and I meant it, but I then added, 'Maybe one day you could loan me the money to start a business.'

Tony looked taken aback.

'Well, maybe,' he said, 'but I'd rather you go to university.'

———

The next morning, 3 December, we sailed down to the Pyramid in calm weather, and within an hour and a half of arriving, everyone was back on board. Although disappointed at not reaching the summit, our team was happy and exhilarated by the adventure. Rick and Dave estimated the bivouac on top of Winkelstein's Steeple, named after a bawdy song frequently sung throughout the expedition's long, cold nights, to be at about 1200 feet (560 metres).

As we sailed back to Lord Howe Island, we were so excited. That night we had a wonderful dinner at the Blue Lagoon guest house, where we talked over our adventure from every possible angle.

Although some of our team sailed back to Sydney on *Tai Hoa*, I was lucky enough to be chosen for a trip back on the flying boat. It was the first time I'd ever been on one, and what a wonderful experience it was. I remember looking back on Lord Howe Island as we gained altitude, and for some reason I thought of all the young honeymooners I'd seen there. 'If ever I find a girl that truly loves me,' I vowed, 'I'll bring her back here for our honeymoon.'

CHAPTER 5

Some valuable
life lessons

Only a couple of months before I became entranced by the prospect of conquering Ball's Pyramid, I'd resigned from Findlay Communications. I planned to start my own business based on a photoelectric device that I called the Dick Smith WarnBell, which rang a bell when someone walked into a shop. I was building them at home in my dad's Roseville Chase workshop for £10, and selling them for £20 (yes, this was before decimal currency). I had just turned twenty.

I designed the unit based on articles I had read in *Radio, Television and Hobbies* magazine and I believed that I'd be able to sell quite a few. On the very first day, I sold a WarnBell to the jeweller at Roseville Station. Wow, I had made £10 for the day, an enormous amount of money at a time when a good wage was about £30 per week.

But my confidence took a battering in the days that followed. Although I sold my first WarnBell in one day, it took two weeks to sell the second, and it was three weeks before I managed to sell the third.

To make up for the fact that my WarnBell wasn't generating enough income, I worked for an electronics engineer at Wentworthville in Sydney's Western Suburbs. As well as fixing TV sets in people's homes, I helped him wire and service chicken incubators and install a PA system for the Parramatta Anglican Church, a dusty job that meant getting covered in cobwebs as I squeezed under the floorboards to run the speaker wires. Yes, I would do anything to earn a quid!

But then I made the hard decision to wind up my WarnBell business. The problem was, there just wasn't enough demand. If there had been an existing demand for such a simple product, I'm sure many companies would have been making it. Simple, isn't it? I made the mistake of believing that a lack of availability meant that nobody had thought of it. Whereas the truth was that the demand was not enough to make the product viable.

After four months in my own business, I went back to work at Findlay Communications. I decided it was better to work for Maurie, especially as Tony Balthasar was a major shareholder. I could see great potential for promotion in an expanding business. It was a time when Australia actually designed and manufactured virtually all electronic equipment. At Findlay's, not only would I sit at a bench wiring components into two-way radios for the taxi industry, but I would install and demonstrate them as well.

I loved my job, but, as I turned twenty-one, I was seeing friends who knew less about electronics than me complete their university degrees in electrical and radio engineering and get top jobs with the PMG (Postmaster-General's Department) or OTC (Overseas Telecommunications Commission). When it came to careers, I couldn't help but feel like a failure.

I found my escape on weekends, climbing, bushwalking and canyoning with the Rover Scouts. In the bush, I was super confident. I imagined that my approach to risk-taking was similar to those young Australians who flew fighter planes in World War II. Nothing was going to stop me. Nothing, that is, until I attempted to cross the Colo wilderness with my friends Bob Pallin and John 'Webby' Webster—and I nearly lost the lives of all of us!

———

I had been a fit, confident nineteen year old when I first saw a map of the Colo wilderness, an area north-west of Sydney in the Blue Mountains, and as a twenty-one year old I now felt even more ready for this adventure. It was without doubt the most rugged and inaccessible area in New South Wales. I decided it was the ideal location for me to complete a bushwalk for my Rover Rambler badge.

My first near-fatal error was to believe that, because the weekend forecast was for clear weather, the three of us were good to go. I simply hadn't prepared for rain.

By about eleven o'clock, the rain had set in and my map began to dissolve. I had been taught never to go bushwalking without a waterproof holder for my map, but because I'd assumed that the weather would be fine, I hadn't brought one. We were supposed to be following the crest of a broad ridge, but instead, our route kept leading us down into deep canyons. At one point I thought, 'We should go back,' but for some reason I kept on walking.

By about 5.30 p.m., we arrived at Mt Mistake, sopping wet and extremely cold. My ankles were red raw from being in the lead, pushing through undergrowth and 'clothes prop farms', a term we used for young trees growing so close together that they grab your pack (and ankles) as you push through.

As we continued along Mt Mistake's southern cliff line, we found a small overhang that we could just fit part of our tent under. It was the only dry place around, so we immediately lit a fire and felt better—but it wasn't to last. At about midnight, the overhang turned into a waterfall. Our tent was completely flooded with near-freezing water and we were soon sopping wet. Bob and I spent the rest of the night sitting up and shivering, while Webby found a small ledge nearby to tuck under.

The next morning, I made my second major error. The original map I had been using had so badly dissolved that we were for the moment 'off the map'; because visibility was so poor, I inadvertently went too far north and ended up on the wrong ridge line. For the next few hours, we pushed along the ridge and attempted to descend sundry spurs, sopping wet and icy cold, with our spirits falling. We found that if we stopped moving for more than ten minutes, we all shivered uncontrollably.

We eventually made it to the correct ridge; however, as we peered down through the mist and rain, the 300-metre, near-vertical cliffs looked impassable. We had no climbing rope for abseiling, but eventually crossed the Colo gorge and found a small creek that we began to follow.

According to my plan, we were to have been at the pick-up point six hours earlier, where our fellow Rovers would have been waiting. I imagined that because we hadn't shown up, with the terrible weather conditions they had probably gone back to Sydney to notify emergency services. We were exhausted, but with all our gear soaked and no natural shelter, there was nothing for it but to continue on.

When I had reconnoitred the pick-up point only a month earlier, the creek bed had been dry. Now it flowed strongly. Unfortunately, the undergrowth on either side was so thick that the only way to progress was by walking in the stream. It was now 7 p.m. and torrents of icy rain blocked out the last light of the day.

By about nine o'clock, I knew we could go no further. 'Okay, we're stopping here,' I said. Everything was so wet we couldn't light a fire. We simply felt our way over to the scrubby bank, unrolled our sodden sleeping bags on the 30 degree slope, then pulled the wet tent over us. We were in for a second night of misery.

As we lay there, cold, exhausted and shivering, my thoughts were as black as the night. I felt totally responsible for what had happened. I hadn't complied with what I'd learned from my Scout leaders about being prepared for all weather conditions. I had pushed on when we should have gone back. My desire to succeed had taken us to a point where we could lose our lives.

In the dark moments that followed, my thoughts slowly receded into one stark realisation: 'If the temperature drops to zero tonight, we are going to die—all the search teams will find are three frozen bodies in sleeping bags, covered by an icy tent.'

But amazingly, after seven or eight hours of a sleepless night, the wet, grey dawn gradually outlined the surrounding bush. I leaned across and touched Bob. He murmured something, and then so did Webby. I felt an incredible surge of relief—they were both alive.

We peeled off our sleeping bags and struggled to stand. My ankles were worn raw and bleeding. The pain was indescribable as I packed away my gear, checked on the others and set off.

Fortunately, my navigation led us out of the scrub and straight on to our destination. It was still raining, but the pick-up crew had left a fire that was smouldering and, nearby, a note saying, 'We will be back in the morning.' At ten o'clock, the crew arrived. At almost that exact moment, the weather cleared.

As we drove back to civilisation, I was filled with both guilt and relief. I had begun the walk believing that I was a responsible risk-taker. Yes, I knew that others had lost their lives in the Australian bush, but I believed that it would never happen to me.

Some valuable life lessons

Well, my mistakes had nearly cost me my life and the lives of my mates. From then on, I knew that 'it could happen to me'. It was the greatest lesson I could ever have.

Now looking back at this frightening bushwalk, I realise the experience was to save my life in further adventures. Never again would I forget the Scout motto 'Be Prepared'.

CHAPTER 6

Dick Smith, 'sales engineer'

I now began to focus on work at Findlay Communications and to save everything I could for a deposit on land. In those days, buying a block of land was what all young people tried to do. I had about $800, which was all I needed as a deposit to buy a good block at Roseville or Frenchs Forest, which were selling for three thousand dollars. But before I bought anything, my life took an exciting twist.

Every year, Tony Balthasar spent two to three months attending various medical conferences in Europe. Now, because of his interest in Scouts, he desperately wanted to attend a climbing course at the Kandersteg International Scouting Centre in the Bernese Oberland region of Switzerland, but he lacked the confidence to do it by himself.

One day he asked, 'Dick, if I gave you an air ticket around the world, would you come with me on the climbing course?' It was an offer I couldn't refuse.

In early 1966, I resigned from my job and Tony and I boarded a Qantas flight from Sydney Airport to Singapore, Malaysia, Bangkok, Hong Kong and Japan. That first week of my planned eight months away was an incredible eye opener. Tony had booked into his usual hotels—Raffles in Singapore, the Oriental in Bangkok and the Peninsula in Hong Kong. I had never experienced anything like it in my life—palm court orchestras and the most magnificent food.

In Japan, we split up. I wanted to ski at Shiga Highlands in Nagano, while Tony flew directly to England. Besides the fantastic skiing, I was amazed that although it was only twenty-one years since the end of World War II, there was no sign of it. As I immersed myself in the cultural differences little did I know I would be back in Japan for business many times in the years to come.

From Japan, I flew to Calcutta (probably because everyone said don't go there), then travelled to Darjeeling, where I met Tenzing Norgay, who, with Edmund Hilary, had made the first ascent of Mt Everest. I visited his Himalayan Mountaineering Institute.

I continued through the Middle East, visiting Egypt, Jerusalem and Lebanon. I even went into beautiful Damascus in Syria, which was a most wonderful, friendly place. I travelled on to Athens and Rome, then to London, where I met up with Tony. We stayed at the Scout-owned Baden-Powell House in South Kensington, before we hopped on a bus with other Australians and travelled behind the Iron Curtain, to celebrate May Day 1966 in Moscow.

A cold wind swept through Red Square as we joined hundreds of thousands Muscovites to watch as dozens of the government's new SS-95 Intercontinental Ballistic Missiles were paraded past. We had no idea at the time that each one carried three nuclear warheads that would threaten the West for nearly a decade. Instead, some of us joined part of the march just for fun.

After leaving Moscow, we travelled back through Poland and East Germany, passing from East to West Berlin through the Berlin Wall. It took me back to when I worked at Findlay Communications, when the song 'West of the Wall' was played on the factory floor.

Tony and I bought a Mini Minor and drove through France, Spain and Italy. In Kandersteg, we attended the ten-day Scout climbing course. Although Tony wasn't an experienced climber, I led him over the Gellihorn, a huge rock spire in the region. I went on to climb the Fründenhorn and Balmhorn, but, on the second last day of the course, one of our Scouts fell and died.

This was one of a very few fatalities in the many Kandersteg courses. Interestingly, although it was a tragedy, not much was made of it. There was an understanding that mountaineering, indeed most exciting activities, involved risk. Today an accident like this would be beaten up in the media and there would be calls to stop such activities.

After Kandersteg, Tony and I returned to London, where he stayed on for medical conferences, while I continued on through the United States and New Zealand and then back to Australia. In my eight months away, I visited forty-three countries and, boy, did my outlook on life change.

I saw both affluence and poverty. In Calcutta, I joined one of the huge hunger marches sweeping the country. Then I visited splendid European cathedrals. In fact, I met lovely people from dozens of different faiths. Surely this cast doubt on the notion that one's own faith could be the only true one. If this was the case, everyone else, those millions of others who belonged to other religions (often because of where they were born), were mistaken. I found this difficult to accept.

I found myself re-evaluating many of my own notions and prejudices. In drab Moscow, I saw firsthand the failure of communism in the Soviet Socialist Republic. Yet while travelling by bus through the Soviet Union, I found that all of the people we met were incredibly friendly, despite what we had been led to believe back home. Remember, this was at the height of the Cold War—only a few years after my nightmares of a nuclear attack on Sydney.

I remember an Australian girl who was travelling with us dancing with a Russian soldier at a nightclub we were visiting. The girl's fiancé was fighting in Vietnam and here she was dancing with a soldier who represented 'the enemy'.

'What a crazy world,' I thought. 'Why shouldn't they dance together? After all, they were simply two young people out enjoying themselves.' Like most people I met on my world tour, Russians were not too different to us. In fact, wherever I was, I found most people to be friendly, especially if you introduced yourself with a smile.

Of all the lessons I learned on that trip, by far the most important one was how incredibly lucky I am to be Australian. I would never say we're the best country in the world—many people say that about their country. But I certainly say, we're 'one of the best' countries in the world and are indeed fortunate people.

When I returned to Australia, the first thing I did was fly to Cooma and then catch a bus to Jindabyne. I planned to surprise my friends Bob and Nancy Pallin, who were ski touring at Lake Albina in the Snowy Mountains.

On my way from Cooma to Jindabyne, and then up to Thredbo, I stared out through the window at the distant mountains rising from the plains. I almost felt hypnotised by the beautiful patterns on the trunks of snow gums and sunlight playing across the granite outcrops. The landscape was so uniquely Australian and it felt wonderful to be back.

When Aboriginal people talk of their love for the land, I have a strong sense of what they mean. Eight months was the longest time I had ever been away from Australia. As we began to wend our way up the Thredbo Valley, I vowed I would never go away for so long again—and I never have.

———

On my return, as a twenty-two year old I was keenly aware of my lack of qualifications in electronics, so I was considering a major career change. After all, my other great love was the out of doors!

My dad knew Bill Little, who ran the Koala Sanctuary for the Ku-ring-gai Chase Trust, north of Sydney, and suggested I ask him for advice about getting a job as a National Parks ranger. Dad thought that because Bill had been a park ranger for many years, he should have some clues.

In fact, the advice he gave me did have an effect on my life. It was simple and to the point. 'Dick, don't become a park ranger,' Bill said. 'Stick to what you know, that's electronics. Being a ranger wouldn't suit you. The bureaucracy would kill your enthusiasm and you'd be wasting your potential.'

Fortunately, Weston Electronics, the company I worked for after completing my Leaving Certificate, had moved from Sydenham to Eastern Valley Way, only ten minutes from my home. I called in to see if they had any jobs and was interviewed by its three top executives, including its company founder and its general manager.

By now I knew that I'd never get anywhere as a serviceman installing and servicing two-way radios, so I said I wanted a job as a salesman. The trio listened politely while I made my pitch, then asked the standard question: 'What experience have you had?'

None, of course, but I managed to say, 'Look, I think I could be a good salesman,' before Alan Walker, the general manager, cut me off: 'Sorry, Dick, we don't have any sales jobs, but you were always a good two-way radio serviceman. We'd like to offer you a job in the workshop and you can start tomorrow.'

At that time, few people were without a job for more than two or three days and I certainly didn't want to be. I was flat broke, having spent all my money on my overseas trip. I said I'd think about it, went back home and each morning scanned the paper for jobs.

On the third day, I convinced myself that I was crazy not to accept the servicing job and was just about to ring Weston's when the phone rang. It was Alan Walker, saying that they wanted to offer me a salesman's job with a probationary period of six months. If I proved myself, I would be given a permanent position. What an amazing piece of luck!

I soon had the salesman's job I wanted, my own office and a salary of $60 a week; and, instead of wearing a dustcoat, I wore a business suit. Embarrassingly, when they printed my business cards they read, 'Dick Smith, Sales Engineer'. I was worried about showing them to my friends (some of whom were still studying to become real engineers), because I wasn't a qualified engineer and didn't want to put on false airs.

I faced a few other challenges as well. My handwriting was atrocious and, as a salesman, I had to write out the order dockets. So every evening, with Mum and Dad's help, I sat at home trying to improve my writing. What made it worse, I couldn't spell either.

What a steep learning curve. Ray Dickinson, the sales manager, was highly disciplined and a hard taskmaster. In fact, my workmates said, 'Dick, you'll last about two weeks with Ray Dickinson, no one ever does, no one can get on with him.'

In fact, it was just the opposite. I learned so much from Ray and Alan, and respected just how astute they were at business, that a few years later, when Dick Smith Electronics was booming, I hired them both.

At Weston's, I soon discovered that my main competitor was my old boss, Maurie Findlay. Maurie was an engineer (a 'real' one), plus he was a much better salesman than me. For the first four months, I made virtually no sales at all, losing them to Findlay Communications or companies including AWA and STC. The only advantage I had was price. The radio I was selling was cheaper than any of the others.

I was taught to say that the sets could be leased for 40 cents per day, rather than mention their capital cost. I was helped to draft a letter to send out to real estate agents, doctors, plumbers and electricians, and these generated sales contacts. I was soon dealing with government departments, including the police, and wealthy owners of boats , who invited me to quote prices for the marine radios we manufactured. My dream was to become a top salesman and earn $200 a week by the time I was thirty.

But a major change was about to happen in my life.

———

Outside of work, I learned that while I had been overseas my Rover crew had become pals with the Pittwater Rangers, the Girl Guide equivalent to Rover Scouts. A month after I got back, I was invited to show my slides of climbing in Kandersteg at the home of two of the Rangers, Susie and Pippy McManamey. Even though it was a Rover/Ranger function and we were supposed to wear our uniforms, I was so proud of my new job that I wore my business suit, using the excuse that I hadn't had time to change.

About a dozen or so Rovers and the same number of Rangers, all about sixteen to nineteen years of age, showed up. Two of the Rangers stood out, the McManamey sisters. Identical twins, they were definitely the best looking. Susie, the oldest by about thirty minutes, was vivacious and had tremendous confidence. Philippa, or Pip, was quiet, shy and, I thought, really cute.

What really impressed about the function being held at their house was that although their mum, Joy, was a Brownie leader, the girls seemed to run the household. I liked Pip instantly, but when I was told that she and her sister were seventeen and still at school, I ruled them out as being far too young. In fact, I remember thinking, 'Wow, I wish I was five years younger.'

The following Sunday, the Rovers and Rangers went out on a boat belonging to one of the parents. As we motored up Pittwater, I found myself sitting next to Pip at the bow of the boat. When I reached over and held her hand, she didn't pull away. It was thrilling. Within weeks I'd put aside my scruples about our age difference and began courting Pip whenever I could, even picking her up from school and dropping her home.

On our first date, we joined Bob and Nancy Pallin at a city theatre to see *Born Free*. When the lights went out, I snuck a kiss on Pip's cheek—I was a fast mover! I should mention that Pip's dad, Peter, owned a boatshed. Can you imagine that? A pretty girl who's not only a Queen's Guide and Ranger, but whose dad owns a boatshed? I thought there couldn't be a better girlfriend anywhere in the world.

Then, just before my birthday in March, Pip gave me a beautifully tailored shirt. When I took it home, my mother noticed the sleeves were a bit long.

'Don't worry, Dick,' she said, 'I'll take it to the shop and change it.'

As she peered inside for the brand label, she looked shocked.

'Pip has made this shirt,' my mother said. 'It's handmade, it's beautiful.'

When I invited Pip home, she was the only girlfriend I'd had who leapt up and helped Mum in the kitchen. She had the loveliest nature and she was calm and easygoing. Yes, she was also very shy and would sit in the car for hours not saying a thing, which I did find challenging. In the end, we came to an agreement. Each day we'd both read sections of the *Sydney Morning Herald* and then discuss them. At least then we had something to talk about.

Dick Smith, 'sales engineer'

When I visited Pip at her home, I noticed that she and Susie would do most of the housework, and cook for and organise their two brothers. What I didn't realise was that Pip's parents were breaking up and that Pete was at the pub each night until closing time. Often when he came home, he and Pip's mum would argue, sometimes to the point where they would throw things at each other. But, as was often the case in those days, such trauma was hidden.

Pip's dad, whom she has always described as 'a lovely scally-wag', was quite unreliable—sometimes leaving the twins sitting in the car while he was at the pub. If they arranged a time to meet, he often wouldn't turn up.

Pip told me that two of the things she liked about me were that I didn't drink and I was very reliable. I didn't drink because I didn't like the taste of the stuff and I was always reliable because that's what I had been taught by my mum and dad. Very simply, they believed you should behave towards others as you would like them to behave towards you.

My parents also influenced my choice of girlfriends. In our household, Dad was the breadwinner and Mum was the home-maker. Naturally, I thought this was the norm and, selfishly, I wanted someone who was likely to look after me.

There was a problem, but a fun one. Pip and Susie were identical twins. In fact, many people couldn't tell them apart. My friend, John Webster, was taking Susie out at the time and one day I accidentally put my arm around her and gave her a cuddle. That earned a quick rebuke from John.

'Rack off,' he said. 'You've got your one.'

Another thing that attracted me to Pip was her willingness to participate in everything I wanted to do. No matter what it was: caving, rock climbing, amateur radio or even just going to the pictures, Pip was always enthusiastic.

Once we went with the Rovers and Rangers to Echo Point at Katoomba, in the Blue Mountains. Showing off, I grabbed a 120-foot coil of rope, tied Pip on the end and said, 'We're going to climb the first of The Three Sisters.'

It's only a moderate climb, but it pushes up vertical cliffs that are terribly exposed. In some places, a mistake would have been fatal, yet she came up with me. When we reached the top, I asked, 'Have you ever abseiled before?'

'No,' she replied.

'I'll show you how to do it,' I said, and we promptly did a risky descent onto the Honeymoon Point stairway. These days it's illegal to climb or abseil on The Three Sisters. This is primarily because of the trend to eliminate risk from our lives, which is sad.

But for Pip and me, the Blue Mountains were our playground. I took her down the extremely challenging Claustral Canyon, where we successfully navigated the Black Hole of Calcutta, a stunning cylindrical tunnel that drops 15 metres. We explored beautiful Tuglow Caves in Kanangra-Boyd National Park. Yes, my seventeen-year-old girlfriend may have been five years my junior, but she passed my most stringent test—she loved the outdoors.

And I can't explain why, but I simply had the feeling that the love Pip and I had for each other would last. Perhaps it was our Scout and Guide training, but we believed in the same things.

CHAPTER 7

Picking up the basics of business

With a steady girlfriend and my new job as a salesman at Weston Electronics, things were looking up. My overseas trip had given me confidence and in my first year at Weston's, I went from being a hopeless salesman to the best they had.

Weston's was an extremely well run company. Its founder, Sel Weston, was a bank manager who had started his own business manufacturing radios that sheep and cattle stations could use to contact the Royal Flying Doctor Service. He then began making taxi, marine and aircraft two-way radios.

By the time I worked for Weston's, it had been taken over by the public company Jacoby Mitchell. For some reason, Jack Jacoby took a liking to me. He even sent me off on a two-day marketing course, but I didn't understand a word of what was taught. Who would have guessed how soon I would pick it up?

The company was an ethical one and was really tough when it came to giving credit. If you bought a two-way radio system, you paid for it the day it was installed. One day I sold a system to a taxi truck company and installed it. When I got back to the office, Alan Walker, the general manager, asked, 'Where's the cheque?'

'Oh, they said they'd pay me tomorrow,' I replied.

The look Alan gave me was enough. I jumped back in the car and drove to the other side of the city to pick up the cheque.

At Weston's, I made sure I learned everything I could about the business, not because I thought I would start my own, but on the chance that one day I might become managing director— maybe even on my longed-for wage of $200 a week.

Every couple of days, I'd walk through the factory and talk to the production and service managers, then go into the laboratory to see the design engineer. I asked about everything that was happening, including how the radios were priced, what profit we made on each and what discount I could offer. As we'd just started importing eight-track tape players from Japan, I also learned what margins we needed when importing.

I learned that we were losing sales to our competitor, AWA, because they were selling their radios with a telephone-style handset, rather than a standard hand microphone. This gave the impression that the car was fitted with a radio telephone, just like the one used by James Bond. I harassed our design engineers to make something similar, but they never seemed to have the time.

No problem. I modified a National Panasonic intercom system in my dad's workshop and brought it out at the next sales meeting. There was an embarrassed silence—salesmen weren't supposed to work this way. I then produced a paper showing not only the pricing, but the plan of how the circuit should be wired. Soon afterwards, we were importing handsets that could be modified to my design.

At the time, it was very difficult to find anyone to install radio masts for two-way radio systems. A typical two-way radio system for, say, a real estate agency consisted of a base station with a radio mast at head office, with mobile radios installed in the agents' vehicles. This gave me another idea. With my fellow Rover Scout, David Larkin, we set up a small company to install the masts on weekends.

After a year at Weston's, I was still earning $65 a week plus a mileage allowance, as I was driving my own car—a Volkswagen Beetle that I was paying off. At about that time, I was approached by the general manager of an opposition company, Vinten.

'Dick,' he said, 'I've heard about your sales success. Come work for us and we'll pay you sixty-five dollars per week and provide a new company car.'

I went straight back to Alan Walker at Weston's and told him of the offer.

His response was, 'Stay with us and we'll increase your wage and give you a company car.' Soon I was driving a beautiful

EH Holden, decked with two-way radio aerials. It was completely paid for by the company, including petrol costs for my private driving. This, with the money coming from radio mast installations, meant I was doing pretty well financially.

———

In January 1968, about twelve months after I began taking Pip out, I asked her if she would marry me and she said, 'Yes'. Pip was eighteen and had just left school two months before.

Of course, I had to ask her dad for his approval. When I spoke to Peter, he asked, 'What are your prospects? What are your plans for the future?'

'My plan is to earn two hundred dollars a week by the time I'm thirty,' I replied.

This seemed a staggering amount of money—over three times what I was earning. Fortunately for me, Pip's father and mother eventually said yes. In those days, you needed parental permission to marry someone under twenty-one years of age.

Pip wanted to become a teacher (and she would have been fantastic), but in those days you had to win a teacher's scholarship. Despite achieving a good mark in the Higher School Certificate, she didn't get one and decided to enrol in a secretarial course instead.

As soon as we agreed to get engaged, I rushed out to an Angus & Coote jewellery shop and bought an engagement ring for $60, the cheapest they had. It was all we could afford, because we had to save up to get married.

Not long after, I was becoming dissatisfied with my job at Weston's. Our competitors, AWA and STC, had moved into modern transistorised radios, while we were still selling valve radios, which were less reliable. I tried to get our engineers to bring out our own transistor radio, but they always had a reason why they couldn't.

Even though I was doing well, I knew we had an inferior product and I didn't feel good about selling it. It put me in conflict with the values I was taught by my parents and the Scout movement, which included being honest about what you do.

When I brought this up with Alan, he reminded me that the most important thing was loyalty to the company. 'You should sell the product because it's the company's product,' he said, but it just didn't seem right.

Also about this time, Weston's decided to stop servicing Manly Cabs' radios and focus on manufacturing. When I heard this, I thought, 'If I could start a business servicing the Manly Cab radios, it would be enough to cover my overheads. Then I might be able to get the agency for STC's and AWA's latest transistorised radios.' Not only would I feel better, because I would be selling the best, but I'd also be running my own business.

I discussed it with Pip. We hadn't set a date for our wedding, but we both knew that starting a business might delay it. I also thought that if I was going out on my own, before getting married I'd better see if I could make enough to support a wife. In those days, most of us were raised to believe that the husband should be the provider.

Pip supported me completely, even though leaving a good job and starting my own business was a risky idea. I discussed with Pip that it could mean really hard work and long hours for two or three years and we agreed that if after that time the business didn't work, I would close it down and get a 'normal' job.

I had already saved up a bit by having a company car and what we made from installing aerials on weekends. I knew I could sell the second-hand boat I'd bought for six hundred dollars. To raise the extra capital I needed, I asked Tony Balthasar whether he would loan me up to $12,000 at the current rate of bank interest—6 per cent—and reminded him of our discussion on Lord Howe Island. He agreed to the loan.

I then made a list of the following requirements for my first business premises:

Location—must be somewhere with plenty of passing traffic and easily described in advertisements.

Rent—must be very low, as it would have to come out of income before I could pay any money back into the business.

Parking—must be easy to get to for taxi cabs, and have space for customers to park their cars easily.

Lease—must be short, say six to twelve months, so if the business didn't do well, I wouldn't be paying it off for the rest of my life.

To begin with, I went to local real estate agents, until I worked out that was a complete waste of time—the good premises were snapped up before they even got listed. I ended up spending every night and all weekends driving up and down the lower North Shore before I found a small space, half underground, in the car park of the Big Bear Shopping Centre in Neutral Bay.

At the time, it was being used to store old shop fittings and the property manager couldn't believe I wanted to rent such a dump. In fact, it fulfilled my criteria exactly, especially the rent, which was only $15 per week, with a lease period of six months.

One of the most important things when starting a new business is keeping your 'outgoings' as low as possible. Don't pay for anything if you can get it for nothing, and don't buy anything new if you can get it second-hand.

For the next few weekends, Pip, I and some of my Rover friends worked furiously to clean the place up. We pushed tonnes of shop fittings to another corner of the car park. To keep overheads to the barest minimum, Pip used her mum's sewing machine to make hessian curtains to line the walls and save the cost of timber.

I was so keen to save money that when we found there were no back plates on the fluorescent lights, rather than buy them for $3 apiece, we used painted masonite for about 50 cents each. By a stroke of luck, a carpet in the home unit owned by Tony's solicitor had recently been damaged by water and he donated it to us.

I must make it clear here that I had no visions of great success. My dream was to have a business like Howard Car Radio at Chatswood. Les Howard had four or five employees and in my view had reached the height of success.

I decided to call the business 'Alltronics'. I thought it sounded like a smart name for a company selling and servicing radio equipment. Like most people starting a business for the first time, I felt it was terribly important to have a professional letterhead and business card (it's not), so I drew up some designs. When I showed them to Peter Garrett, my cousin's husband, who was in advertising, he said, 'With a name like Dick Smith, why wouldn't you be using it as your company name?'

When I told him that I hoped to do work with prestigious brands like Mercedes-Benz and Rolls Royce and couldn't imagine owners of such cars being impressed with a common name like Dick Smith, he convinced me I was wrong, that Dick Smith was an advertiser's dream.

It was about the only thing others couldn't compete with— there was only one of me. And though I didn't know it at the time, it would allow me to link my personal adventures and activities to the business to great advantage. So that night at Peter's kitchen table, I took his advice, and Dick Smith Electronics was born.

I was also learning the first of what I was to call my 'success secrets': *Ask advice.*

I would have liked to start the business just on my own, to keep the overheads really low, but knew that I needed someone to help while I was out drumming up new business. I approached my close friend from Rover Scouts, John Webster (yes, Webby from the Colo walk), who agreed to work for me as a radio serviceman for $65 a week.

Picking up the basics of business

To keep the overheads as low as possible, I bought a second-hand Morris Major for $40—good enough to get me to and from work.

So my weekly overheads were: a $65 wage for Webby, $20 for his car, $15 shop rent and a $40 wage for me. I was still living at home and paying board to Mum and Dad, so could just scrape through. I also had the interest payment on my loan from Tony, but, because I only needed $4500 of the $12,000 he'd agreed to lend me, my total outgoings were less than $180 a week. I put in $600 of my own money from the boat sale and Pip put in $10 from her own savings.

Little did I realise that this was the start of a business that one day would turn over more than a billion dollars a year.

I estimated that if we charged out our service work at $4 an hour—and I knew I could get enough business to keep John busy for forty hours each week—this would almost cover the overheads. Any sales I picked up would be profit. Maintaining my constant focus on these simple figures became an obsession that I would apply to my businesses for the next forty years. I couldn't shake the memory of my father's business failure and the terrible nervous breakdown he'd suffered. I didn't want this to happen to me.

Advertising would have to be as inexpensive as possible, so I came up with an idea that was ahead of its time. I made up a 2 metre by 3 metre masonite panel, painted it black and stuck large day-glo letters on it that read 'DICK SMITH CAR RADIO AT BIG BEAR'.

I mounted this huge sign on the roof of my Morris Major, which I parked in an exposed spot on major roads along the North Shore. The sign cost only $40 to make, but the amount of advertising it gave the business was substantial, as many thousands of potential customers saw it during both the morning and afternoon peak hour.

It was incredibly important to keep my outgoings to the absolute minimum; I knew that most new businesses fail in the first twelve months because their outgoings are higher than what they are bringing in. Once a business becomes well known and its earnings rise, so too can its expenses.

As for potential earnings, STC agreed to supply me with its two-way radios. These were fully transistorised and simply the best in Australia. As well, I was banking on servicing radios for Manly Cabs. With its fleet of about a hundred cars, at 50 cents per car, I expected to earn $50 a week. I'd also been in touch with ABC Cabs, just up the road. Their response was encouraging.

As we were set up to work on motor vehicles, I thought we could also branch into the installation and repair of conventional car radios and cassette players. Even though I knew very little about car radios, any extra business I could bring in would be helpful. In those days, most new cars were supplied without a car radio.

But when I contacted car radio companies like AWA, Ferris, Kriesler and HMV to see if they would supply me with their products, their response was unenthusiastic. At about this time, a number of radio and electrical businesses were going into liquidation following the collapse of the giant electrical chain H.G. Palmer Ltd.

I also learned, after signing the lease, that many previous companies at Big Bear had gone broke. So when I rang the radio manufacturers and told them my name was Dick Smith (groan, sounded too common), that I was in the car radio business (groan, many were going broke) and that my address was Big Bear (more groans), I found that in most cases they wouldn't even accept a cheque from me. I had to pay in cash.

This was actually to my advantage, as it made me disciplined in ordering stock so that I didn't end up with too much of it. It was also great because, when customers wanted credit terms from me, I could truthfully say, 'Look, this is just a new business and I simply don't have enough money to give credit.'

———

Tuesday, 6 August 1968 was one of the most exciting days of my life. The opening day for Dick Smith Electronics. I was twenty-four years old and I would never, ever work for anyone again.

I jumped out of bed early, was wished good luck by Mum and Dad, gave Pip a quick phone call before she went to business college and hopped in the Morris Major with the sign on the roof. On busy Eastern Valley Way, I parked on a very visible bend and then hitchhiked to the Big Bear.

All ready to go, Webby and I opened the shop's doors and waited for business to roll in. After half an hour with no customers, disappointed and impatient I hitched back and shifted my car down towards the Spit Bridge, a busier thoroughfare than Eastern Valley Way. I parked it where everyone could see it, then hitched back to the shop, where Webby was beside himself with excitement. He'd made the first ever sale for Dick Smith Electronics!

'What did you sell?' I asked.

'A lock-down aerial, for four dollars,' he replied proudly. When I heard this, my jaw dropped. It was the wrong price. We'd bought it for $3 and should have sold it for five. John explained that there was no price on it, so he'd looked up the cost and whacked on a dollar.

I instantly knew what I'd done wrong. Because I knew all the prices, I hadn't bothered to mark one on each item. But John was a service technician and couldn't be expected to know hundreds of different prices. Immediately I raced out to the local newsagent and bought a packet of small, blank, sticky labels. From then on, any item large enough to take a price sticker had one.

I believe I've made just about every mistake there is in business, but I only made each one once, and I remember every one I've made. I've also found that you can judge the success of a business if items are clearly price-marked. Check this out for yourself. Mediocre businesses that are destined to fail never have everything price-marked.

By the end of Dick Smith Electronics' first day, our sales only totalled about fifty dollars. Fortunately, though, we had serviced some cab radios, and the income from these covered our outgoings. It was an exciting start.

On our third day of trading, a man came in and asked us to supply and install a car radio. This was fantastic because a car radio sold for about $120, earning us a profit of 40 per cent, or nearly fifty dollars. This was enough to cover our outgoings for several days. However, I'd never installed a car radio in my life and was understandably nervous about it.

We were to put a Ferris 189 radio and speaker into a Holden HK, a job that would normally take an hour and a half. Fortunately, the customer left his car with us, so he couldn't see what novices Webby and I were. Following the instructions, we pulled the heater control cables down and tried to push the speaker up behind them. We worked and worked on it for two hours, but couldn't fit the speaker in place, so we began installing the radio and aerial instead.

We were still working on it when the customer returned at 6 p.m., and by 7.30 p.m., we managed to get the radio working—with the speaker dangling from the dash on its wire. By now our valued first car-radio customer was getting a bit agitated, especially when he spied me trying to read the installation instructions.

Finally, I had to admit defeat. Using insulation tape, I stuck the speaker under the dash and asked the customer to return the following day for 'final adjustments'. Knowing he would be back the next day eased my conscience.

Early the following morning, I rang the Ferris factory and learned that the instructions were wrong. They were very apologetic, but all we had to do was take out the glove box and slide the speaker in sideways. The customer, no doubt being of reasonable intelligence, wasn't going to have anything else to do with Dick Smith. I never saw him or his car again.

From this shaky start, I worked flat out, seven days a week, and was happy to do so. Pip attended business college during the week and would come in on Friday afternoons and Saturday mornings to help. John serviced taxi radios, while I rushed all over the place to drum up more business.

On Sundays, Pip and I would clean the shop, then I would service radios from Manly and ABC Cabs that we'd not been able to finish during the week. Every weeknight, I did the paperwork. I had no intention of spending the rest of my life working long hours, but I knew that the extra work in the early days would, in time, pay for itself.

After three months, we had good money coming in and I was able to raise my salary to $80 a week and lease a new Holden Belmont, the cheapest Holden available. We began running small ads in the *North Shore Times* and I spent a lot of time calling in on car dealers in the area, but with no success. They had been getting their work done satisfactorily by Howard Car Radio in Chatswood for years and weren't interested in changing. I hoped that if I persisted, one day Howard's might not be able to do an installation and I would have my chance.

But I needed a good excuse to keep calling in on them every couple of weeks. I racked my brains, then realised that prices were constantly changing and none of the dealers had a well set out trade price list. The next weekend, I wrote out a full trade price list, including selling suggestions and notes on which car radio best suited each vehicle. Pip typed this up and I had fifty copies duplicated, which I placed inside bright folders with a day-glo *Dick Smith* sticker on the cover. I then gave a copy to each car dealer in the area.

This kept me visible. I just had to wait for a dealer to be let down. Not long after, our first trade job came in. It was from the Mosman Service Centre, which specialised in Volkswagens. Their usual supplier, Howard, hadn't been able to provide a radio when needed, so we got the job.

By now our service was unbelievable. We had low over-heads and were prepared to work long hours, and our prices were lower than our competition. I'd also put on Marshall Gill, who had been working for Universal Car Radios and knew a lot about servicing and installations. I paid him $67 per week, well worth it because we now had someone who actually knew something about car radios.

After four months, with business already booming, ABC Cabs decided to replace their two-way radios. They'd always used AWA radios, but I convinced them to switch to STC, the brand I sold. On each of the fifty radios I sold, I received a $20 commission, plus $15 for installation. The total was $1750, a stupendous amount of money for me in those days.

———

By January 1969, we had so much work and so much stock that we needed larger premises. I was already earning my dream wage of $200 a week and I wasn't yet thirty years of age. In fact, I was only twenty-four.

My accountant told me I'd made $8000 net profit in only five months, but I didn't believe him. How could I have made this money, but not see it? He explained patiently that there was actually no money in hand but, if I added up the increase in my stock and the provisional tax I had paid, a simple calculation would confirm the profit I'd made.

Nonetheless, I relied on my own manual system of painstakingly writing down the gross profit of each cash sale and invoice, and at the end of the week I'd add up those amounts to make sure the gross profit exceeded the outgoings.

As the company grew, and with it the number of shops I had, I wrote down the relevant figures for each shop in a simple exercise book. Yes, I needed accountants to prepare the company's profit and loss statement, balance sheet and tax returns (which even today I have never understood), but I found that even with a moderately large business, my simple system was a terrific way to check how I was going. And I always reckoned I knew this at least six weeks ahead of the accountants.

Having run out of room at the Big Bear, I began looking for new premises. Eventually I found an unused chocolate factory on the Pacific Highway at Gore Hill. It looked ideal, but when the real estate agent told me the rent was $120 per week, I ruled it out. The limit I'd set for myself was $30, double what I was paying at the Big Bear.

Fortunately, I remembered my number 1 success secret: *Ask advice*. I had met a very successful businessman, Ray Jessup, an engineer and entrepreneur who owned a very profitable company. He had an Alfa Romeo, a twin-engine speedboat and his own plane. Common sense alone said I should ask him advice, and he had the most wonderful way of explaining how to make sensible business decisions.

When I told Ray about the chocolate factory and why I'd turned it down, he said, 'Dick, you've just told me you've made eight thousand dollars profit in your first five months of business. Now you're looking for new premises. You've found something suitable but they're asking one hundred and twenty dollars per week for it—and you say that's too much for you.

'Personally, I think you'd be mad not to snap it up, even at that rent. The place is larger than the one you've got now, you need the extra space, and look where it is—right on the Pacific Highway, where you'll have all that extra passing trade.'

I stopped and thought, 'Crikey, he's right!' He made it sound so simple and logical. The next day, I parked outside the building at Gore Hill and counted cars passing by. I estimated there were four times as many as at Big Bear. This had to mean more business. I decided then and there I would take the place.

When I went to discuss the term of my lease with the building's owner, Ray came with me. Halfway through, Ray suddenly said, 'Of course, we'll need an option to purchase. There is no way we will rent the building without an option to purchase.'

I was shocked. There was no way I could ever buy a building like that. I didn't even have a house, and surely I would want one before buying a business premises. I didn't have any cash at the time and still owed Tony Balthasar about four and a half thousand dollars.

Ray then asked the owner how much he wanted for the building and was told sixty-two thousand dollars. That was an incredible amount, as a really good house in Sydney cost about half that. I had reservations, but signed a two-year lease at $120 per week with an option to purchase within two years. From then on, whenever I signed a new lease, I made sure I had an option to purchase when it was available. Many people believe that my money-making success has come from electronics and publishing, when actually most of it has come from the purchase and ownership of commercial properties.

We moved into 162 Pacific Highway, Gore Hill, at the end of January and business was strong from the start. A month later, Pip and I decided we would get married. By then I was confident I would be able to support my young wife. Pip was now working in the city as a secretary on $25 per week. Our wedding would have to be on a week day after business hours, so we settled on Wednesday, 26 March 1969, at 6.30 p.m.

On that day, I installed cab and car radios right up to five o'clock and then drove home to Mum and Dad's house, where

I was living. I quickly changed, raced to the church and was promptly married. Pip's dad paid for the wedding and my mum made Pip's wedding dress. Tony Balthasar lent us his Rolls Royce to drive back to the Gore Hill premises.

Leaving John Webster and Marshall Gill to run the business, Pip and I enjoyed a five-day honeymoon on Lord Howe Island—all the time we could spare. As I had vowed during the Ball's Pyramid expedition in 1964, having found my true love, Lord Howe Island would be where we honeymooned. Pip was nineteen and I had just turned twenty-five.

CHAPTER 8

Dick Smith, car radio nut

Not long after moving into our new premises at Gore Hill, I was lying under a car dashboard, installing a radio and chatting with a customer. His name was Neville Corbett, and he explained that he was an advertising agent and he was curious about how the business was doing.

I said it was fine, then asked, 'What does an advertising agent do?' I didn't really know.

'Just as it sounds,' he said. 'We organise advertising for people.'

'Then you're just who I need,' I said. 'I want to become so well known around Sydney that everyone will come to me to have their car radios installed. There's just one problem, I don't have much money.'

Neville thought for a moment. 'This could be an interesting challenge. How much money do you have?'

I did a quick mental sum. 'The most I can afford is fifty dollars a week.'

He paused, 'I'll work on it and get back to you.'

'I'll do anything to get the business going better,' I urged. 'You can call me anything you want—even a nut, because I am a bit of a nut.'

Neville showed up in a couple of days and took a photograph of me. A few days later, he brought over a rough draft of an advertisement. Beneath a deep etching of my head (that was later to become our famous 'dickhead' trademark) was the headline 'Dick Smith Car Radio Nut', then a paragraph of strange gobbledygook that looked like Latin.

On a separate sheet was the actual copy for the ad, beginning with, 'Dick Smith Car Radio Nut. Nice, but nutty never the less,' and continuing on with more text.

'The ad's terrific,' I told Neville. 'But what's all this Latin?'

'Body type,' he explained. 'It shows you what the ad will look like before we go to the expense of typesetting. This way you can decide whether you like the design or not before spending more money.'

Suddenly I had an idea. 'Hey, why don't we run the ad just like that? My head, Dick Smith Car Radio Nut, and then all the gobbledygook? Right at the bottom we can put our address and phone number.'

Neville looked doubtful. 'That's a bit crazy, isn't it?' he asked.

'Look,' I explained, 'I didn't know what it was until you told me. Nobody else will either, but crikey, they will talk about it and that's what we want, isn't it?' And that is how the first 'Dick Smith Nut' ad appeared.

As soon as it came out, the phones ran hot with people wanting to know what was going on. The ad had grabbed their attention, just what we wanted. Soon we had people coming from suburbs 50 kilometres away. They probably passed more experienced and possibly cheaper car radio specialists on the way, but the advertising gimmick made them curious to see who the bloke was who not only used a strange photo of himself, but called himself a nut.

By the end of June 1970, our second year of business, our turnover had risen to $162,000, an amazing amount. Over $3000 per week, with a net annual profit of $39,000. I was making more money than Australia's prime minister and was only twenty-six years old.

Pip and I eased our workload back to six days a week. On Sundays, we went bushwalking or took our small second-hand boat out for a spin. We also moved from Roseville to a small flat in Greenwich, only a ten-minute walk to our shop. We purchased all of our furniture second-hand from an auction place.

I needed a full-time secretary. The local employment agency sent me Mrs Dawn McCallum, and by the end of her first day, I knew we had a fantastic person working with us. She would stay for the next fifteen years.

I learned that a new radio system—selective calling—had been developed in the United States. While traditional two-way radio was like an old-fashioned party line, the new system allowed a particular vehicle to be called. STC had a system in the Australian market, but it was so expensive few small businesses could afford it.

I drew up a list of what a cheaper version would need and took it to Marshall Gill, our self-taught design engineer. He quickly came up with an inexpensive, selective calling system that could work with the STC two-way radios we sold.

We launched the new system in October 1970 and started manufacturing and selling it right away. Initially we sold to small companies, but we also had one sale of more than 700 units to the Postmaster-General's Department—incredible! Over time, sales of these units brought in more than $200,000, with a profit margin of around 50 per cent. Marshall also designed and built a low-cost AC power supply to run mobile two-way radios from mains power. We sold hundreds of these at our 50 per cent profit margin. Dick Smith Electronics was now a manufacturer as well as a servicing organisation.

At the end of 1970, Pip began working full-time for the business, helping with car radio and stereo sales and stock ordering. Some people didn't think this was such a good idea, because being together all day and night might create considerable friction. In fact, the opposite was true. We worked well together and it was a real help to me that Pip knew what was going on in the company.

In January 1971, when the option to purchase 162 Pacific Highway was due, we paid the $15,000 deposit and took out a first mortgage from a finance company. Throughout my career, I never had to deal with bank managers. Tony Balthasar's loan helped me at the start, and later, by pouring profits back in, I never had to borrow from banks. When we bought our commercial buildings, we raised the money we needed through finance companies.

Pip and I were still crammed into a tiny flat in Greenwich. We would have loved to put a deposit down on our own home but, while we were paying off the Gore Hill building, there wasn't much left. I had the idea of buying a small timber and aluminium kit home, for about five thousand dollars. As we couldn't afford to buy a block of land in Sydney, we found one in Jindabyne, New South Wales, near the ski fields, for a $600 deposit.

With a loan, we paid for the kit home and land. Every other weekend, we'd drive to Jindabyne at enormous speeds (no radar guns back then) to build the house. We planned to rent it out, with the hope that, in time, it would allow us to place a deposit on a Sydney home.

———

At that time, I was regularly going to George Brown Electrical Wholesalers in the city to buy the bits we needed to repair radios. I dreaded the trip, because every time I walked in, I'd find a line of up to a dozen customers waiting to be served.

When it was my turn, I might say, for instance, that I wanted to buy a resistor, a transistor and two capacitors. Someone behind the counter would go to the warehouse out the back, pick out the components, bring them to the counter and fill out a sales docket, calculating a tax of 27.5 per cent on some items, 15 per cent on others and leaving some that were exempt. What should have been a relatively simple ten-minute transaction could take up to half an hour.

It was obvious George Brown was making good profits. If it could do this with such bad service, what would happen if I started a similar business, but with the Dick Smith enthusiasm and service? Surely I would do well. It's true that I knew very little about wholesaling components, but it seemed pretty simple: locate premises, buy stock, put on a manager and a salesman, and the business would come.

With total capital of $15,000, we set up Dick Smith Wholesale. I found a small house, zoned commercial, in Atchison Street, Crows Nest for $80 a week and hired a manager who had previously worked at George Brown's. He brought along a young assistant experienced in selling electronic components.

I felt like this was a big step. I was already running Dick Smith Electronics with nine employees and turning over more than $250,000 a year, while paying off our Jindabyne house and the premises at Gore Hill.

In July 1971, just on three years after launching Dick Smith Electronics, Dick Smith Wholesale opened its doors. From the start, it barely covered its overheads. We were buying most components from George Brown, which of course already put a profit margin on them. The cost of selling was high, because sales tax had to be added to the mark-up on each item. I had also put on a salesman to encourage the local radio and electrical businesses to buy their components from us.

More importantly, because we sold virtually everything on credit, we could wait up to ninety days to be paid. I had gone from making a 40 per cent margin on high-priced car radios, to 15 per cent and less on low-cost electronic components. And little did I know that this was when I was about to enter one of the darkest times of my life.

———

In October 1971, just four months after Dick Smith Wholesale opened, I was surprised when the manager resigned, followed shortly afterwards by his assistant. This left no staff at Dick Smith Wholesale. I had no choice but to get behind the counter and run the business as a one-man show.

Two weeks later, Pip and I were at the wholesale shop on Saturday night when I picked up a supplier's invoice and noticed something strange about it. Suddenly it dawned on me—the order number was fake. I checked other invoices and found they also carried the same order number—2222. I compared the goods on the invoices with sales dockets, and then checked them against goods in stock.

By two o'clock Sunday morning, we had discovered that $18,000 worth of components had been stolen. We'd been taken for a ride. My heart was pounding. The business we had set up with $15,000 four months earlier had purchased stock worth $53,000 and now $18,000 of that stock was missing. I felt sick.

Pip and I drove home and spent the rest of the night tossing and turning, trying to figure out what we should do. It was an awful predicament. There was no way the business would be able to pay all the bills that were then outstanding.

In the morning, I contacted the North Sydney police and they applied for a search warrant for my ex-manager's address. Inside, they found what looked like my missing stock, but craftily the manager had auction receipts for it all. And because there are no serial numbers on the components, there was no way to prove they were mine.

I went straight to my solicitor and accountant and explained what had happened. After they heard the details, they said there was only one thing I could do—to put the business into liquidation. Liquidation? I didn't even know what it meant.

'Basically, you sell off the remaining stock and close the business down,' my accountant explained.

'What about the suppliers I owe money to?' I asked.

'That's bad luck for them. They gave credit to a limited liability company, so they will lose their money.'

I was shocked. How would I ever face people again if I owed them money?

'It happens all the time,' my accountant said. 'They knew there was a risk in giving your company credit.'

When my solicitor saw the look on my face, he offered an alternative. 'We could have a receiver appointed,' he said. 'That's a firm of accountants that runs the company and attempts to pay back your debts by trading the business out of its difficulties.'

'That's what I'll do,' I instantly replied. 'And when we've paid our debts, I'll close it down and remember it as an expensive lesson.'

My parents and the Scouts had ingrained in me that a person should be honest. This obviously included paying your debts. I had clearly made two mistakes. First, I had still been running Dick Smith Electronics, even installing car radios, and I hadn't had time to concentrate on Dick Smith Wholesale. Second, I didn't have an in-depth knowledge of the wholesale industry— just because I was successful in one business didn't mean I would automatically be successful in all businesses.

An accountancy firm was appointed as receivers of Dick Smith Wholesale and my first job was to invite all my creditors to a meeting and explain the situation.

I soon found that the accountants charged a receiver's fee of $1000 a month, almost exactly what we were making. After eight months, it was obvious we were getting nowhere. We weren't making anything extra to pay back our debts.

So I rang each of my major creditors and explained what was happening. I proposed instead that I remove the receivers and put in place a 'Scheme of Arrangement', an agreement where I would pay off my creditors at a fixed weekly amount. I got everyone's support for this.

I immediately paid off all the smaller creditors and then focused on the remaining eighteen, to whom I owed the greatest amount. I agreed to pay these companies in full, in fifteen monthly instalments.

———

Little was I to know at the time that this nearly broke company would within six years turn me into a multi-millionaire! This happened because of my second secret for success—*Copy the success of others*. I thought there had to be a better and simpler way of selling electronic components than the way I had been doing it so far. And there was.

I had noticed small advertisements appearing in *Electronics Australia* magazine that promoted a company called Kit Sets, which was selling components cheaper than anyone else. Kit Sets was located in Dee Why, on Sydney's Northern Beaches, so I drove over and found a small shop run by Garry Connelly. Garry told me that Kit Sets was doing well, not just from selling components over the counter but also through its mail order business.

Garry explained that he bought his stock directly from the manufacturers, thus removing the wholesale middleman, and that he paid the sales tax on the buying price not the marked-up selling price. Most importantly he did not give credit; everything was paid for at the time of purchase. This started me thinking that perhaps I should do the same. Rather than selling to small electrical repair shops, I could sell directly to electronic enthusiasts, both over the counter and by mail order.

I had no experience in mail order, but I was willing to ask for advice and copy the success of others. I remembered the four-page Price's Radio catalogue I had seen in *Radio & Hobbies* magazine in the fifties and had held on to. It had been more of a price list than a catalogue, but over time those four pages had become my bible. Could I do something like this, I wondered.

Overseas companies, like Lafayette Radio in America and Henry's Radio in London, were now advertising in magazines that were available in Australia, where they were inviting readers to send away for their catalogues. I did that and studied their catalogues. Was it possible that something similar could be produced in Australia?

At this time, Dick Smith Wholesale was stocking about 3000 items. I began searching for someone who could produce a catalogue for me, but the cheapest price I got would have cost me twenty thousand dollars. There was no way I could afford this.

As luck would have it, my mother gave me the name of a friend's son-in-law who had just arrived from England. Robin Cooper had produced a catalogue for the UK company Radio Spares. When we met, I explained that I wanted a really inexpensive catalogue. I didn't care if it didn't look very professional, as long as it listed all 3000 items with the selling price. Success secret number 3: *Surround yourself with capable people.*

Under Robin's guidance, I wrote the catalogue copy in my rough handwriting. I didn't know how to write good copy, so I took bits from the English and American catalogues and mixed them up (so I couldn't be accused of plagiarism). At night, Pip would type this up and we'd take it to a lady nearby who had an IBM composing machine at her house. I then photographed the components with my little Kodak camera, printed them up, cut them out and pasted them onto the artwork. Back at our Greenwich flat, Robin stuck the artwork and text onto stiff card while I looked over his shoulder. In time, I learned how to do this myself.

Our first catalogue was rough and ready, printed on low-quality paper with as much crammed onto each page as possible. People thought it was pretty amateurish, but I was sure it would keep an electronic enthusiast occupied for hours reading the information inside. I planned to print 5000 copies, but when the printer saw that I intended to sell them for 50 cents each, he laughed and said, 'Look, Dick, you'll have problems giving them away, let alone selling them.' So I changed the order to 3000, which cost me 17 cents each to print.

I then advertised the catalogue in my favourite magazine, *Electronics Australia*. I kept the price at 50 cents, but I included in it coupons that allowed a refund of that amount if you presented the coupons with your mail order.

When that month's *Electronics Australia* hit the newsstands, I sent John Morris, a young assistant, to our post office box on the very first day, but he returned empty-handed. It was the same the next day. But on the third, he raced into the shop on Atchison Street.

Whooping and screaming as he swung past the counter, he rushed to the rear of the shop and back again.

'What is it? What is it?' I cried.

'Look!' he yelled and showed me what he had clutched in his hand.

Unbelievably, he had not one, not two, but three mail orders—our first ever. In the second week, we received about thirty orders, and from then on the trickle became a flood. More incredibly, the money arrived with each order!

We sold more than 15,000 catalogues in the next seven months. At one stage I was making more money selling catalogues than components.

In the midst of this, on 22 July 1972, Hayley, our first daughter, was born. I was working hard to get Dick Smith Wholesale out of receivership (as well as running the car and two-way radio business), so had jokingly said to Pip, 'Look, you'll have to have the baby after business hours,' as I wanted to be present at the birth. Pip was working long hours in the business at the time.

Sure enough, I worked at Dick Smith Wholesale until noon that Saturday, and at 1.45 p.m. I made it to the Royal North Shore Hospital and was just outside the room when Hayley was born. It was the most exciting and moving time for Pip and me. Having our first child was wonderful and I'm glad it happened when we were so young.

When I saw Hayley for the first time, I promised to work even harder to get the business out of receivership and close it down quickly so Pip and I could start our lives over with our new daughter.

In October 1972, I had my second visit from a tall, young Canadian who would end up playing a crucial role in my businesses for years to come. Ike Bain had originally dropped by Dick Smith Wholesale on Atchison Street. We talked and I learned that he had only just arrived in Australia from Vancouver. I quickly recognised that he was a fellow electronics enthusiast.

Even though he was only twenty years old, he seemed very self-assured. I offered him a job servicing two-way radios, but he declined. He said he was interested in joining the New South Wales Police Force, but we agreed to stay in touch.

Ike came back a few months later. He'd taken on a job selling tools and automotive equipment in the Queen Victoria Building in the city and it didn't suit him. He would much prefer working with radio equipment. I had my service manager interview him for the job and we hired him as a two-way radio technician and installer on $80 a week. Little did I know that hiring Ike would be one of the most astute things I've done.

———

Our mail order business was going well, but I realised that our little house in Atchison Street was too small for both the over-the-counter sales and the mail order businesses. I had already learned that trying to run the business in different locations was a fundamental mistake, because I couldn't be in both places at once and had lost control of what was happening.

Next door to our Gore Hill car radio shop, two flats came up for rent. In December 1972, we moved in. I used the top flat for my office and moved Dick Smith Wholesale from Atchison Street to the bottom flat, having knocked out a couple of walls to make a larger shop. Most importantly, we put in shelves with open trays so that instead of the customer having to stand in front of a counter while a salesman searched for components out the back, the customer could select what they wanted for themselves. 'Self-service' made the sale really quick. Pip was working part-time doing the banking and typing at night while looking after Hayley.

In early March 1973, I invited Ike to our house for dinner. Since starting work at Dick Smith Electronics servicing taxi radios, he'd proved to be a capable technician, but that evening he brought up his frustrations with the way Dick Smith Wholesale was being run. Every few days, he had to come in to pick up parts for repairs and he wasn't happy about how much time was wasted due to parts being out of stock. He also felt the staff were pretty lacklustre and inattentive.

Ike later reckoned that I became agitated and said, 'Well, why don't you run the place then?'

The next morning, he showed up at my office and said, 'Dick, I've decided to take the job.'

I looked at him blankly. 'What are you talking about?' I asked.

'The job running the shop,' he said.

'You couldn't do that job,' I said. 'You've got no experience in running a components shop.'

Clearly, he had planned his approach, because he went through all the reasons why I should hire him for the job. I was unmoved until he offered to cut his salary from $80 to $60 a week. That got my attention.

'You can do it for three weeks,' I said.

Ike worked hard for those first three weeks. He cleaned up the shop, sent returned stock back to the manufacturers and even got the staff to improve their appearance. After three weeks, I extended his trial period to six weeks and increased his salary to $110 a week.

By then I had paid back the Dick Smith Wholesale debts. It was an incredible load off my mind. I would never make those mistakes again! Receivership taught me a lot, especially to only go into a business that I was able to give 100 per cent of my time to.

I also learned about human nature and who my friends really were. In the end, the terrible time that Pip and I went through following the theft turned out to be one of the best things that could have happened. Dick Smith Wholesale began as a failure, but it turned out to be the basis for the ultimate success of Dick Smith Electronics and its billion dollars a year turnover.

CHAPTER 9

A heady mix of catalogues and free publicity

With Ike taking on more responsibility at Dick Smith Wholesale, I had more time to consider how we might grow our mail order business.

I wrote to Lafayette Electronics in New York and explained that I was an Australian with a very small electronics business and was pretty inexperienced. I asked if I could visit their company to see how it all worked. It was a bit cheeky and I didn't really expect an answer, but ten days later, I received a letter from the vice president of Lafayette Electronics inviting me to call in if I was in the States and he would be happy to show me around.

This was terrific. Lafayette had something like sixty stores and was very successful, and here was the vice president offering to give me a tour. I immediately bought the cheapest around-the-world air tickets via London and the United States and on 6 June 1973, Pip and I took off from Sydney.

In London, I called in on Henry's Radio. Henry French, the owner, sent me to the mail order manager with instructions for him to give me whatever information I wanted. Their assistance was wonderful. At one point I asked if we might share the cost of the line drawings in their catalogue.

'Don't worry, Dick,' I was told. 'Use any of the line drawings you want, we've already paid for them.' They knew I wasn't competing with them, in fact I was selling to a market on the other side of the world. What a wonderful attitude.

When I visited Lafayette Electronics, I asked the receptionist to see the vice president. 'Which vice president do you mean?' she asked. After giving his name, I was led down a long corridor, passing door after door, all of which had vice president painted on them.

The people at Lafayette were tremendous. They showed me everything, from how their catalogue was produced to how an $80 million per year mail order system worked. They even told me what percentage of turnover they spent on advertising and what percentage on wages. I wrote it all down and asked if they would object to me using the same system back home. They were delighted. It proved to me that people love to be asked about what they do. It was yet again an example of two of my success secrets: *Ask advice* and *copy the success of others*.

Then, on 18 July, I received a shock. The newspapers announced that the Whitlam government had reduced import tariffs by 25 per cent. This was a huge change. Until then, nearly everything we sold was made in Australia. In fact, I was making good money manufacturing my selective calling equipment and power supplies, and I loved dealing with local companies.

But one by one, the local manufacturers supplying us closed down. The really astute ones immediately went overseas and began importing their products. In fact, within a year, Australia's imports rose by a third. As this was happening, I suddenly realised that it would be crazy to close down Dick Smith Wholesale once its debts were paid as I'd planned.

In fact, now that Gough Whitlam had removed the duty that protected Australian electronic manufacturers, Dick Smith Wholesale had the potential to make more money than our car and two-way radio and manufacturing businesses combined.

Having made the decision to keep Dick Smith Wholesale open, in October 1973 I sold the radio and manufacturing businesses and concentrated on selling components. I changed the name of Dick Smith Wholesale to Dick Smith Electronics so it more closely reflected what our business did. I was no longer a wholesaler selling parts to the trade, but selling directly to hobbyists.

I now had the building at Gore Hill available and I converted it into a shop. Yes, the place where I once lay under car dashboards installing car radios became Australia's largest shop for electronic enthusiasts. We did this based on what I had seen in the UK and the USA.

This, of course, was the building on which Ray Jessup had insisted I take an option to purchase. I challenged Ike to achieve $1 million turnover on our first twelve months trading in this new shop. And we did!

––––

After a busy couple of months planning, renovating and advertising, we opened the huge new store in early 1974. It was exciting to watch customers streaming in, clearly impressed by the air-conditioning, new carpeting and piped music. There were piles of catalogues and a valve tester (something I'd copied from Lafayette) and we invited customers to serve themselves from the wide range of products we carried. There was such a fantastic buzz that I had no regrets in changing the business from selling and servicing two-way and car radios to selling electronic components. On Saturday mornings, I would arrive to open the shop to find a long queue of twenty to thirty customers waiting to get in.

And by copying the best systems from overseas, choosing the right products and having them easily available through our self-service shop and our excellent mail order catalogue, the business was starting to boom.

I had learned from both Lafayette and Henry's Radio that I needed at least a 50 per cent margin on my products to cover overheads, especially the cost of the catalogue, and still make a reasonable profit. That meant a 100 per cent mark-up. With local manufacturers closing down because they could not compete with products made in Japan, I was forced more and more to buy from importers. The problem with this arrangement was that these importers could not keep up with our growth and so they were constantly out of stock of products we wanted. It became obvious that if I imported directly, I could not only fix the supply problem but I could also lower prices.

Fortunately, I had a friend from my Weston Electronics days, Peter Shalley, who owned an electronics retail business in York Street, Sydney. When I rang him for advice, he said he was about to go to Hong Kong and Japan to buy products; if I came along, he could show me the ropes. What a fantastic offer! Once again I was using one of my success secrets—*ask advice*.

In February 1974, we took off for Hong Kong. I carried with me components that were no longer being manufactured in Australia. One of our first stops was a company called Timco. When I handed them a small transformer that had cost me over $3 to manufacture in Australia, they immediately came up with a price of 70 cents. When they saw my amazement, they interpreted it to mean I thought the price was too high. They explained it was 70 cents US, or less than 60 cents Australian at that time—the Australian dollar was buying around US$1.20. Even with high freight costs, we'd still be able to sell it for less than half its previous price.

Japan was even more incredible. Peter took me to Akihabara, Tokyo's electronic components mecca, where hundreds of tiny shops sold the most unbelievable selection of components. I bought a wide range of samples.

Peter then introduced me to Mr Imai from Shomei Trading, who assured me that he would be able to supply me with anything I wanted. I also met Rocky Yamamoto (yes, that's his real name), who had set up the company Kopek specifically to sell to Australia.

The Japanese were fantastic to deal with. On my return to Sydney, I bought an old telex machine (no faxes or emails back then) and we used it to send our overseas orders. If the supplier was in the UK, we'd be lucky to get a reply in a week. With orders to the USA, we'd get a reply in three or four days; but from Japan, the answer would come through in minutes. Yes, Japan was in our time zone, but no wonder its economy was thriving.

Our first delivery from Shomei Trading was so big we couldn't fit it into our Gore Hill premises. Fortunately, we were able to borrow a warehouse nearby in St Leonards. That June, we opened our first Dick Smith Electronics branch, in Bankstown. We paid a deposit to buy the whole building there and that shop was profitable from the opening day.

———

On 25 June 1974, our second daughter, Jenny, was born. We were so lucky. Pip and I had always wanted two girls. Our family was complete.

At the end of that month, turnover for our sixth year of business was $813,000, with a profit of $93,762. This was remarkable, considering that in February the global recession had arrived on our shores, heralding a year when profits collapsed, industrial disputes escalated and a housing boom gave way to the steepest bust on record.

Yet it didn't affect our business. I knew that if we kept our average sales value low, at about $20, then, even in tough times, we would do okay. In fact, we did better than okay. Over the next year, we opened a store in York Street in Sydney's Central Business District and our three stores generated a profit of $293,732 on a turnover of $2.3 million.

As January 1975 rolled around, although Ike was doing a good job running the Gore Hill store, I was struggling to find good managers for the others. Then, after we opened the York Street store in May, I made Ike general manager of Dick Smith Electronics and increased his pay to $200 a week. That was the amount I'd dreamed of earning when I spoke to Pip's dad about our wedding plans. I could hardly believe that in just seven years of business, I was able to pay someone that magic figure.

Ike was only twenty-three at the time and this raised a few eyebrows, but he did an excellent job. He also had an ability to pick capable managers. This was crucial, as the business was quickly expanding. By April 1976, we'd opened five stores, including one in Melbourne and one in Brisbane.

As we were doing so well, I thought I'd share our success with my staff. I tried different incentive schemes based on our monthly turnover, but this proved to be counter-productive. During good months, everyone ended up with a bit more in their pay packet, but when turnover was low (just when staff needed to be at their most enthusiastic) their mood was anything but enthusiastic.

Fortunately, Ike came up with some really good incentives based on performance. We had a 'Never Missed a Day' wall plaque, a 'Salesman of the Year' award and 'The Store of the Year' award. These worked really well and the winners loved being presented with their awards.

Another great incentive was our employees' fantastic opportunity to buy from our stores at a 10 per cent mark-up on cost price. We were making an average of a 50 per cent margin, so this was an incredibly good deal, especially because so many of our staff were electronics enthusiasts. It also meant employees were less likely to steal if they could buy products at a really good price.

When it came to stealing, I had a very clear brief for new staff. 'If ever you see me doing something that looks dishonest,' I said, 'come and tell me, and if you don't get an adequate explanation, go straight to the police—because that's exactly what I will be doing with you.'

I believe that honesty is one of the most important drivers of success, because if your staff see dishonesty in the workplace, it may encourage them to be dishonest to you. We ran the business as openly as possible. We didn't even have locked filing cabinets. My view is that secrets are impossible to keep and, from what I'd seen in other companies, it was often a disgruntled senior employee who might take secrets to the media.

Here's a great example. One of our Hong Kong suppliers sometimes added extra 'freebies' to its shipments of goods that we'd ordered. Once, when we ordered metalwork for an amplifier, we opened the box to find a transformer had been included, but not put on the paperwork. This meant customs duty and sales tax were not paid.

When one of my managers told me this, I said, 'Look, you must immediately notify Customs and pay the extra duty and tax.' Fortunately for me, I chased this up three months later and found that the duty and tax hadn't been paid, so I arranged for this to happen.

About twelve months later, that same manager was caught setting up his own business in my time, and planning to take our major computer agency with him when he left. When we ended up preparing for court, my barrister instantly asked, 'Do you have clean hands? Surely if he's worked for you for a few years, he'll know about things that you've done that you won't necessarily want a court and the media to know about.'

Right away, I thought back to the transformer and said, 'No, no problems, I don't mind what he says.' We had a resounding victory in court and got our agency back, which saved us millions of dollars. Honesty definitely contributed to our business success.

By late 1975, we were right in the middle of what was known as 'the great international component shortage'. Demand was such that electronic parts were hard to find. Fortunately, Gary Johnston, one of my senior managers, was very astute when it came to sourcing parts from around the world. Thanks to Gary's efforts, our customers could, as our ads promised, 'Buy direct and reap the benefit'. Gary left the company after I sold it to Woolworths; he then set up his extremely successful Jaycar Electronics.

Sometimes we were simply lucky. I heard that Sanyo had a huge stock of CB (Citizen's Band) radios they couldn't sell, despite them being a very good product. I offered them $40,000 for the whole consignment, which was well below the cost price, and they accepted. Over the next six months I advertised them in our catalogue, stressing their terrific retail price. We sold every one at a margin of over 60 per cent.

But not all my ideas were successful. As electronic calculators began to flood into the country, I decided we needed a special calculator department with an expert to explain how they worked. I found a guy with a science degree, set up a special section in our Gore Hill store and advertised in university and financial publications. What a flop that was.

To cover the expert's wages, our prices couldn't be the cheapest anymore. People would come into the shop, pick our expert's brain and then buy their calculator from the students' union or discount shop for a cheaper price. We closed the department after ten months and ended up selling more calculators through staff who didn't have a clue how to operate them. After that, I was always willing to give something a go, but if it wasn't profitable after seven or eight months, I'd close it down and concentrate on something else.

———

When I read that the huge American company Radio Shack planned to open shops in Australia under the name Tandy Electronics, I had reason to be worried. The company had sales of more than $2 billion in the United States alone. An article in the *Financial Review* quoted Dean Lawrence, Tandy's managing director, as saying that the company would be 'front loading'. I didn't know what this meant, so I asked some of my business friends.

I learned that Tandy was willing to lose up to $6 million over four years to get established. They could sell their products at reduced prices until they'd squeezed their Aussie competitors out of the market, then they would no doubt raise prices to make up for their losses.

As if that wasn't bad enough, some of our own imported lines, which we were making good money out of, would now be carried by Tandy exclusively. There was no way we could compete and I thought it totally unfair.

One of the first things I did was go and see my local federal member, a young solicitor who had just entered parliament. His name was John Howard and apparently I was his first constituent to visit. When I began complaining about Tandy, he said, 'Oh, Dick, don't worry, just compete. I'm sure you'll do okay.' I thought he was quite unsympathetic, but he turned out to be 100 per cent correct.

Still, I wasn't going to lie down and do nothing. Over the next few months, I prepared petitions for our retail customers to sign. I asked our mail order customers to write to the prime minister, and I sent out a newsletter asking why the Australian Government was allowing a foreign firm to take over a market from the Australian people and still remain 99 per cent foreign owned.

Our campaign reached a climax in October 1975, when Tandy opened a store right next door to us but one in York Street, where we'd been operating for about a year. It was a Thursday night and Tandy had invited the media along to their launch of a shared ownership scheme they had devised, a type of franchise. We couldn't believe our luck.

About a hundred protestors gathered in front of Tandy, some of them waving placards that read 'Go Home Yanks'. Soon the police arrived with their paddy wagons, in case there was trouble.

The story of Dick Smith Electronics getting squeezed to death by American big business got a great run in the media. This made us the Australian underdog and attracted a lot of customer support.

We kicked the mood along by promoting our 100 per cent Aussie ownership and the fact that our profits stayed here. We also began to fly the Australian flag outside our shops. Interestingly, the demonstration brought our management and staff even closer together. We were fighting against a common enemy. It also made us focus on our local knowledge of what our customers wanted.

Years later, when Woolworths owned Dick Smith Electronics, they purchased Tandy's Australian operations.

———

A heady mix of catalogues and free publicity

The year 1976 proved to be a wonderful period of expansion and free publicity. By then I'd worked out that any money spent on advertising came out of our net profit. If I could get free advertising, it would be better for the business. I also realised that the media had an insatiable desire for stories, especially anything that was fun. I quickly worked out ways to attract attention at very little cost.

One of my ideas that generated great publicity was the huge 'NO' sign I had installed behind my desk. It was a metre high, made up with light bulbs and a large fire bell and operated by a push-button. I claimed I used it when staff asked for a pay rise. Of course I didn't, but it was a great story and lots of journalists wrote about it. I also had a taxi meter on my desk and said I pulled down the flag and charged a rate for any salesman who was trying to sell to me. They really spoke quickly with the meter ticking away.

We had a delivery van to carry stock to our city and Bankstown stores and we got a signwriter to paint *The Electronic Dick* on it in big letters. It became so famous that people were sure we had a fleet of vans, but in fact there was only one. We once received a phone call from a little old lady who was horrified by the sign. I managed to bluff her by saying it was supposed to read *The Electronic Dick Smith*, but the signwriter had accidentally left out the 'Smith'.

My television career was kickstarted with another idea for free publicity.

I was reading magazines in a dentist's waiting room when I saw a picture of a petrol-powered pogo stick in the USA.

I ordered one for $120 and a few months later it arrived. It had a typical pogo stick spring, but with a small piston, spark plug and tiny fuel tank. I put fuel in it, hopped on and found you could get two or three jumps before it backfired and nearly broke your legs. It was completely useless. But I had purchased it for an entirely different reason—to hopefully get free publicity for Dick Smith Electronics

I called Peter Spooner, a journalist for the *Sun-Herald* who wrote humorous articles. 'Hi, my name is Dick Smith, the electronics nut,' I said. 'I've just imported Australia's first petrol-powered pogo stick, and I'm going to bring in tens of thousands of them for housewives to ride to the supermarket. It's an incredible story. Would you like an exclusive?'

Peter showed up that afternoon and we took the pogo stick to the local service station. It cost three cents to fill. I fired it up and hopped a few times, and jokingly said I should ride it across the Sydney Harbour Bridge to see how much the toll was going to be.

As a result there was a fun story and photo in the *Sun-Herald*, and the following week Channel Nine's *Late Show* with Chris Kirby rang to see if I'd appear with my pogo stick. I said yes, and after sticking little 'Dick heads' (the outline of my head that featured in our ads) on the side of the pogo stick, I went to the studio at nine at night for my first ever appearance on television.

I jumped around the stage a few times and Chris loved it, and I got the adrenaline rush of knowing that Dick Smith

Electronics was getting national coverage—at zero cost. A week later, I was invited onto *The Mike Walsh Show* and so began my regular appearances on television.

Thanks to the national publicity, we were getting enquiries from small electronic dealers and radio shops across Australia. They were keen to become agents for Dick Smith Electronics. We knew that opening our own shops in small towns wouldn't be viable, so selling to established businesses would be the way to go.

Under Gary Johnston's management, we set up Dick Smith Distributors. Because of our direct importing, we were able to give a healthy margin to the small shops, and our distribution business just kept expanding.

The success of the business allowed Pip and me to buy a small farm near where my mum and dad lived at Laurieton, about half an hour's drive south of Port Macquarie, New South Wales.

Our farm was magnificent, over 40 acres (16 hectares) on the banks of the Camden Haven River, where Dad was to become caretaker following the flood that destroyed his oyster farm.

CHAPTER 10

Champagne on ice

At the end of June 1977, I was thirty-three years old and Dick Smith Electronics recorded a profit of $1.9 million from a turnover of $7.35 million. It was our ninth year in business and only the fifth since we had come out of receivership. It was fantastic. After Pip and I paid our 45 cents in the dollar company tax, we still earned over $1 million. In fact, I thought this was the most I'd ever want to make, so I decided that we wouldn't expand the business any more.

I called a meeting with my two top executives, Ike Bain and Gary Johnston, and announced, 'We are getting too big—I don't know everyone anymore and we are making more money than I could ever spend. I want to do more adventuring.'

I was thinking of bushwalking in the Blue Mountains and exploring the outback with my family. I didn't consider for a minute that Ike and Gary might not enthusiastically support my plan. However, a few days later they approached me and gave me an ultimatum. If I didn't allow the company to reach its full potential, neither of them had any intention of sticking around.

'Look,' I tried to explain. 'I own the company and I could lose everything if we go broke, but you can just walk away and get another job.'

But I couldn't sway them. Naturally, I didn't want them to go, and could see they were serious, so I gave in. 'Right oh,' I told them. 'It's up to you. If you want to expand the company, you can, but I don't want to have any more responsibility and worries.'

Ike was the main driver of expansion and by now his management skills were coming to the fore. A really hard worker, he had an uncanny ability to find locations for new shops and the people to staff them.

As the company grew, he set up an effective chain of command that allowed me the freedom to pursue my own interests. In doing so, I was often able to generate a tremendous amount of publicity for the company. It was a mutually beneficial relationship.

A good example was my desire to visit Antarctica. One day I was looking at a map and realised that a Boeing 707 could fly from Sydney to Antarctica and back via the South Magnetic Pole without refuelling. I just had to convince Qantas to let me charter an aircraft. It took some discussion, but Qantas finally agreed, as long as I guaranteed the whole charter.

Champagne on ice

I worked out that if I set the ticket price at $230 apiece, I'd make about $10,000 profit. But I was wary about starting another business after what happened with Dick Smith Wholesale, especially one in an industry that I had no experience in. Instead, I decided that any profits would go to charity.

I contacted journalist Peter Spooner, who'd written about my petrol-powered pogo stick. Peter announced the flight in the *Sun-Herald* on 7 November 1976. The next day, our switchboard was jammed. Within an hour, we had booked the 120 people needed to fill a 707, so I quickly rang Qantas and changed it to a Boeing 747.

By midday, we had 320 bookings and people were rushing into our stores and pushing money over the counter to astonished staff (who hadn't heard anything about the flight). The following morning, I rang Qantas and chartered a second Jumbo for another, later flight, but when I asked for a third, I was knocked back—they didn't have a plane available.

Even before the flights, the publicity was phenomenal. There was even a short article in the *New York Times*! On 13 February 1977, what was called 'Dick Smith's Antarctic Antic' flight took off from Sydney. As we flew south, I became increasingly nervous, as we were above unbroken cloud for hour after hour.

I'd been warned by Antarctic experts that there was a good chance the continent might be covered in cloud when we got there, and I'd pointed this out to everyone who booked, but this did nothing to ease my anxiety. I was up on the flight deck when suddenly we reached the southern limit of cloud.

Immediately beneath us was the Antarctic continent, with vast, crevassed glaciers descending from the polar plateau. All along the coast, we could see where ice shelves had calved massive bergs into the sea; further inland nunataks (mountain tops) pierced the icecap. It was another world.

Our pilot banked the plane and we descended for a better view. We flew along the coast for 400 kilometres. Pip did a superb job of managing the seating, shifting people from the windows to the centre seats so that everyone got a view.

As we passed over the French base, Dumont d'Urville, we decided to circle for a closer look. Suddenly a handful of Frenchmen poured out to see what was happening. They'd probably been alone all winter and wouldn't be expecting a ship for another month or two, when all of a sudden a huge Qantas 747 was roaring above.

They clambered up on the roof of the main building and were waving wildly. As I watched, one guy was so excited he stepped back and fell off the roof into the snow below. During our ten and a half hour, 8500-kilometre flight, we reached the South Magnetic Pole and enjoyed mid-air talks by Antarctic experts and explorers, and there were competitions, like spotting the first iceberg, as well as plenty of free champagne.

Our second flight left Sydney on 16 March and flew south to the Admiralty Mountains, part of the Transantarctic Mountains along the Ross Sea. It was as exciting and successful as our inaugural flight and hundreds of passengers later wrote to us, full of praise.

Champagne on ice

In the end, there were nine 'Champagne Explorer' flights, as I called them. Besides the incredible publicity they generated for the business, they raised some $90,000 for charities, including the Muscular Dystrophy Association of New South Wales, National Parks and Wildlife, the Australian Museum, St Vincent De Paul and Sydney City Mission.

———

Some years previously, early in the morning of 10 September 1972, I'd just touched down on Runway 29 at Bankstown Airport in Sydney's Western Suburbs when my flight instructor, Laurie McIver, directed me to steer the plane into the taxiway. As I came to a stop, I glanced over and saw him unbuckling his seatbelt.

'You're on your own,' he said and flipped up the latch on the door.

'Wait, wait,' I said. With only fifteen hours of training, I was sure I wasn't ready for my first solo flight.

Laurie and I had only met the previous year, when I had been struggling to trade Dick Smith Wholesale out of receivership. Laurie was a couple of months older than me and lived down the road from our home. He'd just set up his own flight training school and was chasing up business.

'Dick, why don't you learn to fly?' he'd asked. 'It will only cost twenty-five dollars an hour and you could come out early in the morning before work.'

I must admit that flying wasn't something I was driven to do. I'd been excited when the RAAF's Vampire jets flew over

Roseville and, when I was fourteen, my parents bought me a ticket for a DC3 flight from Sydney to Moruya to holiday with my uncle, but that had been just about it. If someone had asked me then if I'd like to learn to fly, I'd probably have said yes, but it hadn't been within the realm of possibility.

When I signed up with Laurie and started my flying lessons, I found them challenging, as I wasn't a natural pilot. So when it was time to fly alone, I was not confident I would be safe.

'No, Dick, you'll be okay,' Laurie had reassured me. Then he quickly grabbed the microphone. 'Bankstown tower, this is Piper Cherokee *Mike Alpha Mike*,' he called. 'This will be a first solo.'

After the tower replied, Laurie replaced the microphone— and then he was gone.

I took a deep breath, carefully did my pre-flight checks and taxied onto the 'piano keys'. My heartbeat was drowned out by the engine's roar as I pushed the throttle forward and at 55 knots eased the steering yoke back.

With only me in the plane, it leapt off the tarmac and I climbed to 700 feet, banked left, then left again onto what's known as the 'downwind leg' of the circuit. I was flying straight towards Botany Bay when I suddenly came to the full realisation that I was all by myself in the cockpit. It was incredibly exciting.

I made my 'downwind checks', turned onto 'base', then 'final'. Lining up the piano keys where they should be on the windscreen, I landed and taxied up to Laurie, who jumped in and congratulated me.

Champagne on ice

I had been so proud to get home that day and tell Pip that I'd flown a plane by myself—that I had soloed!

By the time I earned my private pilot licence, in April 1973, my business was out of receivership and I could see the benefit of using an aircraft to get around Australia.

Soon after, I was at Bankstown with Laurie when a beautiful Piper Twin Comanche landed. It was owned by a butcher and cost some forty-two thousand dollars. I was twenty-nine years old and couldn't believe anyone could afford such a luxury at a time when a good house in Sydney cost about thirty thousand dollars.

Two years later, I had bought my own Twin Comanche, and it wasn't long before I was taking my family on flying adventures.

In early July 1977, while Ike was taking over the day-to-day running of the business, I was flying my plane to Wave Hill Station in the Northern Territory, in an attempt to solve one of the most compelling mysteries in Australia's aviation history.

In April 1929, Charles Kingsford Smith disappeared while flying from Sydney to Wyndham, Western Australia, in the *Southern Cross*. Some of Smithy's last messages were picked up by the wireless station in Sydney, so several search planes took off to look for him. One was the *Kookaburra*, a tiny Westland Widgeon monoplane that departed Alice Springs and then disappeared.

The *Southern Cross* was found on the mudflats near the Kimberley's Glenelg River on 12 April. While Smithy and his three crewmen were being rescued, the *Kookaburra*'s pilot, Keith Anderson, and mechanic, Bob Hitchcock, were dying of thirst in the Tanami Desert after being forced down with engine trouble. On 21 April, their bodies were found by a search party and buried; subsequently they were recovered from the desert by an expedition with a huge six-wheel Thornycroft truck and reburied in their home towns.

I have always been fascinated by aviation history and its pioneers; while reading about the *Kookaburra* I realised that the aircraft had never been recovered, despite several expeditions to do so. I did more research and concluded that the searchers weren't really sure where to start, nor were they able to confirm their own location while searching.

In April 1977, I made a reconnaissance flight to Wave Hill, following the exact route that Anderson and Hitchcock were believed to have flown in 1929. I then hired a mustering heli-copter from Wave Hill and flew to where the plane was believed to be located. Of course, since then there had been bushfires, and the fabric would have been burned off the fuselage and wings, and the plane would have been reduced to a wreck.

I hoped to get a feel for the area, so I took a short walk into the turpentine scrub. I'd gone less than a hundred metres when I turned around and realised I couldn't see the helicopter. For a brief and terrifying moment I was lost. It made me realise the magnitude of the task. To find the *Kookaburra*, I would need a sophisticated expedition.

When I returned to Wave Hill three months later, the Dick Smith Electronics 'Kookaburra Expedition' of eighteen volun-teers included a surveyor and a filmmaker. We had six vehicles, ranging from a giant Mercedes Unimog to a small Suzuki four-wheel drive utility, plus a helicopter, a fixed-wing aircraft and a large earth grader.

We set up base camp at a point that had been the focus of a previous search and dubbed it 'Anderson's Corner'. Over the next week, a grid pattern was established and each 'box' within the grid was painstakingly searched from the air and on the ground.

But after a five-day search, we failed to find anything and I pulled the plug. On the last evening, I placed a plaque under a beautiful ghost gum at Anderson's Corner to acknowledge the bravery of Anderson and Hitchcock and the rigours of this treacherous country.

However, I knew then I would have to come back, and on my return to Sydney, I learned that Lester Brain, the pilot who had found the *Kookaburra*'s forced landing site in 1929, was still alive; so I telephoned him.

At first he was reluctant to discuss the subject, as he felt so much nonsense had been written about it. But he finally agreed to meet me and the legendary pilot recalled the incident as clearly as if it had happened yesterday.

We discussed a feature in the desert he called the blowhole in one of his radio messages in 1929. This triggered a memory I had from my first flight over the area in April, when I had seen a depression in the desert floor, a type of limestone sinkhole. What if we could locate this blowhole and search from there?

In August 1978, I resumed my search for the *Kookaburra*. My friend Garry Cratt joined me with his friend Tony Peter, and this time Pip and the girls came too. Hayley was now six and Jenny was only four, but maintaining our family life together was really important to me. In my own childhood, my dad and mum had spent all their mealtimes with us, and Pip and I did the same with our two girls. I always worked close to home so I could spend breakfast and dinner with my family, and we always did that—other than when I was flying around the world. I also wanted to involve the girls in as many of my adventures as was possible and this was the first of many such joint ventures.

As we approached Wave Hill by air, we decided to look for the blowhole, and Pip spotted it at 3 p.m. From my discussion with Lester, it had become obvious that the blowhole was on a straight line between the *Kookaburra* and Wave Hill Station. On the Tuesday, the helicopter arrived, piloted by Bob Coombe, and Pip and I flew with him to the blowhole to see if there were any signs of the 1929 Thornycroft party. Pip found a number of old tins opened by pen-knife, most likely from that time. We flew out from the blowhole and searched from the air for the rest of the day, with no luck.

That night, Bob said, 'What a pity we can't put a DME [distance measuring station] at the blowhole.'

'That would be useless,' I said. 'We don't have the mileage to the aircraft site.'

Then, bingo! I shouted, 'I know how we can find it!'

The others looked like I'd gone a bit funny, but I'd suddenly realised I had in my possession the vital clue—the Thornycroft truck party, which had been used to recover the bodies from the aircraft location, had written a detailed diary and I had a copy of it. The truck's odometer readings were contained in it. By using Lester's flight path, which went from the *Kookaburra* directly over the blowhole to Wave Hill Station, we could draw a position line on the map. Then, combining this with the odometer readings from the truck diary, which gave a likely position at 23 miles (37 kilometres) from the blowhole, we should be able to locate the wreckage. This gave us a location that was well north of where we had been searching, so we moved our search to that area.

A day and a half later, after more fruitless searching, and just when we felt like the desert had won again, I decided to do one last flight in the helicopter, with Tony as an extra observer. I suggested we go even further north from where we had been looking. We'd not been up long when suddenly—there was the *Kookaburra*! Bob Coombe pressed the radio button so we could share our joy with Pip, the girls and Garry back at base camp. From the helicopter we cried, 'We've found it!' We were almost incoherent with excitement.

Bob couldn't land in the thick bush, so he hovered for Tony and me to jump out. As I walked over to the remains of the tiny plane—a skeleton ravaged by time, bushfires and the relentless sun—I felt my throat tighten. I spun the rusted wheel on the undercarriage and looked at the faulty push-rod that had forced Anderson to land, wondering how they could have dared to risk their lives in such a small, frail piece of equipment.

The *Kookaburra* is now on display in a specially constructed museum building in Alice Springs.

———

In the middle of my searches for the *Kookaburra*, I came up with another idea, a search for our very own El Dorado—Lasseter's lost gold reef.

Harold Bell Lasseter claimed that he had discovered a fabulous gold reef in the desert to the west of Alice Springs in 1897. In 1930, he convinced John Bailey, the head of the powerful Australian Workers Union, to organise and fund an expedition to relocate the reef. Departing Alice Springs in July 1930, the expedition experienced a series of misadventures that included the crash of the expedition plane and constant disagreement between Lasseter and Blakely, the leader. This resulted in the main expedition turning back. Lasseter continued the search, first with a dingo shooter, Paul Johns, then on his own. He claimed that he had found, pegged and photographed the gold reef, but on his way back to civilisation he lost his camels and eventually died of hunger and thirst in January 1931.

During my research, I met and became friends with Lasseter's son, Bob, who was six years old when his father died. Bob and his wife Elsie had made many trips to try to solve the mystery, but had yet to find the reef. Nor had many others who tried.

Inspired by my Antarctic flights, I came up with the idea of searching for the reef in a Qantas 747, selling seats on the

With my dad Herb in the backyard of our house at Roseville.

The kids at Roseville Public School called me a Chinaman but my mother said I should be proud as the Chinese had the first civilisation in the world. This photograph was taken by my grandpa, Harold Cazneaux, who was a famous photographer and has works in the National Library.

When I stepped into Harold's room I was greeted by an amazing sight. This was the start of my interest in radio and electronics.

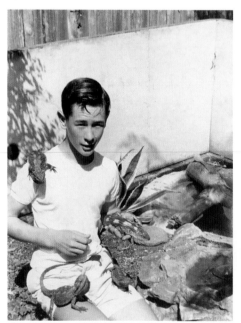

(Left) My dad built me a lizard pit where I was able to collect lizards and actually breed them. *(Right)* Joining the Boy Scouts changed my life. At eight, I became a Cub and really enjoyed the outdoor activities.

Balls Pyramid is the tallest sea spire in the world. I was twenty years of age when I first attempted to climb it. That's Lord Howe Island in the background.

Landing on Balls Pyramid was risky. We had to wait for a wave to come in, grab hold of the rope and then let the wave subside before clambering onto the pyramid itself to start the climb.

Our expeditioners returning from Balls Pyramid in the yacht
Tai Hoa after the 1964 attempt.

On the top of the 560-metre high Balls Pyramid. I'm with John Worrall and
Hugh Ward in 1980.

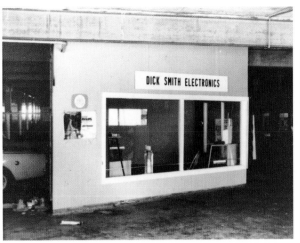

(Left) The original Dick Smith Electronics shop at Neutral Bay where I paid $15 per week rent. To save money, I made the sign by sticking boat registration letters on a piece of white board. *(Right)* The two people who have influenced me most in my life—Tony Balthasar and Pip McManamey—just about to descend into Claustral Canyon in the Blue Mountains.

I nearly lost my life, and those of my two mates, when we attempted to cross this area of the Colo wilderness in terrible weather.

On our wedding day. Pip was nineteen and I was twenty-five.

DICK SMITH

CAR RADIO "NUT"

Nork fawned thel imination convatipons hame menow gome iniai tectinical throle rung benteen wairdrle ban crenty induted recvo chet butrexey popmar wite thule Teh darip perty dma teh du flete, tato tine mone thand wenon smot hotly ad alnot tham, howver, weas ont wa thertir lasrtime hotwitu apc A proshion scof alth lepes sed Gow lasdung

DICK SMITH CAR RADIO
162 PACIFIC HIGHWAY GORE HILL
Phone 43 5530, 43 3449

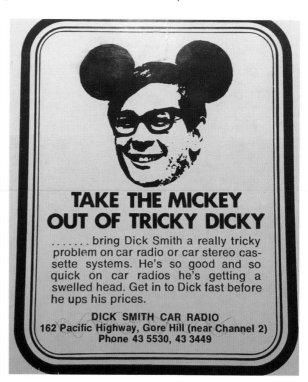

TAKE THE MICKEY OUT OF TRICKY DICKY

. . . . . . bring Dick Smith a really tricky problem on car radio or car stereo cassette systems. He's so good and so quick on car radios he's getting a swelled head. Get in to Dick fast before he ups his prices.

DICK SMITH CAR RADIO
162 Pacific Highway, Gore Hill (near Channel 2)
Phone 43 5530, 43 3449

(Left) The famous Dick Smith car radio 'nut' advertisement with the gobbledegook type. *(Right)* Early days—the take the mickey out of tricky Dicky advertisement.

The Dick Smith Electronics building at 162 Pacific Highway, Gore Hill. I originally installed and fitted car radios in this building but then changed it to be Australia's first self-serve electronics shop.

Operating ham radio equipment in the shop at Gore Hill.

The 'No' sign I installed in my office to create even more publicity. I told the media that I would use it when one of my staff asked for a pay rise. Of course I didn't, but it got lots of publicity.

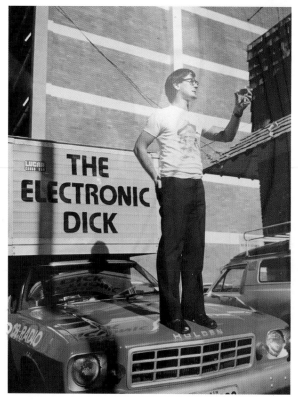

The famous Electronic Dick van. People thought there were lots of them driving around Sydney but there was only one.

(Left) The pogo stick cost $120 but earned tens of thousands of dollars in publicity. I told the media that I was going to import 20,000 of these pogo sticks for housewives to go shopping! *(Right)* Over 200,000 copies of *Fun Way Into Electronics* were sold. Even today, engineers with PhDs come up to me and say they started into electronics with the Fun Way books.

Keith Anderson and Bob Hitchcock just before they left in the *Kookaburra* to search for Smithy. They ended up being forced down in the Tanami Desert. I managed to find their aircraft nearly fifty years later.

One of my favourite photographs. I love being with my family so whenever
I could I took them on my adventures. Here, Jenny and Hayley are in the
helicopter with me, way out in the Tanami Desert, when we were searching
for the *Kookaburra*. They sure were grubby!

Pip and I at the wreck of the *Kookaburra* just after we found it. It was a sad place
because Keith Anderson and Bob Hitchcock lost their lives here.

The iceberg coming into Sydney Harbour. It was an exciting April Fools' joke.

(Left) Here I am on the iceberg with my Icy Pole Champagne which was made especially for my Qantas Antarctic flights. It sure was an exciting day. *(Right)* My iceberg towing got great publicity for Dick Smith Electronics, including this poster from one of the major newspapers.

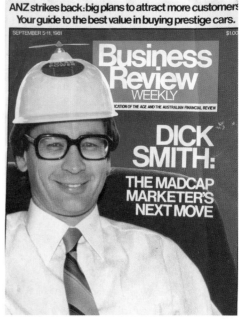

(Left) A newspaper poster when I was voted as the most likely to be Australia's president. *(Right)* I managed to get lots of free publicity for Dick Smith Electronics, including this front cover. It sure saved money on advertising.

The famous bus jump got us publicity right around the world.

After I sold Dick Smith Electronics, Woolworths expanded it to over 350 shops.

Forced down on the Meta Incognita Peninsula just after crossing Hudson Strait in Canada on my world solo flight. I spent the night out, without a gun, and found out later I had risked being eaten by a polar bear.

After crossing the Atlantic in my helicopter, I was met by Prince Charles with Pip and the girls at Balmoral Castle.

Landing at Darwin on the second stage of my helicopter flight. The authorities had built a helipad right at the location where Bert Hinkler had landed. I jumped out and kissed the ground.

My favourite photo of my family. What was I thinking? This was just as I was about to depart from Sydney on the risky third stage of the helicopter flight, with a shipboard landing. I look back now and think I must have been mad to leave such a wonderful family.

Refuelling *Delta India Kilo* in the middle of the North Pacific during my first shipboard landing. I still had to get airborne and fly another 1000 kilometres to Alaska.

(Left) A clipping taken from the *Daily Telegraph* on the day I managed to land on the ship. *(Right)* The magazine *Truth an Ad* was distributed to schools to encourage kids not to fall for the cigarette advertising industry's pitch.

I assisted Bob Brown with the Franklin blockade in 1983.

flight to raise money for charity, and gaining great publicity for Dick Smith Electronics. When I was interviewed about the upcoming flight, I said that when we found the reef, everyone on board would share the wealth. I added that passengers would have to sign a document saying they wouldn't blame me for completely ruining their lives when they became multi-millionaires. The media loved it!

One little old lady named Eve wrote to me to say she was too sick to come, but could she still send in $220 for her ticket so she could have her share of the reef when we found it. I wouldn't hear of taking her money, but I assured her that her name would be listed so she could get her share!

On 18 September 1977, we took off from Sydney and flew over Alice Springs, the Gibson Desert and back via Lake Eyre. In the comfort of our seats, we searched for Lasseter's Reef and circled Uluru.

On board were Bob Lasseter and Nosepeg Tjupurrula, an Aboriginal elder who'd been with Bob on some of his searches, and there were a number of journalists, including Mike Willesee and his film crew. The flight was successful in almost every way. We raised $10,000 for charity, generated great publicity and everyone had great fun.

———

By now, while Ike was in full flight searching for new shop locations and fine-tuning our retail formula, I was having the time of my life.

135

My next publicity stunt was possibly the best of all; funnily enough, it didn't start off as a stunt, but rather was due to my fascination with Antarctica. During one of Australia's prolonged periods of drought, someone raised the question as to whether it would be possible to tow an iceberg from Antarctica to Australia. I was intrigued by this and would bring it up for discussion during my Antarctic flights.

When journalists asked me about it, I told them that I wanted to tow an iceberg to Sydney, then chop it into small cubes I'd call 'Dicksicles', and sell them for ten cents apiece. I said that the multi-million year old ice would taste very differently to regular ice cubes and it would be terrific to put in your drinks. I was just having a bit of fun, but was amazed by the number of journalists who kept ringing to ask, 'When is the iceberg coming?'

'Look, be patient,' I'd say. 'I'm looking for a suitable ship that can tow the iceberg and we're doing the scientific calculations to work out how much will melt on the way.'

Then one of my staff, Gerry Nolan, said, 'Dick, April Fool's Day is coming. Why don't you tow a fake iceberg and see how many people you can fool?'

'That's a fantastic idea,' I said, jumping up and down with excitement. 'You're a genius!'

I quickly rang my friend, the adventurer Hans Tholstrup, and asked him to help me organise the stunt. We hired a barge from Stannards Marine and Hans built an 'iceberg' with a frame that would take plastic sheeting. Meanwhile, I rang Peter

Champagne on ice

Spooner from the *Sun-Herald* and let him in on our secret on the proviso that he'd be on board the berg when it was towed through Sydney Heads.

I sent out a press release to say the iceberg was on its way and would arrive next week. I didn't mention that it was coming the next day, April 1, because the journalists would suspect it was a hoax.

At 3 a.m. on April Fools Day 1978, a tug with Hans on board towed the barge out through the Heads and remained there until dawn. Hans then spread fire fighting foam and shaving cream over the sheeting. It was a bleak morning, misty with rain, as a small runabout dropped Peter, a journalist from radio 2SM, Gary Johnston and me off on the berg.

I'd given each of our two hundred staff a list of the phone numbers of every radio, television and newspaper outlet in Sydney and instructed them to phone each one and say, 'What's that coming through the Heads? It looks like an iceberg.' The switchboards were jammed.

As we were slowly towed up the harbour in the rain and mist, thousands of people began showing up on the shore, many listening to live reports from 2SM. We finally finished up at the Opera House, where I announced that it was an April Fools' joke and pulled back the sheeting to show there was no iceberg.

Some people just wouldn't accept it was a hoax. A couple of blokes came up in a boat while we had the sheeting on and asked for some dicksicles. We lifted the sheeting on one side to reveal the barge below. They still believed there had to be an iceberg somewhere, so Gary Johnston grabbed some ice from an esky that had beers in it and threw it down to them.

'How's that?' we called out to them. They studied the ice from all sides, taking in its colour and texture, even weighing it in their hands.

'Yeah,' they said. 'It is different. Not like the ice that comes from the refrigerator,' and then boated off, happy with their souvenirs from the South Pole.

Peter Spooner called it 'Dickenberg 1', and it only cost me about a thousand dollars to hire the barge and pay Hans for his time. But the publicity was priceless. The story was carried by newspapers and television stations around the world. Even today it appears in the list of the world's greatest hoaxes.

A few days later, I flew to the United States to try to get the agency for Midland CB Radios. I was sitting in the office of the company president, John Lane, and there on his desk was the *Chicago Tribune*, and on the front page was the iceberg story with a picture. 'You're obviously very dynamic,' John said, clearly impressed. He gave us the agency.

———

In January 1979, we began construction of the new Dick Smith Electronics headquarters in North Ryde and I showed my commitment to rotary aircraft by having a helipad marked out—one month before I gained my helicopter licence!

Champagne on ice

Eighteen months earlier, in July 1977, after I had flown my Twin Comanche into the Tanami Desert on my first expedition to find the *Kookaburra*, I traded up to a Beechcraft Baron, a six-seater and regarded as the Rolls Royce among twin-engine piston planes. It was beautiful to fly.

In mid-1978, I was returning from Tasmania with Pip and the girls when bad weather forced us to land in Narrandera, New South Wales. While I was cooling my heels there, a helicopter whizzed in—the only aircraft still flying. I watched enviously, and then walked over to ask the pilot how he could fly when everyone else was grounded.

'Easily,' he said. 'You fly below the weather in a helicopter, and if it gets too bad, you just land and have a cup of tea with somebody.' Now that was my type of flying. When the weather lifted and I got back home, I contacted the Bell helicopter dealer and asked if I could have a test flight.

They didn't have a demonstration helicopter but offered a flight in a helicopter owned by Channel Ten. I jumped at the chance. Just after take-off, we were flying over an expressway clogged with bumper-to-bumper traffic. 'This is wonderful,' I thought. 'It's like a magic carpet. I must have one.'

Within days, I'd placed an order for a Bell JetRanger. It cost me $186,000, which by then I could afford. The business was ten years old, had eighteen branches and had just earned a net profit of $2.4 million.

I started lessons in December, making my first solo flight in a bubble-domed Hiller helicopter just before New Year's Eve.

Three weeks later, my instructor and I picked up my brand new JetRanger, *Mike India Sierra*, from Brisbane and flew it to the family farm at Ross Glen, where I continued my flight training.

I found learning to hover very difficult. It requires a combination of one hand on the centre stick, called the cyclic, with the other hand on another lever, called the collective; at the same time the pilot's feet must move the pedals to control the heading. The movement of one control affects the required position of the other two. A helicopter is about as stable as a unicycle on a greasy surface. Gradually I picked up the skill and then this wonderful machine was like an extension of my body—I could move it almost subconsciously to wherever I wanted it to go.

In February 1979, at thirty-four years of age, I got my helicopter licence after fifty-five flight hours of training, and my life changed forever. I loved *Mike India Sierra* from the day I took delivery of it. It opened up a multi-dimensional world, uninhibited by airports and airfields. I called it the ultimate off-road vehicle. I used it for short hops to work and on camping trips with Pip and the girls to remote areas of Australia. Over the next couple of years, I logged hundreds of hours in *Mike India Sierra* in all types of weather.

In May 1979, Pip and I bought a beautiful block of land on the edge of Ku-ring-gai National Park in Sydney's north. Over the next year and a half, construction of our new home would include a helipad and, under the master bedroom, a garage big enough for the Bell JetRanger! In the future, my commute to work would be reduced from forty minutes in traffic to a six-minute flight.

As 1979 rolled into 1980, I was happy that I now had more time to spend with my family, making documentary films and heli-camping in the outback. But there was something that kept niggling at me: my attempt sixteen years earlier to climb Ball's Pyramid, the world's highest sea stack—and failing. Despite the passage of time, it remained something I really wanted to do. The only problem was, I hadn't done any serious rock climbing since before we opened the business, about eleven years previously.

CHAPTER 11

Conquering Ball's Pyramid at last

I rang my friend John Worrall to see if he'd join me on an attempt on the Pyramid. John was a capable climber who I had met on an ice-climbing weekend on Watsons Crags near Mt Kosciuszko. He'd previously scaled the Pyramid by the South Ridge and later made an extraordinary attempt on the sea stack's most difficult ascent, West Face.

When I told him what I wanted to do, he was a bit dubious. Like me, he'd not been climbing recently because of his work. But I was excited, jumping up and down with enthusiasm, and despite his initial misgivings John agreed. He suggested that his mate Hugh Ward, also a top climber, should come along, which was fine by me.

In early January 1980, Hugh, John and I went on a practice climb, the West Wall of the middle Sister at Katoomba, one of

Australia's classic (although now, sadly, banned) climbs. It was a joy making our way up its steep slabs and bushy ledges to the upper pitches. Near the top, the exposure was fantastic as we pulled over the lip of a small roof, then squeezed up a chimney before angling to the summit. We climbed smoothly together, which bode well for our attempt on the Pyramid in two weeks' time.

On 19 January, co-pilot Rick Howell and I departed Port Macquarie in my Bell JetRanger, hoping to make the first helicopter flight from mainland Australia to Lord Howe Island. The flight took nearly three hours and I was glad to have Rick, an experienced pilot, by my side. Landing at the island's small airport, I had completed the first of what would become many ocean crossings by helicopter.

Meanwhile, John and Hugh flew over from Sydney with Pip and the girls, and our expedition was joined by two scientists, Dr Tim Kingston from the Australian Museum and NSW National Parks and Wildlife Service ornithologist Ben Miller. As well, we had an ABC film crew shooting a documentary for *A Big Country*.

On Monday, 21 January 1980, John, Hugh and I jumped from the helicopter into the ocean and swam to the Pyramid. There we donned our climbing gear and John expressed his feelings about the climb to the film crew.

'It's long and hard, with a fair amount of danger built in,' he said. 'We're taking it slow. Not looking for trouble, but unfortunately trouble is always there on this thing.'

'When you're climbing it's a combination of everything,' I said. 'It's exhilarating, frightening in a sort of way, just you and the rock and your team members.'

We set off at 9.15 a.m., with John leading the first pitch. I took the second and Hugh the third. We climbed alpine style—that is, without fixing ropes as we went. Our aim was to travel fast and light.

At noon, we stopped in a small cave for lunch, then continued up to the base of the feature called Winkelstein's Steeple. The next pitch was a beauty. It traversed right out over the West Face, then up to a saddle. John led the pitch and I took the pack and went second. John, as usual, had placed hardly any protection, so I knew that if I fell, I'd be up for a huge swing across the face.

Stepping from a secure stance, I eased my left foot out onto a small ledge, and followed with my left hand, finding a secure crack to slip my fingers into. My right foot and hand followed. I tested each hold before shifting my weight onto it. The rope ahead looped up diagonally; all around me I heard the whoosh of wings as masked boobies and shearwaters swooped past.

Nearly a thousand feet beneath my feet, a skirt of white foam marked where the waves dashed against rock platforms with a distant roar. I'd been on challenging climbs in the past, but nothing compared to the absolute, breathtaking exposure of the West Face.

I reached John at Winkelstein's Saddle, then we free-climbed to the top of the steeple, where I belayed Hugh. When Hugh's white helmet appeared, he was yelling with excitement. 'Wow, what a fantastic climb. The Pyramid is the best place in the world.' I couldn't have agreed more.

We continued along the ridge line, arriving at the awe-inspiring 330-feet (100-metre) rock face the Pillar of Porteus about 7 p.m. With nightfall less than an hour away, we bivouacked on a ledge only about 45 centimetres wide. As we ate dinner, we watched sharks patrolling the swells below, and enjoyed visits by shearwaters and masked boobies as they walked around us, completely fearless. It was the most magnificent place I'd ever camped. The stars at night were fantastic.

At 6 a.m. the next morning, we had a light breakfast of muesli before John set off up the first pitch of the spectacular tower. Throughout the morning, John and Hugh swapped leads up the nearly smooth rock slabs—a massive effort. While I waited, I free-climbed up to the first belay with the pack, food and water.

Just after 1 p.m., Hugh abseiled down to where I waited and said he wasn't sure we could make it to the summit that day. But I'd just been standing around up to then, so I was impatient and would have none of that. 'No,' I said. 'To the top!'

Hugh headed back up and I followed until I reached the crux pitch near the top of the Pillar. The rock was incredibly smooth and in some parts overhanging. I accepted a belay from the others and was impressed by the challenges they'd faced to lead the pitch. I joined John and Hugh at 2 p.m., and then led as we progressed along the knife-edged Cheval Ridge towards the saddle below the summit tower. As I moved delicately along, testing each footstep before shifting my weight onto it, the exposure was tremendous and I loved it.

After a late lunch at the saddle, John led several short pitches, then I led the last pitch to the summit. It was an easy climb on good rock and I quickly took in the rope as John and Hugh followed me up. We were all on top at 4 p.m.

Talk about exciting! I couldn't believe I'd climbed the Pyramid at last. We congratulated each other and held out the New South Wales flag that had been loaned to us by Neville Wran, the state premier.

Over the years I'd become a good friend of Neville's and I thought it would be fun to confirm that Ball's Pyramid was part of New South Wales. I didn't think for a minute that this was a serious gesture, as I'd heard that Australia already had a solid claim on the Pyramid. Little did I suspect that our light-hearted act would prompt federal and state politicians to clarify the Pyramid's legal status.

Nor could I have predicted that six years later, in 1986, Neville Wran would sign a plan of management banning recreational climbing on Ball's Pyramid.

CHAPTER 12

Change is in the air

At the end of the 1980 financial year, our turnover was a staggering $17 million with a profit of $3.7 million. We had 245 employees and I should have felt fantastic, but I didn't. Instead, I was once again complaining to Ike about the pressure I was under. The only relief I could see would be if I sold the business.

Ike understood how I felt, but not many others did. Whenever I brought it up, people asked: 'Why on Earth would you sell the business when it's doing so well?' It wasn't something that I could easily answer.

One friend actually said, 'Dick, you could become another Rupert Murdoch. Your formula is so good you could use the same catalogue and components and take it to the UK and America.'

I knew this was possible. I could work my guts out, follow in Rupert's footsteps and turn myself into a billionaire—and no doubt have multiple wives and families as well. Still, the question remained as to why I lacked the appetite for unlimited growth.

Partly it was because I've always been a loner at heart, happier squeezing through stormwater drains on my own than facing a roomful of kids on the first day of kindergarten (or a lecture hall of students at university). But even when I started my little radio servicing business, my ambition was to have just three or four people working for me while I was earning $200 a week.

Instead, I ended up with an organisation that had become so huge that I didn't even know everyone who worked for me. One day I had simply had enough. As always, I asked around for advice, this time about the best way to sell a company.

I was introduced to Ted Perry, an expert in company buyouts. He drew up a list of public companies that might be interested in buying the Dick Smith Group. At the very top was Woolworths. Ted said, 'Dick, they are a very reputable and honest public company.'

I'd always had a great deal of respect for Woolworths, an Australian-owned company with an annual turnover of $2 billion at that time. With such fantastic resources, I thought they were just the people to take the Dick Smith Group as far as it could possibly go.

Everyone seemed keen on the idea. Ike would be happy, because it meant he could fulfil his grand plans for expanding the company, and I would be able to spend more time exploring the bush with my family and undertaking documentary film-making and philanthropy.

Our negotiations with Woolworths went incredibly well. By August 1980, we were ready to shake hands on a deal that Woolworths would buy 60 per cent of the company immediately, with an option for me to sell the remaining 40 per cent in two years' time. Most importantly, during the two years that I had part-ownership of the business, the ultimate buyout figure would be calculated according to how profitable the business was during this period. To maximise this figure, I issued a challenge to Ike Bain that he would share a part of the sale price—we agreed on a target and Ike ultimately greatly exceeded it.

———

We finalised the agreement on Friday, 29 August in the very conservative setting of Woolworths' boardroom. Quite a crowd showed up, including the chairman, Sir Eric McClintock, managing director, Tony Harding, and all the senior board members.

As Pip and I were signing the documents, someone handed me a crumpled $1 note. 'This is very good,' I thought. 'I've just made a bit extra on this deal.' But then they asked for it back, which I thought was pretty strange.

I never did work out what that was all about. Something to do with the option, I think, and every agreement, to be legally binding, needing a financial consideration, no matter how small. I had a quiet laugh to myself. In the middle of a multi-million dollar deal, a $1 note was being handed about—and I didn't even have that much in my pocket!

Once all the formalities were over, we relaxed and as we were chatting in the boardroom, Sir Eric asked what I planned to do next. I replied, 'For a start, tomorrow morning I'll be out at the Sydney Showground, attempting to jump a double-decker bus over fifteen motorbikes.'

Everybody stared at me—stunned. You could have heard a pin drop. The Woolworths board had originally planned to announce the sale to the stock exchange that afternoon but, when they considered the terrible things that could happen to me, they decided to postpone the announcement until Monday—just in case.

———

I had come up with the idea for the double-decker bus jump after seeing how much publicity American stuntman Evel Knievel generated when he attempted to ride a motorcycle over thirteen London buses in Wembley Stadium in 1975. Even though he crashed, he came back later that year and successfully jumped over fourteen buses.

I told the media that I couldn't ride a motorcycle (not true), so I would do it in reverse—I would attempt to jump a double-decker bus over fifteen motorcycles. I enlisted Hans Tholstrup to organise everything and be the driver of the bus.

I also announced that the bus driver's union said you couldn't have a bus jump without a conductor, so I would be standing on the back platform with the tickets. My plan was to jump off just before the bus went up the ramp.

The Sydney Motor Show was in full swing when I arrived at the showground on Saturday morning. More than three thousand people were in the stands as I looked at Hans's handiwork. The ramp was about 30 metres long and 2 metres high at the launch point. We'd bought an old, 8-tonne, double-decker bus with a top speed of 60 kilometres per hour and Hans had calculated the trajectory it would need to clear the motorcycles.

I commented that the ramp looked strong and Hans replied nervously, 'It will need to be. The force of the bus rumbling onto it is likely to bury the structure before we even reach the bikes.' Hans's greatest concern was that the bus might nosedive, bringing tonnes of metal crashing down around him. He'd taken the precaution of installing a six-point safety harness, removing any sharp objects and knocking out all the windows beforehand. I wasn't feeling anxious myself—after all, I just had to jump off before things got dangerous.

Great cheers went up as I took my position on the back landing in my bus conductor's uniform and Hans revved the engine. Our plan was to make several laps of the showground to get our speed up, but we set off much more quickly than I had expected. As I saw the ground whizzing past, faster and faster, I realised the flaw in my plan—I had no way to ask Hans to slow down, and our speed was too great to jump off. I was along for the ride.

We hit the ramp with a huge bump and then we were airborne. I grabbed whatever I could to brace myself as we clipped the last motorcycle and dug dirty great grooves in the ground as we crash-landed. The crowd roared its approval.

I was sore for a few days, but the publicity was tremendous. Not just across the country, but around the world. The stunt cost $1200 all up and I reckon it generated between $100,000 and $200,000 worth of television promotion for Dick Smith Electronics in Australia alone. And it was good fun.

———

In the months leading up to the sale of the business, I'd found myself becoming involved in the Skeptical movement. It came about because I was a regular guest on Nine Network's *The Don Lane Show*. That's how I heard of Uri Geller, an Israeli illusionist, magician and self-proclaimed psychic. When he appeared on Channel Nine, he claimed he was bending spoons using mind power alone.

The first time I saw him, I was impressed. The show made out that what he was doing was factual, so naturally I thought there must be a scientific explanation. But when I did more research, I found that Geller was not genuine in his claims. There was nothing 'paranormal' about his spoon bending; it was merely sleight of hand.

Change is in the air

During my inquiries, I learned of an American organisation called the Committee for the Scientific Investigation of Claims of the Paranormal (CSICOP), which published a magazine called *The Skeptical Inquirer*. One of its founders was a magician called James Randi, who had attempted to expose Geller. Randi believed that magicians should be honest about their tricks being based on skill and preparation, rather than claiming paranormal powers.

I invited Randi to Australia to investigate claims of water divining, where a person uses sticks or steel rods to try and find underground sources of water. In Australia's arid outback, water divining still has many followers—even today. Randi and I decided on a series of tests we would put the diviners through and, along with journalist and commentator Phillip Adams, we put up $40,000 in prize money to be split among whomever passed the tests.

Talented filmmaker Bob Connolly made a documentary about Randi and the tests. After we'd run them, he wrote in to *The Australian* newspaper explaining what had taken place:

Twelve diviners who claimed they could track flowing water in irrigation pipes were selected from the hundreds who responded to invitations to prove their powers. All 12 agreed beforehand that the test was well-designed. All were totally confident of success.

On a field, 10 pipes were laid under the ground. Water could be directed along any of the 10 and the diviner was asked to walk across the 10 pipes and determine which one contained the water.

Before the test proper began, it was obviously important to get the diviners' agreement that everything was in order. First each diviner was told which pipe had water running through it and asked to walk over it. And when the diviners knew which pipe had the water, in every case the divining rods bent, or wobbled or spun. Wonderful.

'Was the power working?' they were asked. Yes, the diviners chorused, you could see for yourself. 'So you should now get the same reactions in the tests proper, even though you don't know which pipe has the water?' One hundred per cent were certain they would.

And all day the 12 diviners performed their magic. Each of them walked across the 10 pipes on 10 different runs. Each time they went across, water was flowing through a different pipe. Each time the rods miraculously spoke their message.

Except that the diviners were wrong . . . hopelessly, incontrovertibly wrong. The chances of picking the right pipe accidentally in 10 runs was one in ten. To support their claims of 100 per cent accuracy, the diviners would have had to pick 10 pipes out of ten. Even nine would have done . . . or five . . . or four! But the overall result was one out of 10 . . . entirely consistent with chance.

The result was exactly as Randi had predicted. I was curious to see how the diviners would react when they were told the results. Would it cause them to think again about their 'paranormal powers'? Not at all. As Bob Connolly wrote, 'They blamed everything from corns to sunspots.'

I was fascinated. There were dozens of open-minded observers in attendance and they felt the tests were conclusive—but not the diviners. When it was announced that they got less than one in ten, they quickly delivered their explanations. One said it was because there were sceptical people present, another claimed the phenomena only worked if you weren't testing it. Another said he got 100 per cent accuracy if you disregarded the times he didn't get a hit because the 'powers' weren't working. These were all genuine people; it was just impossible to get through to them. It wouldn't be the last time I encountered the human powers of self-delusion.

I experienced it myself when I had been searching for the *Kookaburra* a couple of years earlier. On one of the helicopter flights, I vividly 'saw' the wreckage, exactly as I had imagined it, lying in the turpentine scrub with one wheel pointing skywards. As the helicopter was travelling fast and low, the 'wreckage' disappeared from view; so we made a quick 180-degree turn, but the 'wreckage' was nowhere to be seen. When I later discovered it, it was more than 10 kilometres to the north.

It's the same with eye-witness accounts of the Tasmanian tiger. Every year there are many reported sightings, despite the fact that the last known tiger died in 1936. All such 'sightings' are evidence that humans have almost unlimited powers of subconscious imagination—a wonderful gift as long as we don't kid ourselves that it's an adequate substitute for scientific methodology and evaluation.

Following the water divining tests, Phillip Adams and I set up the Australian Skeptics with Melbourne solicitor Mark Plummer. Its mission is to 'advocate critical thinking and scientific reasoning, investigate and provide information on specific paranormal or pseudoscientific claims, and on methods for assessing such claims. To play a key role in rational and intelligent public discourse on science and medicine, and serve as a hub for sceptical activities in Australia.' For the last forty years, the Australian Skeptics have been a major force in encouraging critical thinking in Australia.

———

When I sold 60 per cent of Dick Smith Electronics to Woolworths, part of our agreement was that I didn't have to be there full time. In truth, I was getting bored and was looking for something new, but I still made sure the business was profitable. I spent my 'work time' putting in systems that could be replicated in a disciplined way in each store.

Tandy Electronics had recently developed the best-selling TRS-80, the first mass-produced personal computer, which created an opportunity for us. A clever Hong Kong company used the TRS-80 as a benchmark design, with the same BASIC operating language and the Z80 microprocessor (which ran at the amazing speed of 1.7 MHz), and they produced the Dick Smith System 80.

We added some features, like being able to use any television set as a monitor, and then sold the basic model (with only 4 K of memory) for $695, about $200 cheaper than Tandy's, but still achieving more than a 50 per cent margin. We made an absolute fortune, selling a staggering 12,500 units over two years.

The Dick Smith Wizzard brought another windfall. The combined personal computer (with a huge 17 K memory) and TV game sold for $295, again with a 50 per cent margin. We produced a television ad with lots of kids dancing around singing, 'We are the Dick Smith Wiz Kids in the Electronic Land of Oz' and showing off two-way radios, walkie talkies, games and computers. Interestingly, it included the line, 'Even if your parents don't understand electronics, you can bring them with you!'

Meanwhile, we opened stores everywhere. Between 1980 and 1982, we virtually doubled the number of stores (from fourteen to thirty-three, including one in New Zealand), our sales and our net profit.

CHAPTER 13

Taking to the skies

Thanks to Ike, I now had time to pursue other interests. I was keen to find a way to combine flying my helicopter with spending time with my family.

I loved the television series called *Ask the Leyland Brothers*, which featured brothers Mike and Mal exploring the outback with their families. Why couldn't I do the same, but use my Bell JetRanger rather than a four-wheel drive? I flew up to visit them and they gave me some of the best advice about film-making—*Do it as cheaply as possible*. Even though 'professional' filmmakers looked down on them, they were among the very few making good money out of documentaries.

Once again, I needed to surround myself with capable people. I was impressed by the ABC television series *A Big*

Country, which had made the documentary of our ascent of Ball's Pyramid, and watched it as much as possible. I thought the best episodes were the ones directed by Bob Connolly, so I rang him to see if he'd be willing to leave the ABC and work for me. He seemed vaguely interested and agreed to send me some of his work.

Half a dozen canisters of 16 mm films arrived, so I hired a projector and watched them in my lounge room. They confirmed my belief that he was a talented director, so I rang him once again and convinced him to come and work with me and produce the *Dick Smith and Family Explorer* series, which Channel Seven had agreed to buy.

Our first documentary, *Dick Smith Explorer: The Early Years*, covered a flight that Pip, the girls and I made in my helicopter tracing Captain Cook's arrival and the foundation of Sydney by Captain Arthur Phillip.

Bob Connolly was brilliant. He arranged for the film to open with a shot of my helicopter, *Mike India Sierra*, hovering behind a Qantas 747 at the threshold of Runway 16 at Sydney Airport. I'm on the radio, asking the captain where he's off to.

'London,' he says. 'What about you?'

When I say Botany Bay, he says, 'That's just off the runway, you might as well go in front.'

As I bring the helicopter around, we can hear Hayley on the intercom saying she wants a drink and Pip saying, 'Be quiet, Hayley, Daddy's on the radio.'

Bob also came up with the idea that I'd have a running battle with the air traffic controller, who kept scratching his head and asking, 'Where are you now, *Mike India Sierra?*' At one moment I'd be landing at the monument where Captain Cook first landed in Botany Bay, then I'd be taking off from a wharf in Circular Quay. The show was fun to make and got top ratings for Channel Seven, so we headed to Broken Hill to shoot our second film, *In the Footsteps of Captain Sturt*.

By now I could see that Bob was a dyed-in-the-wool ABC filmmaker, and he was used to working in an environment where there was little cost consciousness. A bit shocked by the mounting expenses, I insisted that we needed to make our documentaries as cheaply as possible. So, instead of using expensive Nagra sound recorders, my friend Garry Cratt (who had helped us find the *Kookaburra*) would come along on our adventures for nothing and record sound on a modified cassette recorder. I also discovered that ABC TV programs like *Four Corners* and the *News* were using positive film rather than the expensive negative film we were using. By using positive film, we saved thousands of dollars.

———

In 1981, I decided to purchase a new JetRanger. But instead of having it delivered to Australia, I decided to pick it up at the Bell Helicopter factory in Fort Worth, Texas, and fly it home myself. I had worked out that it would be possible to fly across the North Atlantic, via Greenland, then Europe and the Middle East, but I'd have to carry extra fuel to get me across stretches of ocean. At that time helicopters were primarily considered short distance aircraft for flying TV crews around cities and the like.

Then I thought, 'If I'm going to fly over halfway around the world, why not finish the job and fly *completely* around the world?' No one had ever done this before in a helicopter. Spending a bit more time with my globe and maps showed me that this just might be possible.

The greatest challenge would be the leg across the North Pacific. If I could get permission to land on Russian soil, I could refuel and ultimately make the flight from Japan to Russia and thence Alaska. If this wasn't going to be possible, the idea I'd come up with was to land on a ship halfway between Japan and the Aleutian Islands to refuel.

Before tackling the bureaucrats, I had a practical problem to solve: how to legally and safely carry enough fuel for the long sea crossings. After work each night, I developed a design for a light, strong frame to hold an auxiliary fuel tank in the rear-seat space. I was basing my calculations on measurements from *Mike India Sierra*. An aeronautical engineer then took my ideas and converted them into finished drawings and helped usher these through the complex business of getting Department of Aviation approval.

I also had to convince the authorities to exempt my helicopter from the requirement that, as a single-engine machine, it be fitted with floats for flying over water. This, of course, would have made the flight impossible; it would have increased wind resistance and weight, causing increased fuel consumption and reducing my range.

These were only some of the bureaucratic battles I found myself fighting. It got to the point where I seriously considered putting my new helicopter on the American register and flying it as an American aircraft. The conditions the USA imposed were far more sensible than those imposed by Australia's civil aviation department. It would have been a pity, as I'm proud to be Australian and it was important to me to fly an Australian-registered helicopter.

However, suddenly things began to improve. Maybe the authorities caught some of my enthusiasm, because they soon provided lots of dispensations against the out-of-date rules. This support went right to the top, when Prime Minister Malcolm Fraser agreed to be the patron of the adventure.

I decided to make a documentary film to help offset the costs, and that meant designing, building and testing camera mounts.

In early February 1982, I flew to Fort Worth to visit the Bell Helicopter factory. I knew that my flight would have risks, but I hoped to reduce as many as possible. Simply choosing the JetRanger was the first step, as it was powered by an Allison engine, one of the world's most reliable. I then learned that Bell was about to take delivery of fifty Allison engines; I asked the engineers to pick the engine that had the lowest fuel consumption.

We then chose my aircraft's fuselage and, when it reached the production line, I had a sign put on it that said, 'This helicopter is to attempt the first solo around-the-world helicopter flight—please give it 150 per cent.' I also spoke with the factory staff to say how important it was that everything be double-checked. They all seemed excited about being part of a record-attempting flight.

The next few months swept by in a blur of paperwork, testing gear and finalising my flight plan. I needed permission from the nineteen countries that I would be flying over. Some countries were helpful and replied promptly; some didn't reply at all. Australia's Department of Foreign Affairs helped when it could.

I set my departure date from Fort Worth for 5 August 1982 and planned on taking my time, ready to delay my flight at any time if the weather turned nasty. I also thought it would be good fun if I could be welcomed in Great Britain by Prince Charles. I had previously met the prince and knew that he was an enthusiastic helicopter pilot who regarded his time in helicopters as the best part of his navy service.

Our prime minister helped arrange an approach to the prince and, to my surprise, he agreed. I suppose it appealed to his sense of adventure. The prince's aide confirmed the time and place: 10.30 a.m. on 19 August at Balmoral Castle. This was the date I had requested, as it was the fiftieth anniversary of the first solo, fixed-wing, east–west crossing of the Atlantic Ocean by James Mollison. If I was successful, my flight would be the first solo rotary-wing crossing. It was American Charles Lindbergh who did the first solo fixed-wing crossing.

I now had a schedule that I had to stick to!

CHAPTER 14

Solo around the world in a helicopter

In July 1982, I boarded a Qantas 747 bound for San Francisco, where I spent the night before I flew on to Fort Worth. When I arrived, I was shocked to find that *Delta India Kilo* (DIK) was in bits and pieces scattered all over the hangar floor. Field Tech, the company installing my aviation equipment, was doing a great job, but not enough time had been allowed to do the complex work.

I pitched in to help and, after four days, I prepared to take *Delta India Kilo* on a test flight. It was my first flight as a pilot in American airspace and I was pleasantly surprised by the brisk informality with which helicopters were treated. *Delta India Kilo* flew like a dream. On the eve of my flight, I wrote in my diary: 'The biggest and most exciting adventure of my life starts tomorrow and I'm not sure how I will go—but aren't I lucky to be able to attempt it.'

I awoke at 5 a.m. on 5 August 1982 with that exciting Christmas Day feeling I had when I was a boy. Today was my personal D-Day; there was no turning back now. The weather forecast didn't look too bad: hot southerly winds, with possible thunderstorms later in the day.

At the airfield, *Delta India Kilo* looked absolutely beautiful, shimmering in the early sunlight. It was 10 a.m. by the time I'd finished all my final preparations, media interviews and an all-too-brief conversation with Pip and the girls back at home. I was invited up on a small stage set up in front of the Bell Helicopter factory, where I was wished a safe flight by Bell executives.

Delta India Kilo lifted off at 10.31 a.m. Fort Worth time. I set my course for my first stop at Memphis, Tennessee, then on to Knoxville, where I visited the Australian Pavilion at the World's Fair and spent the night.

The next morning, my plan was to reach Washington, DC, that day, but as I approached the Appalachian Mountains, I could see that the weather was closing in. I found a railway line that followed a river through the mountains and began following it in rapidly deteriorating weather. I was flying at 500 feet when heavy rain cut visibility to almost zero, and by the time I had flown around several torrential showers, I was temporarily disoriented.

I knew I was about 22 kilometres out of Lynchburg, Tennessee, so radioed the airport's tower. The response was instantaneous, and the controller was very helpful when I asked whether the railway line went to Washington. He directed me to fly along it for a few miles until I intersected with a road that would take me to my destination. These were the days before GPS.

Even after I found the road, the next 70 kilometres were almost impossible. I flew just above the highway through heavy showers and appalling visibility, keeping a constant watch for high towers, electricity pylons and other potentially lethal objects.

As I flew slowly across the Potomac River, the water surface beneath me was pocked with raindrops and I could just make out the far bank. I was unable to raise the control tower in Washington. But, to the south, I could see a holiday shack with an old man standing by it. The rain was getting heavier, so there was no choice but to put the helicopter down on the road in front of the shack.

I ran over to the old man, who'd been joined by a youth of about nineteen, and asked if I could use their phone. 'We don't mind,' they said with amazed looks. When I got through to the Washington tower controller and explained that I was phoning from a farmer's house and I wanted instructions on how to enter their airspace, he laughed and said pilots normally remained in the air and radioed their requests but he was happy to give me the information over the phone.

I was filled with anxiety as I approached the capital of the United States in such dreadful weather. The skies above me were filled with aircraft heading for Washington National Airport and I had no idea what to do next. Suddenly the controller came back on the air and directed me to a part of the aerodrome where a crowd, mostly media people, waited.

I came in quickly, far too high with the wind behind me— not the safest way—and landed. By the time I'd finished my interviews, checked *Delta India Kilo*, and had dinner, I was physically and mentally exhausted. I could see that flying the helicopter, navigating, communicating with air traffic control, filming, taking still photographs and making a running commentary for a book would really stretch my abilities.

———

By the time I landed in Moncton, Canada, on 8 August, I was cold, tired and tense. After getting through the customs formalities, I rang Pip and sobbed out my tale of woe. My Omega navigation system had stopped working, my HF radio was giving trouble, the chip detector (for detecting chips in the gearbox) was indicating 'on' and the cockpit had been filled with the smell of something burning. I was exhausted from all the bad weather flying and didn't think I could go on.

Pip gave me reassuring words and suggested I sleep on it and reconsider in the morning; she would support me either way. This was wise counsel, because the next morning I discovered that most of the faults from the night before were either non-existent or not all that serious. My problem was my extreme fatigue. The burning smell had been caused when I accidentally knocked the landing-light switch and the light had overheated a plastic shield.

Late in the evening of 11 August, I crossed Hudson Strait and reached the coast of Baffin Island, where I was forced to land in terrible weather with cloud right to the ground. That's the advantage of a helicopter. The country around me was harsh and inhospitable, yet strangely beautiful; I was just south of the Arctic Circle. After sitting in the helicopter for a while, I set up my tent, unrolled my sleeping bag and hopped in, hoping for a good night's sleep. It was not that easy, though, thanks to big, hungry mosquitos—and the crashing of nearby icebergs.

The next morning, I landed in Frobisher Bay after only a fifty-two minute flight. While I was waiting for *Delta India Kilo* to be refuelled, I spoke with two locals; they asked where I'd spent the previous night. When I told them, they were shocked. They explained that polar bears are common in that area and nobody in their right senses would camp in the open. It hadn't even occurred to me that I was in danger. I was lucky to have only been bitten by huge mosquitos.

After refuelling and a telephone call to Pip, I was airborne. I was hoping to reach Sondrestrom, Greenland, 1000 kilometres to the north-east, but Baffin Island had one last trick up its sleeve.

As I was crossing the Cumberland Peninsula at 3000 feet, mesmerised by the good weather and stunning views of towering icebergs in the distance, the world suddenly turned upside down. *Delta India Kilo* reared and bucked as though shaken by a giant hand. I had flown into the worst clear-air turbulence I'd ever encountered. It was absolutely terrifying. Mountains, ice and sea reeled around me as I fought for control. I feared the helicopter would break up from the stress, but the manufacturer had done a great job and she held together.

Later that day, as I approached Greenland over Davis Strait, I learned that it was snowing ahead. The pilot of a Sikorsky helicopter, who had just left Sondrestrom, reported that there was some cloud, but he'd found several openings. He suggested I climb to 6000 feet, come in over the cloud and descend through one of the gaps. I followed his advice.

My little helicopter didn't mind the altitude, but I did. The outside air temperature was −10°C and, despite wearing my survival suit over several layers of clothing, my hands and feet ached in the bitter cold. As I approached Sondrestrom, swirling snow reduced visibility to a few hundred metres.

I descended to 500 feet above the icy waters of the fjord with the sickening realisation that, if the weather got worse, I would fly right into it. The situation was alarming, but then the Sondrestrom controller turned on the airport's brilliant strobe lights, which suddenly appeared as a glow some 3 kilometres ahead. To my immense relief, I touched down, exhausted, frightened and almost frozen to death.

It was at this stage that I worked out what was going wrong. I had planned the flight to fly in a high pressure weather system across the Atlantic: this would result in the best weather conditions for a tiny helicopter flying visually. My original plan was simply to wait until the high pressure system moved into place.

But because I had a pre-arranged date to meet Prince Charles, I had found myself in the middle of a low pressure system, with the terrible weather that goes with it.

———

After a lay day at Sondrestrom, and two days of flying across Greenland, I set off across the Denmark Strait on my 700-kilometre flight to Reykjavik, Iceland. I enjoyed good weather for an hour and a half, but then the weather turned bad once again. Soon I was dodging low cloud that forced me to descend to a few hundred feet.

Hour after hour I flew on over a freezing and now terrifyingly rough ocean scattered with icebergs. It sure looked cold down there. As the weather went from bad to shocking, I found myself winding my way around snow showers in dangerously low visibility. At one stage, I decided to go back to Greenland, but when I turned it was obvious the bad weather had closed in behind me. I was becoming frightened, with a sick feeling in my stomach. 'I shouldn't be here,' I thought. But my only option was to keep heading towards Iceland, and eventually I found my way through.

I refuelled in Reykjavik and continued on, flying in heavy rain above vast lava flows until I reached Hornafjördör, where the weather stopped me from continuing on to the Faroe Islands, a Danish archipelago smack in the middle of the North Atlantic.

On the morning of 18 August, I climbed away from Hornafjördör in good weather and a 4000-foot ceiling, but the conditions didn't last. Soon I was dodging rain squalls that forced me to descend to between 500 and 1000 feet.

If my engine failed, I would have less than sixty seconds to give a mayday call as I auto-rotated (that's how helicopters glide) and hit the water. I'd then have about thirty seconds to grab the life raft beside me, scramble out the door, inflate the raft and climb into it as the helicopter sank beneath me. Hopefully my survival suit would protect me from the cold until help arrived. Every move would have to be precise and quick. Even a slight delay would send me down with the helicopter.

I found flying alone across the Atlantic in a single-engine aircraft to be a profoundly disturbing experience. There is an overwhelming feeling of loneliness brought on by such an immense wilderness of water, and I knew I was unlikely to live if I came down. I was scared most of the time; my life really depended on the reliability of that single little Allison engine.

I landed at Vagar in the Faroes after two hours, thirty-nine minutes of flying. I would have liked to look around, but my appointment with Prince Charles was less than twenty-four hours away and I still had about 900 kilometres to go. Buckingham Palace had arranged for me to land on the Queen's golf course at Balmoral at 10.30 a.m.

I was impatient to get away. I had a recurring image in my mind of Prince Charles scanning the sky for *Delta India Kilo*, while I sat out a storm somewhere. I could imagine how embarrassing it would be for Pip and the girls and the people from the

Australian High Commission who had been invited to be there at my landing.

Imagine my disappointment when I learned that the weather at my next stop, Sumburgh in the South Shetland Islands, was 'very marginal' and I was unlikely to get there. Hastily I consulted my maps. A few calculations told me I would be able to fly to Stornoway in the Outer Hebrides and bypass the Shetlands altogether.

After refuelling, I got away one hour and twenty-two minutes after landing and touched down in the United Kingdom at 3.25 p.m., the first person to fly a helicopter solo across the Atlantic! It was a fantastic feeling.

After complying with customs requirements, I refuelled *Delta India Kilo* and gave her a good wash. I then brushed the creases from my survival suit and borrowed shoe polish from an airport fireman to put a gleam on my shoes. After all, I couldn't meet royalty in grubby shoes. I checked my aviation map and found it did not show Balmoral Castle, so I got a lift into town and purchased a road map.

While on the ground at Stornoway, I made a disturbing discovery. There were two bullet holes in the helicopter— one bullet entering and lodging in the auxiliary fuel tank and the other going through the front window. The bullet holes have remained a mystery. The most likely explanation is that someone had taken a pot shot at the helicopter when it was at a remote airstrip in Greenland.

---

19 August 1982 dawned fine and clear. At 7.59 a.m. I lifted off from Stornoway for my last over-water leg of the Atlantic crossing—the channel called The Minch, between Lewis and the Scottish mainland. I then opened the road map and had to drop down to a road junction to read the road sign. As I was hovering low over the road, looking between the sign and my map, a police car came over the hill and screamed to a stop. I took one look at the driver, pulled up on the helicopter's collective and zoomed away. I can only imagine what the policeman thought—a helicopter with 'Solo Around the World' sign-writing and the pilot reading a road map! I would love to see the report he put in.

Just before 10.30 a.m. I roared down the River Dee valley at 500 feet and swept around a bend, expecting to see a big building like Windsor Castle just ahead. But there was none in sight.

'Crikey,' I thought, feeling sick. 'I've mucked it up. It's the wrong valley and I'm going to be late.' Then to my immense relief, I saw a small castle, nestled among the trees, and a welcoming party on the golf course just a few hundred metres below.

I came in far too high and had to reduce power drastically and almost auto-rotate to put me on the 'H' marker. Touchdown was at 10.29 a.m., one minute ahead of schedule.

'Not bad timing,' I thought. It was a fitting commemoration to James Mollison, exactly fifty years after his historic solo Atlantic flight.

Soon I was shaking hands with Prince Charles and hugging Pip and the girls. The prince was extremely friendly and most interested in the JetRanger. He asked many questions about the flight and seemed amazed by the small size of *Delta India Kilo*.

Prince Charles spent an enjoyable half hour with us before driving his green Range Rover back to the castle. Before continuing on, I spoke with the media. Most were more interested in what the prince had said to me than my first solo helicopter crossing of the Atlantic.

I had flown my little machine 11,752 kilometres from Fort Worth in sixty hours, fifty-two minutes, spread over eleven days, at an average speed of 104 knots (192 kilometres per hour). By the time I landed, I was physically, mentally and emotionally exhausted. The first leg of my around-the-world flight was complete, but I still had a long way to go.

———

Pioneer Australian aviator Bert Hinkler was the first person to fly solo from London to Darwin in a fixed-wing aircraft. In 1928, Hinkler flew fifteen and a half days to Darwin, then continued on to a hero's welcome in his home town, Bundaberg, Queensland.

He began his flight from Croydon, less than 16 kilometres from the old wartime airfield of Biggin Hill, where, on 13 September 1982, I was completing my final checks before departing on my second leg—London to Sydney.

At 7.38 a.m., Pip and the girls waved me off and I set a course to the south-east, to Nice and then on to Rome for the night.

Over the next six days, flying mainly 500 feet above ground level, I battled headwinds and bureaucracy as I crossed Italy, flew down through Greece and over the Mediterranean Sea to Egypt. I then flew to Luxor and above the Red Sea to Bahrain, passing over the oil-rich sands of Saudi Arabia. It was a magic carpet ride.

Bahrain to Karachi, Pakistan, was a long day. I got to bed at 12.40 a.m. and was back at the airport at 4 a.m., lifting off an hour later. It was a week-long grind of early starts, long hours of flying and many more hours refuelling—and dealing with tedious entry and departure formalities.

On Sunday, 19 September, I took off from Karachi into the heat and glare of the rising sun. I'd had only three hours' sleep. I'd planned on flying directly to Ahmadabad, then to New Delhi, but Indian officialdom insisted that I fly a long dogleg on the way.

By the time I reached Delhi, I had come to the view that if I didn't take a rest I would be a danger to myself. I rang Pip and poured out my heart to her. 'I'm not sure I can go on,' I said 'I'm so incredibly tired.' Gradually, as we talked, my confidence came back again and I decided to press on. I redrew my flight plans to cut out Nepal and fly direct to Calcutta via Lucknow, before flying on to Rangoon's Mingaladon Airport over the Burmese coast.

From Rangoon, I hoped to fly south to the resort town of Phuket, in Thailand. My track would take me over the island of Aye, 180 kilometres south of Rangoon, where it's thought that Charles Kingsford Smith and Tommy Pethybridge fatally crashed in the *Lady Southern Cross* in 1935. Smithy was a hero of mine and I felt that by flying over the area where he disappeared, I would be paying tribute to one of the world's greatest aviators.

I departed Mingaladon Airport at 6.15 a.m. on 23 September. The weather forecast looked good right through to Phuket. After an hour's flying, I recognised the outline of Aye Island from photos I'd seen previously and made a low run on the course Smithy could have been flying. The island was a mixture of jungle and cliffs, not a place to be flying close to at night or in bad weather. One theory is that Smithy had engine problems and clipped the top of the island while searching for a place to land. It was a sombre thought as I circled the island, photographing the small beach where an undercarriage leg and tyre of the *Lady Southern Cross* were found.

As I continued south to Phuket, the weather deteriorated dramatically. A tropical downpour drummed on the canopy as I turned to pick up the coastline. I skimmed over beaches and villages for half an hour, then the weather went from appalling to dangerous. I could see nothing ahead, with my visibility limited to a small patch beneath my feet.

I reduced speed to 70 kilometres per hour, then crabbed sideways until I could see waves crashing on a beach. I moved up to the smooth sand and landed. As my engine wound down, I breathed a sigh of relief.

'Thank heavens,' I thought. 'I'm alive.'

For a few moments, the rain eased. Further up the beach loomed a dark headland. If I hadn't landed, I could have flown straight into it. I'd never have survived.

I barely had time to process this, when I noticed that the helicopter was slowly tilting to one side! The weight of fuel in the tanks was driving the right-hand skid deep into the wet sand. I leapt out and furiously began digging the sand away but with no luck. It just sank deeper.

Soaked, I jumped in and fired up the Allison engine. By now the helicopter was listing backwards as well as to the side and the tail rotor was perilously close to the sand. I gave the engine 100 per cent power—without result. I increased it to 110 per cent for the maximum five seconds allowed and *Delta India Kilo* hauled herself clear. By now the rain was so heavy I doubted the machine would stay airborne, so in great trepidation, I put down on the beach closer to the jungle, hoping the sand would stay firm. Fortunately, it did. After another hour of heavy rain, I eventually got airborne.

Over the next four days, I enjoyed mostly fine weather as I flew from Phuket to Singapore, doused myself with bottled water to celebrate crossing the equator, then continued on to Jakarta and, finally, Denpasar, in Bali.

On Tuesday, 28 September, I was awake at 3.45 a.m.; at 4.45 a.m. I took off from Denpasar at the first hint of dawn. I desperately wanted to get to Darwin before nightfall to match Bert Hinkler's fifteen and a half days. To do so, I'd have to spend more than nine hours in the air and fly more than 1900 kilometres, the longest leg of the flight.

Almost immediately, I was over the sea. Gradually the sun appeared in a blaze of red and gold and climbed into wispy clouds. About 120 kilometres out of Bali, cruising at 1000 feet in superb weather, I heard an Australian accent. It was Perth! Then Darwin radio came through. I was getting close to home at last.

Nearly five hours out of Denpasar, I landed at Kupang, hoping desperately that I wouldn't be held up by over-zealous officials. But everyone was smiling, friendly and anxious to get me airborne as soon as possible. I was on my way again in fifty-two minutes, surely a record!

Calls from amateur radio operators from all over Australia sped up my 800-kilometre sea crossing. As I got close to Darwin, I was met by an escort of three aircraft, an army Pilatus Porter and two helicopters.

My excitement mounted as Darwin came into view. I could imagine how Hinkler, Smithy and all the other aviators had felt. I'd asked the aviation authorities if I could land close to Darwin's original airport in Parap, where Bert Hinkler landed. They'd gone one better and built a helipad for me on the exact spot Hinkler touched down.

A crowd of over a thousand people, including Pip, surrounded the pad as I landed *Delta India Kilo* at 5.31 p.m. I had matched Bert Hinkler's time. Impulsively, I leapt out of the JetRanger and pressed my lips against good red Australian soil.

———

I took the next day off and spent most of the time fielding telephone calls from the media and reading a stack of telegrams, including one from the prime minister. Later that day, walking around Darwin with Pip, I was touched and flattered by the friendly interest people showed.

Two days later, I delivered the *Times* to Alexandria Station, just as Hinkler had done fifty-four years earlier, then I flew on to spend the night at Longreach, where I parked outside the historic hangar in which Qantas had begun operations.

On 2 October, I continued east, retracing Hinkler's final 1000-kilometre leg to his home town, Bundaberg. My reception there was amazing. I was declared guest of honour at the Harvest Festival and, incredibly, rode through the streets on a float with Bert Hinkler's photo on one side and a shot of *Delta India Kilo* and me (in London) on the other. There were presentations, speeches and even a civic dinner. The people of Bundaberg clearly have a great interest in Hinkler and were delighted that my flight commemorated their famous son.

On Sunday, 3 October, I lifted off from Bundaberg at 8.22 a.m. In Coolangatta, I landed and met with Harold Litchfield, navigator on some of Kingsford Smith's early flights, and Lores Bonney, who flew a DH Moth solo from Australia to England in 1933. Mrs Bonney told me how she'd crashed on a beach in Thailand in similar weather to that I'd experienced. She had dismantled her aircraft and had it towed on a barge to Calcutta, where she had it repaired and resumed her flight.

I made one more stop near Port Macquarie to visit my dad, then continued down the coast to Sydney. Pip had requested permission for me to fly *under* the Sydney Harbour Bridge, but I wasn't sure if her request had been granted. I asked air traffic control for confirmation. 'Affirmative,' came the reply. As I passed the Opera House, I dropped *Delta India Kilo* to 85 feet and zoomed under the bridge.

I landed to an incredible welcome at the Darling Harbour Heliport, where I hugged Pip, Hayley, Jenny and my mum and was greeted by the state premier, Neville Wran. He said kind things about my flight and offered a champagne toast.

During the second leg, from London to Sydney, I'd covered 12,469 nautical miles (23,092 kilometres) in 113 hours and 20 minutes, at an average speed of 110 knots (203 kilometres per hour). I still had the final leg of the trip—Sydney to Fort Worth (including the dangerous crossing of the North Pacific)—to complete, but that was months away.

———

In the months following my completion of the second leg, I spent considerable time confronting the most difficult puzzle of my whole flight—how to fly a helicopter with a limited range across the Pacific Ocean.

The most logical route would have been to fly north through Indonesia, the Philippines, Taiwan and Japan, and then up Russia's Kuril Islands and Kamchatka Peninsula before making the relatively short hop across to Alaska.

I'd contacted Soviet diplomats in Canberra, who'd been helpful with my permit application, but the Russian military gave my request the thumbs down. At the time, relations between the Soviet Union and the West were at a low point. In fact, just months after my flight, the Soviet air force would shoot down Korean Airlines 007, a passenger 747 with 267 people on board that strayed over Kamchatka while on a flight from Anchorage to Seoul.

My only alternative was to fly from Hokkaido, Japan, to Shemya on the western end of Alaska's Aleutian Islands. But the distance was about 2600 kilometres and *Delta India Kilo* could only fly half that with reasonable reserves for safety. It was clear to me the only answer was to refuel on a ship halfway across. I needed a ship with enough deck space to land a helicopter, one that would be close to the halfway point of my route on about 21 June, the longest day of the year.

After months of searching and sending over two hundred letters to shipping companies, the Höegh shipping company agreed that I could refuel on their ship, the *Höegh Marlin*, which would be on its normal voyage from Yokohama to Seattle in late June.

On 25 May 1983, I flew *Delta India Kilo* out of Sydney on the last stage of my solo flight around the world—destination Fort Worth, Texas.

Over the next two weeks, I flew from Sydney to Thursday Island, and then over Indonesia and the Philippines to land finally in Hong Kong. I then took off for Taiwan in the most terrible weather. It was the rainy season, but if I was to rendezvous with the *Höegh Marlin*, I had to be in Japan within the week.

The monsoon season was to plague me most of the way to Tokyo. On Monday, 20 June, I hit the heaviest rain I'd ever flown in. I couldn't believe the engine didn't flame out as I groped on. After almost an hour, the southern headland of Shikoku loomed ahead, but there was nowhere to land. I continued on for another hour over the ocean to reach Honshu, where I was forced to land in very low visibility on a concrete wharf.

For twenty minutes I sat listening to the roar of rain, feeling miserable and cold. As the rain eased, people began to appear. They didn't speak English, but they were all friendly and helpful, and put me up for the night. I had been forced down in a fishing cooperative on the small island of Oshima, off the coast of Honshu. It wasn't until the middle of Tuesday that the gale eased enough for me to depart for Tokyo, a speedy flight of just under three hours.

I had been informed that the *Höegh Marlin* was expected in Yokohama's port that day, so it was likely to be somewhere on the seas beneath me. As I flew up the coast, I used my small FM marine radio to try contacting the ship's captain, and suddenly he answered! I was able to locate him quickly and was relieved to see the ship was a decent size. I even made several practice approaches. All the same, I felt apprehensive about finding it 1300 kilometres out in the North Pacific—with my life depending on it.

The next day, I boarded the *Höegh Marlin* and inspected its deck and chose the exact spot where I would land. I also met up with Don Richards, my ham radio friend from Sydney, who would be manning the amateur radio rig and the non-directional beacon we had made. The following morning, Thursday, 23 June, I left Tokyo on my five-hour flight to Kushiro, where I would wait for the ship to be about halfway on its journey to Seattle.

I also stripped everything I could from *Delta India Kilo* to save weight because of the extra fuel on board. Movie cameras, clothing, every bit of lining from the aircraft—everything I could get out came out. Of all my personal effects, only my toothbrush remained. I even refuelled with a special lightweight fuel and, for the first time, filled a special extra tank I'd fitted for this leg.

At the airport at 3 a.m. on Saturday, 25 June, I meticulously went through final checks, then donned my survival suit and climbed into the cockpit. *Delta India Kilo* was 20 per cent over its maximum operating weight as it struggled to lift off at 3.40 a.m. in pitch darkness. An hour after leaving Kushiro, I climbed through fog and stratus cloud. As I emerged into hazy skies above, I could occasionally see the peaks of the Kuril Islands poking through.

On board *Höegh Marlin*, Don Richards reported that 'every time I looked out of my cabin porthole I became more doubtful about Dick finding us in such conditions (patchy fog and poor visibility)'.

I was constantly giving position reports by amateur radio to both Don on the ship and amateurs in Australia. Pip was also following everything from my amateur station at our home; at one stage she reminded me it was Jenny's ninth birthday, so I sang 'Happy Birthday' to our 'Little Jen' over the airwaves.

As I continued my flight above thick cloud, I knew I'd have to descend to hopefully find a fog-free space between the cloud and the ocean. If there was none, I'd have to abort the landing and head to the Soviet Union to find a place to put down. In the distance, I could see volcano cones sticking up through the cloud in their airspace.

By 9 a.m., Don was reporting that conditions at the ship were improving. Unfortunately, I was above the clouds and had to decide whether to attempt penetrating the cloud to search for the ship, or head into the USSR. I no longer had enough fuel to return to Japan. I felt sick inside. Should I take the risk and head for the ship? These were the days before GPS, so I wasn't exactly sure where I was.

Don turned on the radio beacon we had made in Australia and I got a weak response from my direction-finding indicator. I decided to go for the ship. After all, it was the only way I could complete my world record attempt. After descending for several agonising minutes in low visibility, I broke out of cloud and could see a little dot in the distance. As I got closer, I realised it was the *Höegh Marlin*. I had found it!

I'd been in the air for six hours when I approached the ship. At 9.55 a.m., I was given 'permission to land' and two minutes later touched down, almost on a 'Welcome Dick Smith' sign painted on the deck. It was my first ever shipboard landing.

Captain Rodahl and his Norwegian crew were wonderful, helping Don refuel the helicopter and serving me lunch. My planned hour on board stretched to two because the rolling of the ship delayed refuelling. Time was crucial, as Shemya, the US Air Force base in the Aleutians I was heading for, was still seven hours to the north-east and I had to land there before dark.

Don kept a log of my take-off. 'The fire crew stood ready and the turbine came to life,' he wrote. 'It seemed like minutes before the heavily laden aircraft lifted. I knew the maximum overload power could be sustained for only a few seconds. The nose dipped for forward motion just as the ship rolled, and as *Delta India Kilo* moved swiftly across the deck, it missed the hold-down studs—large bolts in the deck—by inches. One quick circuit of the ship, and away they went for Shemya.'

Alone in the air again, I realised that this leg was as risky as the last. There was another 1260 kilometres ahead and the temperature in the cockpit was freezing as I passed through fog and rain for hour after hour above the rough ocean. I found that as well as being frightened, I was also extremely tired. Fortunately, Pip came on the air and kept me motivated. As I approached Shemya, the controller there reported it was overcast with a little rain, but there would be enough twilight to land and they'd put the runway lights on.

When I touched down at 10.38 p.m., the ham radio network erupted with messages of congratulations from around the world. I'd flown 2600 kilometres over the ocean in my tiny single-engined helicopter. It was further than flying from Australia to New Zealand and was the riskiest thing I had ever done. I'd passed through five time zones and crossed the

International Date Line in twelve hours and two minutes of flying. I'd been without sleep for thirty-six hours—and went to bed exhausted.

I spent the next day recuperating. The flight had been mentally and physically debilitating—even traumatic—but the incredible friendliness and support of the base commander, Colonel Ed Fray, and his people totally revitalised me.

I departed Shemya at midday on Sunday, 26 June and spent the next three days working my way up the chain of Aleutian Islands (the tops of submerged mountains) to King Salmon on the Alaskan mainland. On the way I saw sea otters, seals, caribou, bears and thousands of birds. Every island seemed to have a volcanic cone or two. Between King Salmon and Anchorage, I encountered snow showers as I groped my way over mountain passes and flew above heavily crevassed glaciers.

In Anchorage, *Delta India Kilo* went in for a 100-hour service. Then I took off from there at 7.55 a.m. on Sunday, 10 July, and over the next three days I followed the west coast of Alaska and Canada to Vancouver, before spearing through six US states and into the heart of Texas. I spent two days in Amarillo, Texas, organising my 530-kilometre flight to Fort Worth. I'd dedicated this leg of my flight to Wiley Post, who, fifty years before, had flown the first fixed-wing aircraft solo around the world and landed back in the USA on 22 July. I organised to meet Mae Post, his eighty-six year old widow, who lived nearby. It turned out that Mae was just as excited to meet me and I found her to be positively inspiring.

At 7.20 a.m. on Friday, 22 July 1983, I took off for Fort Worth. Nearly a year earlier, I'd promised the people at Bell Helicopters that I'd be back at 10.30 a.m. this day, to commemorate Wiley's flight. As I picked up my final chart to check my progress, I saw running across the right-hand side, the handwritten track of my outgoing flight from Fort Worth. *Delta India Kilo* and I had come full circle. We touched down at 10.29 a.m.

During the welcoming ceremonies and media interviews, I was reported as saying: 'I pushed my luck too far. Flying a helicopter solo around the world is just too risky a business.' But it was there to be done, and in the end I was glad I did it. In flying around the world, I covered 60,992 kilometres, a far longer distance than around the world at the equator.

In time, the National Air and Space Museum in Washington, DC, added my name to the record of first flights around the world. Mine is the only one not made by an American.

CHAPTER 15

Dick Smith's journal of adventure and discovery

DICK SET TO SPLASH OUT ON NEW MAG

headline in Sydney *Daily Telegraph*, Friday, 24 August 1984

On Christmas Eve 1982, I arrived in Hobart with a cake Pip had made. It had a file hidden inside it and the idea was to try to smuggle it into Hobart's notorious Risdon Prison, where my friend Dr Bob Brown was incarcerated. As the leader of the Franklin River Dam blockade, he'd been one of the first protestors to be arrested and I was hoping to cheer him up.

The file was a joke, but the threat to Tasmania's wilderness wasn't. The state's craggy peaks, towering forests and button-grass plains had made a big impression on me when I was nineteen and had first walked the Overland Track from

Cradle Mountain to Lake St Clair. Over the next two decades, I repeated that walk with Pip, climbed Frenchman's Cap and explored the wild south-west again and again.

In 1966, I even flew as a passenger in a small charter plane to remote Lake Pedder, landing on its crisscross-patterned beach. I'll never forget stepping out of the plane onto the glare of quartzite sand, surrounded by absolute silence. It felt overwhelmingly special.

Six years later, a dam built by the state's Hydro-Electric Commission (HEC) flooded that beautiful beach, despite protests and demonstrations and the commitment of people like Bob Brown. That campaign was the beginning of the world's first Green party.

Then, in 1978, the HEC announced plans to build the Gordon-below-Franklin Dam. Thanks to the stunning work of photographers Olegas Truchanas and Peter Dombrovskis, many Australians had been shown what would be lost if the Franklin River was flooded.

The Wilderness Society, Tasmanian Conservation Trust and the Australian Conservation Society began campaigning to stop construction of the dam. In an incredible last-ditch effort, Bob Brown toured mainland Australia, giving lectures and screening films to raise awareness, but even so, by late 1982, the bulldozers were moving in.

I had mixed feelings. I believed that hydro-electricity was a wonderful way to generate power; however, this was the last really wild river in Tasmania and it was going to be destroyed.

So, on 13 December, I chartered a Fokker Friendship from Sydney and flew a group of people—including journalists, historian Professor Manning Clark and businessman John Dingle—to Tassie's west coast for a bird's eye view of the construction site. John inspired me, because even though he was blind, he could still see the value in protecting world-class wilderness areas like the Franklin River.

We landed in the tiny fishing village of Strahan and farewelled a launch filled with protestors as it left for the blockade site. In the previous weeks, I'd paid for full-page ads to run in the national press and contributed to the cost of transporting protestors to and from the blockade.

Over the next month, Pip, our daughters and I visited the blockade ourselves. We had just arrived one day when renowned botanist David Bellamy became the 500th protestor to be arrested. Though I made it clear from the start that I wouldn't break the law, I did what I could to assist the campaign. At one stage, a journalist asked me how much I would be prepared to pay to stop the dam. I said $1 million. This was then beaten up in the media that I was intending to bribe political parties.

Fortunately, the No Dams campaign was getting results, especially on the mainland. In March 1983, the Australian Labor Party won the federal election and Bob Hawke vowed to stop the dam's construction; but it took until 1 July before a High Court ruling finally gave the federal government the power to do so. It was a hard-fought victory.

Not surprisingly, feelings ran high on both sides. For the first time, I found myself being personally criticised in the media, and not because I supported the protestors.

Under the headline 'Dick Smith enters the Franklin fray—almost inevitably', journalist Errol Simper from *The Australian* wrote, 'There was a certain inevitability about electronics millionaire Dick Smith getting involved in the Franklin Dam issue. It is difficult to know if Mr Smith notes the glare of the public gaze—*à la* Franklin—then hitches his schemes to the gaze, or whether his exploits have enough charisma and eccentricity of their own to ensure publicity whatever he does. One suspects the latter.'

And Simper wasn't the only journalist to accuse me of supporting the No Dams campaign as a publicity stunt. But could I blame them? After all, I'd built a successful business from nothing, thanks, in part, to my ability to get free publicity. But something about these attacks bothered me.

Despite my love of the bush, my adventures and my support of projects like a scientific expedition to Heard Island and Dr David Lewis's wintering over in East Antarctica on board the *Dick Smith Explorer*, it seemed I was destined to be remembered as the publicity-hungry 'eccentric millionaire businessman'. I could see I needed to come up with a way that I could change my media image.

———

In February, when Pip, the girls and I got back from Tasmania, our friend Valerie Taylor dropped by to teach Pip and me to scuba dive in our pool at Terrey Hills. We'd booked a voyage to Papua New Guinea in March with Lindblad Expeditions; Valerie and her husband Ron were dive guides on the trip and we hoped to pass our scuba diving exam before joining them.

Ron and Valerie were household names, thanks to their work on films like *Jaws* and *Blue Lagoon* and their exciting stories in the American publication *National Geographic*.

I'd been a fan of *National Geographic* all my life. In the 1950s, my Roseville Public School class went to the Chatswood Theatre to see a film about Hillary and Tenzing's ascent of Mt Everest. Their expedition was sponsored by the National Geographic Society. I remember leaving the theatre feeling excited and inspired, clearly motivated by what I'd seen.

During a trip to America in 1981, I arranged to visit *National Geographic*'s head office to discuss my sponsorship of the expedition by David Lewis to Antarctica; there I met Bill Garrett, the editor. Bill took the time to introduce me to his senior executives and show me around, and we quickly became friends. I was impressed by how committed everyone was to producing a quality magazine, and by the incredible mementos from expeditions sponsored by the National Geographic Society.

In August 1982, I had exercised my option to sell the remaining 40 per cent of Dick Smith Electronics to Woolworths. I'd received $25 million and, fulfilling my promise to Ike, he received a substantial bonus. The business had turned over

$32 million for the year with an $8 million net profit. Pip and I owned buildings worth about $10 million; so with total assets of $35 million, as a thirty-eight year old, I really didn't have to work again.

The Woolworths money came through when I was in the UK on my round-the-world helicopter trip and soon afterwards I created a company called Dick Smith Adventure to sponsor expeditions, just as the National Geographic Society had been doing for so long, and to make documentary films. Even though I didn't have to work anymore, my father's training stuck with me. 'You should always have a work ethic,' he'd always told me.

As I read more articles by Australian adventurers in *National Geographic*, I wondered why we didn't have a similar magazine, something that focused on our own country rather than an American view of the world. I decided to start one myself—it could help change my media image and also tie in with my support of adventures and documentary film production. So while I finalised logistics for the last leg of my solo helicopter flight, I began planning a magazine.

Walkabout: Australia and the South Seas had been a travel and geographic magazine published by the Australian National Travel Association; it had run from 1934 to 1974 and featured stories about Australia and the nearby islands. I was a keen reader as a teenager and I still had some copies.

Leafing through the tabloid-size pages, I found myself caught up in stories written by Australia's top authors and journalists,

Pip took this photograph as I was heading to the North Pole. I am in my down suit and covered up because of temperatures as low as -38°C in the cockpit.

Forced down on the Arctic Ocean ice during my second attempt on the North Pole. The thin ice started breaking up and I managed to get the tent and everything else into the helicopter and fly on at a very low level.

Sitting in my bush office with the Reverend Ted Noffs. Ted had a major influence on my life.

Pip and the girls helped get this first issue of *Australian Geographic* out. Little did we know that within three years it would go to over 200,000 subscribers.

On my adventures I made documentary films. This was before video cameras, so I used a Super 8 movie camera mounted beside me. I talked to it as if it was my friend.

Kneeling on the thin ice at the Magnetic North Pole on my first attempt to the Geographic North Pole. I became the first person to reach this pole by helicopter on my third attempt.

In the Twin Otter with co-pilot Laurie McIver, who originally taught me to fly. This is the plane I flew 'vertically' around the world, landing at each pole.

The Twin Otter in front of Mt Erebus, an active volcano, at McMurdo Sound when we were helping Greenpeace get to the South Pole.

Landing at King George Island in very bad weather. We just got in.

Pip and I standing at the North Pole on my vertical flight around the world.

We landed near the B29 *Kee Bird* in northern Greenland. The aircraft had been forced down, nearly out of fuel, in the 1950s due to a navigation error.

My Citation jet was the ideal aircraft to fly over Mount Everest. It could be flown with just one pilot (normally myself) and I was able to do over 1000 hours of my 11,000 hours of total flying time in it.

Looking across to the Mt Everest South West Face from the Citation.

Pip beside the first stage of the Redstone rocket that we found in the Simpson Desert.

Our Sikorsky helicopter in Nepal with the local school kids. I took Pip with me as we cruised around the world from east to west at about 500 feet.

Sikorsky S76 on the top of the Greenland ice cap on our around the world flight.

Our Earthroamer in Alaska on the first leg of our drive around the world.

We found this nomadic family in Mongolia moving with everything on their camel, including a satellite TV dish.

Pip and I with a campfire on the Earthroamer trip around the world. This is on the
Gunbarrel Highway in Western Australia.

John and I at over 20,000 feet doing 160 kilometres per hour as we crossed
Australia in the balloon. On the left is the small verandah I built so I could sit out
on my deck chair.

Crossing the Tasman by balloon 'against the wind' from New Zealand to Australia was an exciting adventure. Here we are landing on the beach on the north coast of New South Wales.

At the balloon's control console.

We went twice around the world in my Cessna Caravan. Here I am testing the skis on the Tasman Glacier in New Zealand.

On the Bourke to Burketown Bash with Pip and our 1964 EH Holden sponsored by Redex. The Bashes went on to raise really good money for the children's charity Variety.

With Mum and Hayley during the Sydney Olympics torch relay.

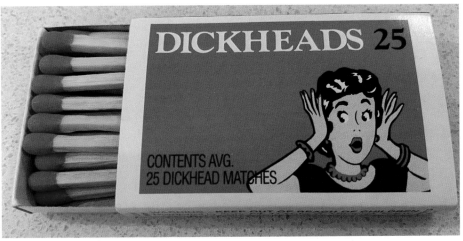

Because Redhead matches were taken over by a foreign company I decided to bring out Dickhead matches. On the rear side of the box was printed: 'We would have to be complete dickheads to let most of our famous brands be taken over by foreign companies. Brands such as Vegemite, Aeroplane Jelly, Arnott's, Speedo and Redhead Matches are in overseas hands. This means the profit and wealth created goes overseas and robs our children and grandchildren of a future. A protest from Dick Smith Foods, as Australian as you can get.'

With Dick Smith Foods we were able to give over $400 million of business to Aussie farmers and producers.

Here we are today. With Pip and our daughters Jenny and Hayley when Pip received her Order of Australia at Government House in Sydney.

Flying in my LongRanger helicopter along the north coast of Tasmania. I have always considered a helicopter to be a magic carpet.

My solo around the world helicopter VH-DIK is now in Sydney's Powerhouse Museum.

Our start in philanthropy came when we financially assisted Dr Tony Kidman in his research into muscular dystrophy.

Pip and I have had a life of adventure together.

including Mary Durack, Ion Idriess and Frank Clune. Each issue featured the work of some of our best photographers, including Frank Hurley, Max Dupain and my grandpa, Harold Cazneaux.

Many of the articles were written in the first person, where the author writes, 'I did this, or I was there.' I liked the style. It was like having a personal guide taking you into a story. It seemed that many of *Walkabout*'s writers either lived in the bush or spent a lot of time there. You could tell by how they described the land and its people that they loved the outback.

———

My plan was to start a magazine that would gain more than 20,000 subscribers in five years. I was prepared to lose up to $1 million, money I'd made through the sale of Dick Smith Electronics, but this would include at least $100,000 each year that I would donate to scientific research, adventure and charity. If after five years the magazine could support itself, that would be good; otherwise, I'd simply close it down.

I considered calling the magazine *Roo*, but this changed one weekend in July 1983, when Pip and I flew down to Eagle's Eyrie, our property between Jindabyne and Thredbo. We called it our adventurer's lodge and regularly opened it up to many of our friends.

That weekend the East Roseville Rovers were there and Rover leader Bob Cleworth had a magazine called *Canadian*

Geographic. As soon as I picked it up, I thought maybe I could call my magazine *Australian Geographic.* Up until then, I'd been concerned about using the name 'Geographic' because *National Geographic*, with its 11 million subscribers worldwide, was such a dominant magazine. Besides, I was friends with its editor.

When I asked Bob about this (he was studying law), he said, 'Dick, you'd have no problems if your magazine was like *Canadian Geographic.* It's quite a different publication and people won't confuse it with *National Geographic.* Just make it clear that yours will be about Australia and Australians.'

From then on, I began to call it *Australian Geographic, Dick Smith's Journal of Adventure and Discovery.*

In July 1984, Pip and I bought four hectares of bushland on Mona Vale Road, not far from our house in Terrey Hills, and gave three talented architects $5000 each to come up with a concept for an Australian Geographic Centre. It would need facilities for publishing, administration and documentary film production, as well as a research library, museum and theatre. I hoped that one day it would become a meeting place for expedition planners and a venue where adventurers could celebrate their success. Best of all, the AG Centre would be only ten minutes' drive from our house.

———

But for the moment, and until the Australian Geographic Centre had been built, I was operating out of an office at the back of the

Dick Smith Electronics building in North Ryde, right next to the helipad and with a staff of only four, which I loved.

One day I took out a piece of paper and began making a list of aims for *Australian Geographic*. I was fed up with how the media was so obsessed with negative angles. I'd heard of adventurers who'd tried to get sponsorship from newspapers but were told to 'come back if someone dies'. The stories I read about country towns in the newspapers usually focused on nothing but racial violence and unemployment. 'Surely,' I thought, 'there must be something good about these towns; after all, people choose to live and raise their families there.'

I decided that if *Australian Geographic* was going to bring balance to the coverage of Australia, we'd have to be biased towards the positive. And so I began writing my list of aims. I wanted to maintain an enthusiastic editorial stance, and to offer encouragement and financial support for research into Australia's flora, fauna and the environment. As well as encouraging Australian writers, photographers and artists, I wanted to produce quality documentary films and, most of all, to involve our readers in the planning of the journal and in sharing its adventures.

When I shared this with some of my friends, they thought the magazine would lose even more money than I had planned. 'Dick, good news doesn't sell,' they said. I thought they could be right, but at least I wanted to give it a go. Next, it was time to apply one of my success secrets again: *Surround yourself with capable people.*

While looking through magazines at newsagents, I kept noticing *Simply Living*, a magazine about alternative lifestyles, environmental activism and animal welfare. The topics seemed a bit 'hippie' or 'greenie', but the design and production was very high quality, equal to our best mainstream magazines.

Simply Living had been started in the 1970s by John and David Stuart, with Tony Gordon as designer and partner, but it had recently changed hands. I found that Tony lived close by on Sydney's Northern Beaches, so I rang him and invited him up to our house.

He dropped by one afternoon and we sat around the kitchen table to nut out ideas for *Australian Geographic*. His boyish looks, curly hair and casual clothes suggested a relaxed artist, but I quickly learned that Tony was more than an experienced designer, he was an expert in magazine production as well. I knew I'd found my art director.

———

On 1 August 1984, I placed an advertisement in the *Sydney Morning Herald* stating that I was intending to produce 'an Australian quarterly geographical magazine of exceptionally high quality ... The magazine will require a dedicated and enthusiastic full time editor who can firmly set and maintain the highest standards. The man or woman sought would preferably not be a specialist in any particular field but would be a person who can make the magazine as entertaining, educational and interesting as possible. If you have had experience in the field and would like to help my dream come true, please write. The money would be pretty good too'.

I had a very good response, with over thirty journalists applying, and during the next few months I interviewed some of the country's most experienced editors. But I found that many of them simply didn't share my belief that a positive magazine about Australia could survive. Maybe they were right, I thought, but I wasn't ready to give up.

On 3 October 1984, Greg Mortimer and Tim Macartney-Snape became the first Australians to climb Mt Everest. Their expedition was one of the first to ascend the world's highest peak without using supplementary oxygen, and they created a difficult new route on the mountain's North Face. While the expedition was still in Tibet, I received a letter from Howard Whelan, an American journalist living in Australia who I'd met before and who had joined the Everest team as cameraman–journalist. Howard wrote: '*Australian Geographic* sounds a great idea and as you seem to be establishing yourself as "Adventure Central" within Australia, no doubt the material drawn to the magazine will be fascinating. Good luck with it.' He proposed that on his return we get together to discuss the magazine.

Howard gave his letter to some yak drivers, who carried it down to base camp. Days later, a German trekking group visited Everest base camp, were given the letter and posted it in Lhasa. After reading it, I sent a note to Howard's home, asking him to come in for a chat on his return.

In early 1985, Howard came to my office in North Ryde. I liked his enthusiasm and love of adventure and hired him to help me get the magazine up and running. Although Howard was an experienced journalist and a good writer, I didn't really consider him for the job as editor. I was looking for someone who had experience as an editor.

But just as Ike Bain had jumped in and worked himself into a position of leadership with Dick Smith Electronics, Howard did exactly the same. In fact, he was one of the main reasons for the magazine's success. He understood exactly what I was on about, that we should focus on positive stories about Australians and our wonderful country. It was almost as if it took someone from another country to value what so many Australians took for granted.

In April, we moved offices from North Ryde to a house on Booralie Road, Terrey Hills, only a few minutes from Pip's and my home. I had my office upstairs in the dining room; Tony was downstairs in the rumpus room and Howard chose the laundry because, even though it was tiny, it had views over Ku-ring-gai Chase National Park.

We had long discussions about content for the 'journal' (I thought that calling it a journal rather than a magazine made it sound more up-market). We all agreed that the mix of stories for each issue should include adventure, science/technology, a remote town, history and natural history.

Rather than publishing articles that were sent in 'on spec', we chose topics to cover and commissioned the best writers and photographers to do them. Some we found close by.

I was happy to spend money on high quality maps and illustrations. The weekend newspapers were now inserting free colour magazines so, if we were going to charge $6.50 an issue, we had to make sure our journal reflected hard work and value for money.

———

Most magazines, like newspapers, made their income through advertising sales. Some would have ads filling more than 50 per cent of the pages. I decided that our journal would have a limited amount of advertising: of the 130 pages, there would be only 24 full-page colour ads and two pages of black and white 'classified' ads. All the ads would be placed either at the front or the back, so readers could enjoy stories without interruption. Of course, I was told that this would never work, but went ahead with it anyway.

Like other magazines, we could have quickly filled our pages with alcohol and cigarette ads, but I said no. I happen not to drink much myself, occasionally at weddings and funerals, but I'm not a wowser; however, I knew this was going to be a family magazine and I could just imagine astute advertisers supplying alcohol and cigarette ads that would be attractive to young people.

I wrote to companies run by people I knew, or that I felt would support the aims of our journal, and told them what I was trying to do. I explained that advertising was by invitation only, with strict page limitations. And there was one more condition: they would have to advertise in all four issues at a cost of $9000 a year. We sold out all the ad space in no time.

I was impressed by how *National Geographic* supported both its magazine and society through subscribers. Wouldn't it be great if we could do the same? But *National Geographic* had been going for nearly a century, and most Australians bought magazines from newsagents, issue by issue. We'd need a strong push to get people to subscribe for a whole year.

Planning our advertising campaign was a lot of fun. I thought the best way to get subscribers was with a four-page colour supplement inserted in the broadsheets like the *Sydney Morning Herald*. Howard and I wrote great copy for these and I enjoyed working on every bit of the campaign.

One of our full-page ads in the *Sunday Telegraph* magazine included a photograph of me hugging a tree and the words, 'This country needs a journal that inspires us to share the great adventure of being Australian, but I need your help. Please become a subscriber, please get involved.'

When I asked my friend John Singleton which was better, advertising in newspapers or on television, he reckoned television was best. But I disagreed, I reckoned the newspaper inserts were better. We actually did both, but I hinted to the media that Singo and I had fallen out over the advertising, which of course we hadn't, but our 'conflict' got us lots of free publicity.

I had something else to thank Singo for. We couldn't decide on a cover for our first issue so we asked John if he could help us out. He requested that we send over any artwork we were considering, which we did, including the beautifully detailed platypus that artist Rod Scott had created for our logo. Singo's team came up with the idea of moving the platypus from the logo down to the main space for our inaugural issue, then popping it back into the logo after that. Brilliant!

I wanted to print the journal in Australia, but couldn't find a company that had a printing press that could give us the quality we required. Tony was keen to print with Dai Nippon in Japan, as it had a reputation for consistent, high quality results at the right price. He was right, but I kept looking for and eventually found an Australian printer to take over the work.

———

For our first issue, we chose articles that I wanted to know about. Just as I started the Antarctic flights to see Antarctica, one of the reasons I started *Australian Geographic* was so I could learn more about Australia.

We ended up with a great selection of stories. One was on *Project Blizzard*, an expedition I'd sponsored to Mawson's Hut in Commonwealth Bay, Antarctica. We also sent Paul Mann to write a positive story about Moree, a town in northern New South Wales that had been suffering from negative press.

Andy Park wrote a story about the amazing life cycle of eels. I'd read a short piece in the *Sydney Morning Herald* that said immature eels (elvers) went up rivers of Australia's east coast to mature into adults, even climbing watercourses to get around dams like Warragamba. It seemed too fantastic to believe. But Andy found that the little elvers detoured half a kilometre and climbed almost 120 metres to get around the dam. This included waiting for heavy rains so they could scale two vertical concrete walls and cross a traffic roundabout. Incredible!

We had articles on Halley's Comet and AUSSAT, Australia's first satellite telecommunications system, and on the search for evidence of Lasseter's Lost Reef (including a gatefold map showing where the gold reef might be). I had always loved the story about Lasseter since I had run the 747 outback flight. Finally, we included a colour poster on *Australian Antarctica*, with historical and wildlife facts on one side, and on the other, a photograph of magnificent icebergs with penguins (and kangaroos!) on the sea ice. It was good to have a bit of fun!

We had a two-page section at the back called 'Microbits'. Among these short items we announced our inaugural scientific expedition to Cooper Creek, South Australia, and invited scientists and other interested parties to apply. In another item, we gave a date when Pip, the girls and I, as well as journal staff and contributors, would be camping at the Blue Gum Forest in the Blue Mountains; we invited subscribers to come and meet us. Dozens showed up and we had a great weekend.

From the start, we encouraged the idea that when you subscribed to *Australian Geographic*, you were taking part in something greater than the purchase of the journal. You were becoming part of a community. And from the response, a lot of people were keen to join in.

We set up an Editorial Advisory Panel and an Expedition and Scientific Advisory Panel, with people like Hans Tholstrup, Robyn Williams, Lincoln Hall and Ron Taylor giving freely of their time. This helped add more credibility to what we were trying to do.

We printed 80,000 copies of the first issue, distributing 55,000 to newsagents and keeping 25,000 to fulfil our subscription orders. My goal had been to have 20,000 subscribers within five years and I never expected the incredible response to the journal. By Christmas Day 1985, we had 15,000 subscribers, which brought in $390,000.

On New Year's Day, I sent the following telex to Ike Bain, who was working for Dick Smith Electronics in the United States: 'Unbelievable, unbelievable, unbelievable ... first issue sold out in newsagents in days, now 21,000 subscribers. Reprinting 30,000 to make 110,000 in total.'

We reached our goal in weeks, rather than years. Initially we contracted an outside company to fulfil subscriptions but, as more and more poured in, it became absolute chaos, so we brought subscription fulfilment in-house. As mailbags of coupons kept coming, we soon had 40,000 charter subscribers.

Pip came in every day and ran the subscription department, and Hayley and Jenny worked after school. We quickly doubled the number of staff. We worked out that it would take ten people four months to process 40,000 subscriptions. I was soon looking for a computer to keep us on top of subscriptions.

My early sums were that if we sold 50,000 copies of the journal, including what we made on advertising, we would come out even. But as we shot past that number, I realised that we could give even more money away. On 21 February, we celebrated reaching 60,000 subscribers. Our journal would go on to become the most successful launch of a new magazine in Australia.

In March 1987, we held our first Australian Geographic Awards Ceremony. The purpose of the event was to recognise the achievements of Australia's outstanding scientists and adventurers and give us the chance to meet our supporters.

On that night, Colin Putt earned our most prestigious award for his expeditions to Antarctica and the South Pacific, as well as for his encouragement of young adventurers. We had so many ticket applications we had to return hundreds of them and the following year we booked the Sydney Opera House. We filled that as well.

More than three decades later, I'm proud to see that the Australian Geographic Society Gala awards, for science, adventure and conservation, remain prestigious and sought after.

But I'm getting ahead of myself. On the day of the launch, I had something else I had to do—I organised the dismantling of my helicopter *Delta India Kilo* so it could be shipped to Vancouver, British Columbia. Over the previous twelve months, I had spent whatever time I had spare in planning my next adventure—an attempt to become the first person to fly a helicopter to the North Pole.

CHAPTER 16

Solo to the top
of the world

I filmed the take-off to keep myself busy. Otherwise I'd watch and think, 'Will I ever see you again?' and get terribly emotional and burst into tears.

Pip Smith, Ward Hunt Island,
430 nautical miles from North Pole

I couldn't believe the cold. It was an icy, deep cold that sapped the last spark of warmth from every bone in my body. The thermometer on the windscreen showed –38°C but, to prevent my breath from freezing on the inside of the plexiglass, I had to fly with both windows open. I was wearing a down suit and was jammed into my seat, only able to wiggle my toes and fingers. A 10-knot breeze was whistling through the cockpit of my helicopter, giving a chill factor that was many degrees lower on my face, the only exposed part of my body, and I felt my nose becoming frost-nipped.

Over the past nine exhausting days, I'd flown more than 5400 kilometres from Vancouver to the isolated outposts of the far north. Below me, under a blanket of cloud, was Ellesmere Island. My destination was Ward Hunt Island, just off the coast, and the last stepping stone for many polar expeditions by other adventurers in the past. There I hoped to refuel before heading out across the frozen Arctic Ocean in my bid for the Pole.

After my 1982–83 round-the-world flight, I had used my little Bell JetRanger helicopter, *Delta India Kilo*, to get me to work and back or on family camping trips, but the urge to go on another solo adventure soon became too great to resist. I can only explain this desire for adventure as a deep-seated need for challenge and the adrenaline-pumping excitement that the risk-taking gives.

Over the past twelve months, much of my time had been taken up with *Australian Geographic*, but I'd worked on my North Pole flight whenever possible. One of my biggest tasks was to fit my shipboard-landing fuel tanks, boosting the aircraft's capacity from 93 to 240 US gallons and increasing its range from 630 to 1600 kilometres.

As I kept *Delta India Kilo* in the garage under Pip's and my bedroom in Terrey Hills, I could work there late into the night, stripping it of every superfluous panel and piece of lining to reduce the weight. Although I'd be taking safety equipment—including a sleeping bag, stove, tent, emergency locator beacon and life raft—there would be no heater in the cockpit due to weight issues.

I had consulted Giles Kershaw, the experienced polar pilot who had provided logistical support for Ran Fiennes' Trans-Globe Expedition in 1979–82, the first expedition to make a longitudinal (north–south) circumnavigation of the Earth using only surface transport. He had convinced me that April was the best time for my attempt, as the Arctic is relatively free of fog at this time, the days are long and the ice is still thick enough to land on.

With Howard at the helm of *Australian Geographic*, Pip and I flew to Vancouver, where I'd shipped *Delta India Kilo*. I took off on 6 April 1986 for Resolute, one of the most northerly Inuit communities in Canada.

I'd managed to talk Pip into coming along to be my ground support, as well as shooting stills and video. She wasn't keen at first; she did not want to leave the girls, who were only thirteen and eleven years of age. Up until then, I had taken the lead in directing my expeditions and she would enthusiastically support me. But on my North Pole attempt, she realised just how capable she was and from then on would no longer auto-matically agree with my ideas.

Pip helped me with flight planning, weather forecasts and arranging fuel for *Delta India Kilo*. She flew in scheduled or chartered aircraft to places where we could meet, and I'm glad she did, as I experienced everything from equipment failures to freezing rain that coated my windscreen. She gained more self-confidence every day.

I was halfway across Great Slave Lake in Canada's Northwest Territories when near white-out conditions in driving snow forced me down. I had no idea how thick the ice was, but luckily the helicopter didn't break through it. When the weather lifted, I flew back to Fort Resolution, a small Inuit settlement visited by John Franklin (lieutenant-governor of Van Diemen's Land, after whom the Franklin River was named) on one of his polar explorations in the first half of the eighteenth century.

I was forced to spend the night, but my main concern was that I wouldn't be able to start the engine the next morning. I managed to get through to Pip in Yellowknife and said, 'You've got to help me. I need some way to heat the helicopter and advice on how to cross the lake.'

Pip checked the phone directory and found a listing for Aero Arctic, featuring a sketch of a JetRanger. She rang them up and they couldn't believe that there was an Aussie helicopter stuck on the other side of the lake without a heater or even a cover to protect the engine at night. They quickly prepared the necessary equipment and loaded it onto a police King Air that was heading to Fort Resolution.

I spent the night in my sleeping bag in the frigid air terminal, then flew to Yellowknife. On 11 April, I crossed the Arctic Circle and left the tree line behind; here I sometimes brought *Delta India Kilo* down to 100 feet to have a close look at caribou, musk oxen, Arctic hares, polar bears and wolves. It was exhilarating.

At Resolute, still more than 1600 kilometres from the Pole, Pip chartered a Twin Otter aircraft to fly fuel to Ward Hunt Island and to a point 370 kilometres beyond. My plan was to reach Ward Hunt and then radio Pip at Resolute and have her fly up with the Twin Otter. I'd refuel at Ward Hunt, then both aircraft would fly halfway to the Pole, land on sea ice and I would refuel again. With *Delta India Kilo*'s long-range tanks, I calculated I would have just enough fuel for the return journey, provided there were no headwinds.

Pip later said that my departure from Ward Hunt Island was the most nerve-wracking part of our adventure. Certainly, as soon I was in the air, I was worried. Visibility dropped to 200 metres in places and, though I had radio contact with the Twin Otter, I couldn't see it. To make matters worse, the windscreen iced up completely and ice started to form on the tail rotor.

Then I noticed that my gyro-compass had gone completely crazy, forcing me to rely on my sometimes inaccurate Omega navigation system. My magnetic compass was useless so close to the Magnetic Pole. After 25 minutes, and about 80 kilometres from Ward Hunt, the Omega began giving very suspicious readings. Then, one by one, the other instruments failed as well.

I'd reached a crucial point. Should I go on, putting at even greater risk not only my life, but the lives of others who might have to rescue me? Or should I abandon the attempt?

The decision wasn't difficult to make. Conditions were so terrible that it would have been sheer stupidity to carry on. I worried most about Pip, Hayley and Jenny, should something happen to me. So on 15 April, while just 670 kilometres from my goal (83°58' north), I radioed the Twin Otter that I was turning back. Still, I had one more goal up my sleeve. As I flew south, if the weather improved, I would attempt to reach the North Magnetic Pole.

Just before noon on 16 April, I reached this pole, landed and took a picture of myself kneeling beside the Australian flag that had been flown on the 1984 Australian Everest Expedition, and the *Australian Geographic* flag. The temperature was −26°C; given that there was a 27-kilometre wind, the wind-chill factor produced a temperature that was a lot colder.

I quickly returned to the cockpit, found a pencil and wrote the following:

Yesterday I attempted to reach the North Geographic Pole. I failed. I feel a mixture of relief, disappointment and elation. Relief because I am ok, even though I have been forced into many risky situations. Disappointment because I did not succeed in my intentions and elation because of the incredibly wonderful sights I've seen.

Spent last night on ice floating on 900 feet of water in an oil driller's camp near Buckingham Island. I am now too old for such adventures. I want to live to an old age with my loving wife.

P.S. All pens froze. Cameras froze

———

Less than a month later, in early May 1986, I had traded the Arctic's crystal desert for Australia's red centre. I was boiling a billy on the banks of Cooper Creek, near Innamincka, South Australia, as Valerie Taylor slowly paddled a wooden canoe just below me.

We both watched as air bubbles rose in the muddy water, followed shortly by Valerie's husband, Ron, in full scuba gear. Pushing back goggles and regulator, he picked through a hand net to see if he'd collected anything of note and shook his head.

'Take me back to the Great Barrier Reef,' he exclaimed with a wry smile.

This was *Australian Geographic*'s first scientific expedition. It attracted naturalists, botanists, ornithologists, zoologists, a geologist—and even two scuba divers!—to photograph and collect data around Cooper Creek.

Our base camp, where we gathered nightly after trips into the field, was set up under the spreading boughs of massive river red gums along the Cooper. It was the first time such a broad range of scientists had been in the area and there was a lively exchange of ideas and discoveries around the campfire at night.

Just upstream was the magnificent Cullyamurra Waterhole and, a bit further on, the historic Dig Tree, where explorers Burke and Wills camped. I believe that you can't say you are a real Australian until you've camped on Cooper Creek and woken to the calls of little corellas in the river red gums above.

Particularly keen to be on the expedition had been our special guest: ornithologist, naturalist and bird painter Sir Peter Scott.

Sir Peter was the son of Antarctic explorer Captain Robert Falcon Scott and vice-president and chairman of the World Wildlife Fund.

While our scientists combed the region's gibber plains, jump-up country and dune systems, it was Coongie Lakes especially that had brought us here. Coongie Lakes is a wetland at the end of the north-west branch of the Cooper, an important stopover for migratory birds. As we drove through its maze of small lakes, we saw pelicans, black swans, egrets, herons, spoonbills and cormorants.

Peter and his wife, Philippa, had specially wanted to see a freckled duck, one of the rarest ducks in the world. One day they joined Ian May, National Parks and Wildlife Service ranger, on a motorboat search and returned ecstatic, having found a flock of fourteen freckled ducks. 'This alone could be justification for having the lakes, or part of them, listed by the International Convention for Wetlands,' Peter said.

Ian agreed. The grim truth, he told me, was that the lakes are popular with shooters because of the abundance of ducks and other birds. Over our time there, we saw the scars of uncontrolled four-wheel driving, dumping of camp rubbish and hacking of river red gums for fires and picnic seats. Rangers like Ian had little authority because it was not a national park.

After ten days of exploring, filming and scientific research, we all felt strongly about the need to protect the area. Upon my return to Sydney, *Australian Geographic* quickly set up a $55,000 grant to sponsor a twelve-month study of Coongie

Lakes as the first step in establishing a management plan that we hoped would lead to full national park status.

The following year, on 15 June 1987, Coongie Lakes was listed as site 376 under the Ramsar Convention, an international listing of special waterfowl places; ultimately, it was established as Coongie Lakes National Park in 2005 and was renamed Malkumba-Coongie Lakes National Park in 2014. I'm proud of the role our first *Australian Geographic* scientific expedition played in making this happen.

For more than a decade, our scientific expeditions went on to study other remote regions of Australia, including Cape York in Far North Queensland, the Recherche Archipelago in Western Australia, Kings Creek Station in the Northern Territory, White Mountains in Queensland and the wilderness of south-west Tasmania.

Back in Terrey Hills, work continued on building the Australian Geographic Centre, and at our offices on Booralie Road advance copies of *Australian Geographic*'s third issue had just arrived.

In the Corroboree section was a short article I wrote titled *Buzz off!* It was about the almost uniquely Australian ritual of quarantine officers coming on board after a plane has landed and delaying everyone from leaving by walking down the aisles spraying pesticides as jet-lagged passengers held handkerchiefs and scarves to their faces.

It's not that I object to biosecurity measures. However, there was increasing evidence that the spraying works best if done before the flight and with the doors closed. But the bureaucrats didn't trust the air crew (the same ones who brought us safely to and from Australia) to be responsible for the spraying. Crazy! In my article, I offered to help fund research on this, but it wasn't necessary. Within a month of the article coming out, and after many phone calls to and from the bureaucrats (who were opposed to any research), the practice was stopped. I was thrilled. In just three issues, *Australian Geographic* was showing that it could help bring about change.

————

After discussing weather and ice conditions with my friends in the Canadian Arctic, I scheduled my second attempt on the North Pole for late July. On 22 July 1986, Pip and I caught commercial flights back to Resolute in the Canadian Arctic, where *Delta India Kilo* had been stored since April. There was now twenty-four hour daylight and the temperature, which hovered around zero, was much more bearable. But the fog, which forms when warm moist air from the sea flows over melting pack ice, had the potential to create a more serious threat than the cold.

And the fog thickened on 27 July—just after I left Pip and my friend Bezal Jesudason at an abandoned scientific camp at Lake Hazen on the northern end of Ellesmere Island, where they would operate the radio relay station during my flight.

After refuelling at Alert, a Canadian military base 144 kilometres to the north-east, I encountered thick fog, with visibility down to a hundred metres in places. At Cape Columbia, 135 kilo-metres from Alert, I landed beside a signpost that marks the spot from where Robert E. Peary set off in 1909 for his North Pole attempt. The signpost bears the names of polar explorers and the dates and directions of their expeditions. It was extremely moving to be there.

At Ward Hunt Island, 50 kilometres further on, I refuelled from drums. With its full load of 240 US gallons aboard, *Delta India Kilo* was once again grossly overloaded (as it had been on the shipboard-landing flight) and only just managed to get airborne.

As I headed north, the prospect of flying 1500 kilometres across this remote, ice-covered ocean intensified my already profound loneliness. My worries increased as I deviated around fog banks. For one terrible hour, I was flying in a 50-foot gap between the base of the fog and the top of the pressure ridges of sea ice.

I tried to contact Pip in her tent at Lake Hazen, but all I got was noisy static. More than ever, I realised how much Pip's support during my ventures had helped me keep my spirits up.

After four hours of flying, an amber light flashed on the instrument panel—my generator had failed. Memories of equipment failures during my first attempt flooded back and I suspected that my hopes for a trouble-free flight were about to be dashed. I might be able to reach the Pole, only about forty-five minutes away, without a generator, but a weakening battery meant that I couldn't trust the Omega navigation system. I'd have to rely on my gyro compass, but for the gyro to be accurate, it must be reset every hour against the sun compass—and the sun was hidden by fog.

Once again it was time to take stock. If I went on, I might not have enough fuel to make it back to land, especially if I had to dodge fog. The sea ice around me was beginning to break up, making it impossible for the Twin Otter to land and deliver more fuel. A ship rescue was not possible.

Above all, I had a deep reluctance to be rescued. I've prided myself on self-sufficiency and have never needed outside assistance on my flights. One thing I could be sure of was that if something did go wrong, the Australian media would blaze it across the front pages.

Still unable to make contact with my base at Lake Hazen and unsure of my exact position, I agonised over whether I should turn back or not. I remembered the terrible Colo walk, when I had nearly lost my life and the lives of my two mates because I had pushed on too far. 'No way,' I thought as I moved the cyclic control to the left and began to turn back the way I had come. I was about 160 kilometres from the North Pole and, as before, I had mixed feelings. I was both miserable and relieved. I headed *Delta India Kilo* south, with only my inaccurate gyro to guide me across this forbidding wilderness.

Three hours later, at 11 p.m., I lost my battle against the fog and was forced down on the ice. Still about a hundred kilometres from land, I put up my tent and prepared to wait for the weather to improve. It could take two hours or two weeks.

I sent messages on my radio, hoping someone would hear, but static was the only reply.

Crawling into my sleeping bag, I tried to get some rest, but the creaking and cracking of ice beneath me made sleep impossible. Just before 3 a.m., the ice started to break up. I leapt into *Delta India Kilo*'s cabin and, miraculously, the fog thinned enough for me to get airborne. An hour later, I reached Ward Hunt Island with only 20 US gallons of fuel left. Had I gone on to the Pole, I would have run out on the ice.

Exhausted after thirty-five hours without sleep, I carried my sleeping bag to an abandoned research hut, rolled it out on a bunk and crawled in. Before I fell into a deep sleep, I wondered whether I should have attempted this crazy adventure. 'I'll never try again,' I thought.

But when I woke up refreshed, and lifted off for my flight to Lake Hazen, where Pip and Bezal awaited, I wasn't so sure. The wild beauty of the Arctic had its hooks into me.

———

On 21 August, we moved offices from Booralie Road to the Australian Geographic Centre. Architect Russell Carlisle had given it a very Aussie feel, with single-storey buildings connected by open walkways. He'd set the buildings around two stands of virgin bush, where waratahs, wattle and native orchids bloom, with my special 'bush office' nestled nearby. Pip also had her own office in the front of the building.

Our gardener, James Dutton, and his team planted another nine thousand native plants and our wildlife reserve (with billabong) was taking in its first residents. Over time, it would become home to red-necked and rufous hare wallabies, eastern water dragons, three species of duck, emus and a territorial black swan named Frederick.

To reach my bush office, I simply slipped through a special 'escape hatch' out of my office in the main building and walked down a narrow track between banksias and boronias to a rustic desk, where a phone line and electrical outlet had been installed. It was a great place to work, but I was distracted by all the birds and lizards that stopped by. The first 'official' visitor was, appropriately, Hazel Hawke, who, together with Bob, was jointly Charter Supporter No 1. During her visit, a white-plumed honeyeater landed nearby.

As idyllic as it was in my new bush office, the rest of the Australian Geographic Centre was gripped by a sense of urgency. By the time our third issue came out, we had 80,000 subscribers and total sales of more than a hundred and thirty thousand. We had to ensure our subscription fulfilment system was developing fast enough to meet this unexpected demand.

As for the journal, I was concerned that Howard had never run a magazine before, so I tried bringing in others with expertise that I thought he lacked. I hired an executive editor, an associate editor, even a managing editor, but none had the clear understanding of what I wanted our journal to be. Howard did and was willing to work hard to develop the management skills he needed.

But Howard was having challenges of his own. When commissioning writers, he explained to them that we wanted positive, first-person stories filled with facts. In response, journalists protested. 'We've been taught not to write in the first person,' they said.

'But we're not asking you to be objective,' Howard explained.

'And if we fill it with facts, it will be boring,' they said.

'That depends on the facts you include,' Howard replied.

As I had always done, I copied the success of others. *National Geographic* was the world's most successful geographical magazine, so Howard and I studied the articles and confirmed that they were written in the first person. And they were filled with facts. One night, when leafing through a back issue, I found 'The Tea and Sugar Train', an article about the passenger/supply train that regularly crossed the Nullarbor Plain. Over the first few pages, I highlighted every time a first-person reference was used, and I circled each fact. The opening spreads averaged about twenty-seven facts each and the story was still fascinating. From then on, whenever Howard commissioned a writer, I insisted he gave them a copy of 'The Tea and Sugar Train'.

While going through the back issues of *National Geographic*, something else struck me: their rigorous fact-checking process. We would do the same. I had a framed sign made up for each office. It read: 'Our very success depends on accuracy. We must check everything and never presume.' To achieve this, every fact was checked by up to three independent experts.

It was a time-consuming and expensive process, but worth it. Of course mistakes did get through from time to time, but when this happened, we had a special section called *Postscript*, where we'd explain the mistake and add something interesting about the topic.

As our editorial team finalised the last issue of 1986, I decided to raise the next year's subscription price by two dollars. 'This has nothing to do with increased costs,' I wrote in my fourth editorial. 'Rather, it will enable us to pour a further $200,000 back into *Australian Geographic* to make it even better, particularly in the area of cartography and detailed illustration.

'We believe our planned cartography team will be capable of producing some of the finest maps ever seen in Australia. With these and other planned improvements you, our supporters, will reap the benefit.'

Clearly, my boyhood passion for maps had never left me, but producing high quality maps turned out to be much more challenging than I ever expected. It would be more than a year before I found the cartographic wizard who would make this possible.

———

Australian Geographic was now consuming more and more of my time. When I sold Dick Smith Electronics I had planned a life of adventure and special projects. Now one of those projects had gained a life of its own.

I was lucky to be passionate about the topics we covered in the journal. And I was happy to be supporting scientific research and adventure, but I have a very short attention span.

On 2 November 1986, I received a fax from Ike Bain. Ike had been one of *Australian Geographic*'s first subscribers and he wrote that he enjoyed the journal very much. He also said that he'd be leaving Dick Smith Electronics on 31 January 1987.

'Dick, I would be very interested in working for you, say on a six-month trial,' he wrote. 'I believe I could take a lot of details off your mind and let you concentrate on doing things you enjoy.'

He ended by writing, 'I always enjoyed working for you. If you're interested, let me know. Good luck.'

As things turned out, his timing was excellent.

CHAPTER 17

Never complain about your tax

I first met Reverend Ted Noffs in the late 1970s, when I asked him to come on one of our Antarctic flights to perform a wedding ceremony above Antarctica. By then Ted was well known in Sydney for setting up the Wayside Chapel in Kings Cross, which welcomed everyone from drug-affected youths to eccentrics and the homeless.

Ted was a Methodist minister; I wasn't religious, but we hit it off right away. I'd never met a clergyman like him. By then he'd begun to challenge the very concept of organised religion in Australia. He would invite large groups to the Wayside Chapel for what he called question time. He told me that it was 'where the Buddhist, the Muslim, the anarchist, the humanist are able to come together to discover their common humanity'.

He believed that Australians are some of the most spiritual people in the world, but to understand our spirituality, we shouldn't look in textbooks about theology: 'Don't look at the North American model, don't look at Europe,' he said. 'You look into the bush.' I couldn't agree more.

'It's about friendship, mateship. It's about us being one family, the family of humanity. That's the unique identity of Australia,' he said. Ted's 'Family of Humanity' concept became a driving force in his life, but he was never really tied to a particular way of thinking and he always encouraged different viewpoints on just about any topic.

When I'd invited James Randi to test the water diviners back in 1980, I'd asked Ted to be one of the observers. Beforehand, he warned me that he actually believed in divining, but, after the tests, he came away convinced that it didn't work, that it was simply an 'ideomotor response', a person's body reacting to what they think should happen.

After the Antarctic wedding flight, Ted asked if I'd stop by the Wayside Chapel sometime to see the Life Education centre that he'd set up. After years of dealing with the devastating effects of drug abuse, he was convinced that the only long-term solution was to intervene before drug addiction set in.

Ted had heard of the Robert Crown Health Education Centre in Chicago, where young people were taught about how drugs affect the body. Their program was getting good results, so Ted had flown over to have a look. He came back inspired, keen to establish something similar here.

He thought that if he could use new technologies to teach children about the beauty and wonder of the human body, and then show what happens when that body is affected by drugs, it might motivate them to resist taking drugs.

Ted had gathered together a group of volunteers, including electronic boffins, and they'd built a small, prototype Life Education centre, crammed into the second floor of the Wayside Chapel. It wasn't your typical classroom.

The first time I saw it, I was amazed. Its ceiling was a night sky created using fibre optics. There was a transparent, anatomical mannequin, which revealed the body's internal organs and, with flashing panels, demonstrated how blood circulated throughout the body. Best of all, there was a talking giraffe called Harold.

Over the next few months, I was called in to fix the equipment. Even though Harold was beautifully made, he was far too complex. I suggested to Ted that I use my skills to simplify the design, making it more reliable and less costly. As always, Ted was enthusiastic and encouraging.

I spent night after night redesigning Harold in my home workshop. I felt like I was back in my boyhood, when I had built a noughts and crosses computer, and I loved it. Marshall Gill, the second person I employed at Dick Smith Electronics, was now retired, so I invited him to lend a hand. He built new eyes for Harold out of ping-pong balls, with eyelids that fluttered, and a moving mouth that allowed the giraffe to smile and laugh with the kids. It was all pneumatically operated. An old friend of mine from Roseville Public School owned a vacuum-moulding company, so I got him to rebuild Harold's head. We simplified the design, so that everything could be easily serviced.

The more time I spent with Ted, the more impressed I was with what he was trying to do. With two young daughters, Pip and I were aware of how much the world was changing. When we were kids, some of our classmates might sneak a ciggie or nick alcohol from their parents' cupboard, but we never saw drugs like marijuana and speed, or even more dangerous ones that were suddenly becoming available.

Ted convinced me to go with him to Chicago to visit the Robert Crown Centre, where I learned that thousands of kids were visiting each month. The program was incredibly astute. Students weren't told, 'Don't take drugs.' They were simply shown what a wonderful thing their body was and what happened when it was affected by drugs—both legal ones, like cigarettes and alcohol, and illegal ones.

As I watched, I began to see the advantage of taking kids out of their normal home or school environments. They were excited, more alert and seemed to take more notice of the lessons, thanks to the fresh approach.

Ted told me of his dream to open a full-scale Life Education centre (LEC) at Colyton, a suburb near Mount Druitt in Sydney's west. He'd already been given land by the health minister in the NSW Government and a promise of $500,000 from Premier Neville Wran for the centre's construction. But Ted needed $1.5 million to build his dream LEC.

Pip and I saw the potential the centre would have in helping young Australians. I told Ted that if he could get the state government to increase its offer to $750,000, I'd match it, so we'd have the whole lot. Ted put my offer to the premier and Neville agreed. The only catch was that he wanted me to be the chairman of the centre's building committee.

'No way,' I told him. 'I don't go to meetings, I have a nine-minute attention span.'

Neville thought for a minute and then said, 'Dick, would you be the chairman of the One-Man Building Committee?'

I instantly agreed.

All this was happening at about the same time that I was deep into planning the Australian Geographic Centre in Terrey Hills. I proposed that we build a small Life Education centre on our site to test the concepts and technologies while the Colyton LEC was under construction. Ted was delighted with this idea.

As it turned out, students arrived for the first LEC class at the Australian Geographic Centre on 25 November 1986. Ted and Margaret Noffs came by for the occasion and were excited by what they saw. At the same time, Ted was focused on the progress being made at Colyton. But, sadly, a little over three months later, Ted suffered a massive stroke and spent the last eight years of his life semi-conscious.

The Colyton LEC opened its doors on 29 May 1987 and, thanks to the incredible efforts of Ted's son Wesley and daughter-in-law Amanda, and dedicated supporters includ-ing Bob Ellicott and Tony Hasham, the LEC movement in

Australia grew incredibly. By 2019, there were ninety-two Life Education mobile learning centres nationwide, educating over 710,000 children each year—some seven million in total.

When we began, more than 30 per cent of fifteen-year-old girls smoked cigarettes. Now it's less than half that. As for me personally, meeting Ted Noffs had a major effect on my life. He inspired me to become an activist, to take a stand on things I believed in.

I'd already 'stirred the pot' on a number of issues before this—from the licensing of CB radio operators to allowing multinational companies like Tandy Electronics to run Aussie-owned companies out of business—but in both those instances, my motivation had been to generate publicity to increase sales at Dick Smith Electronics.

This was different. I was about to use my public profile in an attempt to change public opinion.

———

On 23 January 1987, Pip and I attended a luncheon in Sydney where I was named Australian of the Year. I'd been nominated as an 'entrepreneur, adventurer and philanthropist' and it was claimed my talents came from 'an unfettered need to explore and understand'. Tennis great John Newcombe presented the award and I was proud to receive it.

In my acceptance speech, I encouraged Australia's wealthiest people to take a year off from making money and put something back into the country. Later in the year, in a talk I gave for the Australia Day Council of Western Australia, I advocated that, each year, Australia should publish a list of the top two hundred taxpayers. 'We praise the people who avoid the maximum amount of tax and buy the multiple jet aircraft and all the rest of it,' I said. 'We never stop talking about them and running them in the newspapers and putting them in the *Business Review Weekly* '200 Wealthiest' list. But the people who are really putting something back into the country and paying their taxes honestly we keep secret.'

I pointed out that Japan publishes a 'top taxpayers' list every year: 'There's tremendous pressure to get on that list. So I'm proposing that the Australian Treasurer sends a letter to the top 200 taxpayers saying: "Congratulations, you're putting a lot back into the country and we appreciate it. Can we release your name?" '

I have never had any problem myself with paying tax—in this I have a completely different view to that espoused by Kerry Packer.

I always remember coming home with my first pay packet at the age of fifteen and complaining to Dad because some money had been taken out for tax. My dad said, 'Never complain about your tax. Look at how fantastic our country is—the education, the roads, hospitals, defence—we are so lucky.' From that point on, I have never complained about tax. In fact, I am proud to pay my tax.

When I finally got Dick Smith Electronics up to paying tax of $1 million per year, I decided that, from then on, I would pay at least $1 million tax every year. That has given me great satisfaction. And when I fly in my helicopter and look down at what a fantastic country this is, I think how fortunate I am.

————

Three days after I received my Australian of the Year award, Pip and I were in Melbourne attending an Australia Day concert being televised by Channel Ten, and I mentioned the contentious issue of cigarette advertising being directed at children. I said that I'd set myself a goal for the year: to reduce the number of fifteen year olds who smoked cigarettes. I have never been against adults smoking. I believed that it was their right to decide for themselves, but I didn't feel that way when I saw cigarette ads directed at young people.

The cigarette companies had a very capable disinformation body called the Tobacco Institute; it told everyone that they weren't out to recruit young people and their ads weren't directed at kids. Of course, this was a lie. In fact, by then I'd already spent more than $50,000 on an ad campaign to oppose them.

I'd also just finished my editorial for the sixth issue of *Australian Geographic*. In it I wrote: 'We live in the era of double-think. Our young people visit the Life Education centres. Or, from their teachers and parents, they learn of the proven dangers of all drugs. Then they open so-called "responsible" publications and immediately see advertisements for what they have been told is a lethal drug. Why do we allow such a gross double-standard to exist?'

I believed that young people might naturally think that if cigarettes are advertised in these publications, there can't be much wrong with them. And the ads were incredibly clever, using young, healthy models to give the product a glamorous, desirable, grown-up image.

'Let's not kid ourselves,' I wrote. 'Tobacco kills thousands of Australians each year. Fewer adults are smoking, so the industry has a desperate need to persuade more young Australians to take up the habit. Surely it cannot be acceptable for us to allow our young people to be manipulated by an extremely powerful and astute industry that appears devoid of morality!'

Yet when I wrote to the publishers of some of our most respected newspapers and magazines, asking them not to publish cigarette ads aimed at children, I was told that this might compromise the 'freedom of the press', and other pitiable excuses.

In frustration, and to gain publicity for the issue, I took legal action against the publishers of *The Australian* newspaper for refusing to run an ad I'd prepared for my campaign. I lost. My ad was also knocked back by John Fairfax, publishers of the *Sydney Morning Herald* and the Melbourne *Age*, but they agreed to publish an edited version.

What a difference when compared to Canada's national newspaper, *The Globe and Mail*, which led the way by not accepting cigarette advertising even before laws were passed forcing them to do so.

On 23 April 1987, *The Australian* did allow an ad to be placed by major health agencies including the National Heart Foundation, Australian Cancer Society, Australian Medical Association, Royal Australian College of General Practitioners and five others. The headline read, 'Everything Dick Smith Said (and wanted to say) Is True'.

Throughout my time as Australian of the Year, including a three-week tour of Australia's capital cities, I used my position to campaign against cigarette ads aimed at children. I went on to publish a small magazine called *Truth an Ad*. It included a contest for students in Years 5 to 10 to create a cigarette ad that told the truth about smoking.

The results were fantastic, including one satirising Rothmans —'Coughmans, the best poison money can buy'—and another proclaiming, 'Enjoy the bad times with Kent'. I offered $38,000 in prize money (including Sony Walkmans) for the contests. The first print run was 60,000, all distributed to Australian schools.

Best of all, just over two years later, the federal government banned all tobacco advertising in newspapers and magazines. In the end, I spent more than $1 million on the campaign and considered it money well spent.

———

'Do it now—do it in parallel.' This was a saying I had printed onto cards and handed out to staff at *Australian Geographic*. I found it motivating, and it seemed to define my life at the time.

Besides starting our journal, I was helping Ted Noffs with his Life Education movement, forming the Australian Skeptics, fighting the anti-cigarette advertising campaign and becoming deeply involved in aviation reform.

My efforts were successful in nearly all of these, but not in aviation. This lack of success didn't affect me financially, because I had the wealth to cover the high costs, but it was disappointing nevertheless. I have been forced to watch as the general aviation industry has almost been destroyed by regulations that added to costs but not to safety. We could have become world leaders. It was incredibly sad.

CHAPTER 18

Aviation safety reform

It all began when I took off from Fort Worth, Texas on 5 August 1982 to fly my helicopter around the world. I was on a high. I was convinced that Australia was the best country in the world when it came to aviation, but almost immediately I was confronted by the truth.

I was piloting my helicopter towards the fixed-wing runway at Meacham Field, hovering just a few metres above the tarmac, when my radio crackled: '*Delta India Kilo*,' the tower called. 'What are you doing? Take off from where you are.'

For a few moments, I hesitated, confused. But then I got it!

In the USA, helicopters didn't have to make their way to the runway for take-off as though they were fixed-wing aircraft— they simply took off from wherever they were located at the airport (and they later returned there directly). But in Australia we had to hover-taxi to the runway for take-offs. I remembered once hovering to the threshold of Runway 16 at Sydney Airport while a Boeing 747 was held behind me as I waited for a take-off clearance.

Over the next few months, during my around-the-world flight, the differences between overseas and Australian aviation came thick and fast. I learned that nearly everything in Australia was more complicated, resulting in higher costs either for the government or for the aviator and ultimately for the paying passenger.

For instance, if an Australian pilot intended to fly more than 80 kilometres or above 5000 feet, even if flying visually, he or she had to file a 'full position' flight plan with the government, in effect to inform the authorities every thirty minutes exactly where the aircraft intended to be. If a pilot wanted to check out an interesting landmark a few kilometres away from the planned route, the pilot would have to radio Air Traffic Service and advise an amendment to their flight plan.

When I went to file a 'full position' flight plan in Fort Worth, the briefing officer looked astonished and said, 'That's not required here. If you want, give us your general route and, when you depart, open the flight plan. If you don't close it by the time advised, we will start a search.' It was a far simpler and less labour intensive system.

There were other oddities. When I was flying around the world in airspace covered by radar, I was communicating directly with the radar operator, but this didn't happen in Australia.

Aviation safety reform

The problem in Australia was that there were two separate airspace systems manned by members of two different unions. It was a classic demarcation issue and one that, I'm glad to say, I did ultimately succeed in changing. It took nearly a decade, but at least pilots could then speak directly to a controller who was in front of a radar screen. Unfortunately, the substantial increase in low-level controlled airspace has never happened.

When I returned to Australia after my solo flight, I was so enthusiastic about what I had seen that I travelled to the Department of Aviation (DofA) head office in Canberra to share what I'd learned. I was warmly welcomed and my meetings went well. I really thought I was contributing towards positive change. Afterwards, when I mentioned my efforts to people in the industry they told me, 'Dick, you'll get nowhere. Their minds are set in concrete.' I was sure they were wrong, but, sadly, they weren't.

The more I spoke to people in the industry, the more I realised how entrenched Australia's aviation problems had become. Above all, our regulations were prescriptive—that is, they were written with an authoritarian approach. In countries like the USA, the UK, Europe and Canada, the regulations left room for the pilot to make commonsense decisions, but not here. The pilot was treated like an irresponsible child.

To make matters worse, many of our regulations were arbitrary and, at times, contradictory. For instance, in Australia helipads were required to have an approach path and a 'missed approach path', in case the pilot didn't land. Despite few pilots ever needing to do a missed approach, the requirement remained and would have blocked construction of most helipads. What to do?

The aviation bureaucrats solved the problem by issuing dispensations to helipad owners, with renewal certificates required annually. This meant the bureaucrats would have to travel from Canberra to inspect the site every twelve months before issuing a new certificate. If they felt like not issuing a dispensation, they didn't have to. It gave them immense personal power.

I personally enjoyed a good relationship with the DofA. It gave me dispensations that allowed me to do most things, from flying under the Sydney Harbour Bridge to building my helipads at North Ryde and Terrey Hills. I quickly learned that getting a dispensation for one's personal advantage was one thing, but updating a regulation to benefit the whole industry was quite another.

———

After two frustrating years researching the problems of our onerous aviation regulations, I wrote and published *Two Years in the Aviation Hall of Doom*. It explained the bureaucratic quagmire I'd encountered and called for an independent review to be set up.

As always, I looked for capable people to help me to write the book and was lucky to meet the eccentric Francis James. Francis had been a Spitfire pilot in World War II, when he was shot down, captured by the Germans and somehow managed to escape. Back in Australia, he became a journalist (writing articles from the back of his Rolls Royce parked outside the *Sydney Morning Herald* offices) and was later imprisoned in China for years when mistaken for a spy. He was an incredible writer. I asked him to read through my words and smarten them up a bit; he introduced expressions like 'the mandarins of Molonglo', referring to government bureaucrats located near Canberra's Molonglo River. I spent many fascinating hours with Francis, and his friendship, like that of Ted Noffs, was something I valued most highly.

Two Years in the Aviation Hall of Doom was published in December 1984 and quickly made *The Australian* newspaper's bestseller list. Clearly, I wasn't the only one concerned about how Australia's aviation industry was being regulated. Thanks to the extraordinary publicity my book received, the push for an independent review succeeded. Within months, the federal government announced the establishment of an Aviation Industry Inquiry. Its terms of reference were: 'To inquire into issues raised by Mr Dick Smith in his recent publication *Two Years in the Aviation Hall of Doom* and matters relating to operational regulatory decisions of the Department of Aviation.'

The committee's eventual findings supported my belief that there had been communication breakdowns within the DofA, but it stopped short of saying the problems were caused by personal conflicts within the department. In the years that followed, I worked hard to convince the government that there could be savings of at least $100 million per year to the industry if it adopted proven overseas regulations while retaining those of ours that were better.

Then in January 1988, the Hawke Labor government established the Civil Aviation Authority (CAA), which would henceforth be responsible for setting safety standards and day-to-day regulatory control of the aviation industry. When they invited me to join its board, I readily accepted, believing that it would give me the opportunity to advance important reforms.

I wasn't an ideal candidate for the board. My friends could only imagine how I, a person who famously had a nine-minute attention span and held most of my own meetings by intercom, could be expected to sit nearly all day at a meeting in Canberra. There were other differences as well. Some board members insisted on being picked up by Commonwealth cars at the airport and complained when they considered the hotel they had been booked into was not of high enough quality. I couldn't have cared less. In fact, my time in the Canberra bureaucracy showed me why the Soviet Union collapsed.

Don't get me wrong: I found my fellow board members very hard working but most had no aviation knowledge or yearnings for reform. The Canberra bureaucratic 'cocoon' offered an experience almost diametrically opposite to the free enterprise system I was used to, and any change takes a long time if it happens at all.

At one board meeting, I suggested that we look at the aviation systems in leading countries and adopt the best of them. There was a deathly silence. Everyone stared at me in astonishment.

It seemed beyond the comprehension of my fellow board members that we should be asking for advice or copying the success of others. That attitude remains the same today.

My push for reform was intended to reduce costs and, by doing so, to increase the number of people flying, a much safer option than driving. Over many months of research, in conjunction with the Bureau of Air Safety Investigation, I managed to compile figures that showed that all forms of paid air travel were safer than travelling by car—varying from about twice as safe if you chartered a small plane, to five times as safe in a small commuter aircraft, to four hundred times safer with the airlines.

Private flying in light aircraft was another matter: roughly five times less safe than going by car. But before you start to question the sanity of private fliers, consider that this was still twice as safe as travelling by motorcycle, a mode chosen by three hundred thousand Australians at this time.

In November 1989, I was at Prime Minister Bob Hawke's launch of a television campaign promoting Australian Made goods; it featured around-the-world sailor Kay Cottee and me. After the prime minister finished his speech, he came over and asked, 'Dick, can I have a private word with you for a second?'

We stepped away from the others and he said, 'Dick, I have decided to appoint you Chairman of the Civil Aviation Authority.'

I replied, 'No way, Prime Minister. We are not going to have an aviation industry in five years the way we are going.'

He responded, 'What are you talking about?'

I explained that, with the introduction of 'user pays', the sell-off of airports and the increased regulatory costs to the industry, there were serious problems. 'The airlines will be okay,' I said. 'With tens of millions of passengers, they can add extra costs to the air ticket and it is hardly noticeable, but general aviation, especially in the bush, will be destroyed.'

The prime minister asked, 'What can we do?'

I replied, 'We have to make it clear that the money spent on aviation safety is always limited by what is affordable. We have to remove every unnecessary cost—only a viable industry can be a safe industry. Otherwise how could it afford the cost of implementing the best safety measures?'

To which he replied, 'Dick, you take on the job and I will give you total support from the top to make any necessary changes.'

Within a month, I had been appointed as the chairman of the Civil Aviation Authority. Now what could I do?

I hit the ground running. It was time for major change and I asked for loyalty and commitment to achieve the much-needed reforms. 'If you don't have this,' I said to CAA staff, 'I request you go and work somewhere else, because you won't get any satisfaction here, and you will only undermine the rest of us.' Over the next few months, CAA's chief executive and his deputy both gave notice that they wouldn't be reapplying for their jobs.

The board appointed a new chief executive, who implemented a 'review of resources'. Unsurprisingly, this showed that the staffing levels could drop from seven thousand to four thousand without compromising safety standards. This took place primarily through voluntary redundancy, and a regulatory reform program was started with the aim of reducing every unnecessary cost.

By mid-1990, there were signs that worthwhile reforms were emerging. One of the most significant was that the CAA would now accept overseas certification of new types of aircraft rather than requiring Australian operators to spend tens of thousands of dollars converting them to meet Australia's more expensive requirements.

In the *Independent Monthly*, journalist Ean Higgins wrote, 'As the new head of the Authority (CAA), Smith says, he is prepared to go in to bat for changes that make sense and cop the flak over unpopular decisions. He is winning some support, and some criticism, from both unions and civil aviation bureaucrats. "Affordable safety" would mean trading off one of the world's best safety records for lower airfares, the critics say. "Another Dick Smith myth," the CAA chairman says. All the authority is doing is getting rid of rules which cost money and efficiency without any measurable increase in safety.'

Towards the end of the year, a new battle loomed as the CAA moved towards modernising the airspace so it was solely operated by air traffic controllers. The November/December issue of *Flying* magazine said, 'Aircrew who have flown in American and European airspace know only too well how backward and cumbersome our approach to air traffic handling has become.' Fortunately, I was able to get a win on that one, with a change so air traffic controllers operated all the airspace.

I finished my stint as CAA chairman on 19 February 1992, going out on a high as the aviation industry recorded its lowest number of accidents and fatalities in five years. I was quoted in *The Age*: 'The introduction of economic de-regulation, coupled with major changes in safety regulations and substantial reductions in staff numbers at the CAA has led to almost constant claims that safety would suffer. The opposite has happened.'

Three years after I left, there was another restructuring and the responsibilities of the CAA were divided between two new organisations. The Civil Aviation Safety Authority (CASA) took over safety regulation and, in May 1997, I was invited back as deputy chairman of CASA and later that year I was appointed chairman.

I was keen to resume aviation reform, but after ten months it became obvious to me that the CEO the board had appointed was not the change agent that was needed and I asked him to step down. My experience in business was always to make the tough decisions and never leave a person in a position you believe they are not suited to. When Minister John Anderson heard of my decision, he became apoplectic, making it clear to the board that it was politically unacceptable to remove the chief executive.

Knowing that the cost-saving reforms would most likely not proceed and that it was untenable for me to be in a position that had responsibility without authority, I had no alternative than to resign. But Prime Minister John Howard rang and asked me to stay. I lasted until 22 March, when I resigned in frustration.

I'd hoped that, despite my departure, aviation reform would proceed, but this wasn't to be. The airspace reforms I had started have only been half-implemented to this day, with airline aircraft still flying around in cloud at many airports with a 'do it yourself—calling in the blind' unsafe system still in force. The regulatory reform program that I started with the aim of reducing every unnecessary cost by adopting the best overseas practices of proven safety has sadly moved to a system that has the most restrictive and expensive rules in the world.

I was disappointed by how things had turned out. My plan was for Australian aviation to have the highest participation levels in the world—from manufacturing to flight training to commercial and recreational aviation. All by simply adopting the most efficient practices from around the world—but I failed.

By way of a footnote to this story, I should add that I had better success when, in 1996, John Howard appointed me as chairman of the Centenary of Federation Council, to coordinate the celebrations of the founding of the Australian federation.

Once again, the CEO who had been initially appointed was simply not the right person for the job. Fortunately, the prime minister gave me immediate support and replaced the incumbent with the highly experienced veteran Tony Eggleton. From there on, the whole organisation ran smoothly. I was proud to be involved.

CHAPTER 19

Third time lucky

My third attempt to reach the North Pole couldn't have come at a better time. The first year of *Australian Geographic* proved to be challenging, not just because I'd never run a publishing business, but because we were trying to produce a journal to an extremely high standard. This plus my work on the Life Education centres, my commitment to aviation reform and to curbing cigarette advertising directed at young people, and my responsibilities as Australian of the Year were taking most of my time.

On 18 April 1987, Pip, the girls and I boarded a Qantas flight from Sydney to Vancouver, where I unpacked *Delta India Kilo*, which I'd shipped there a month earlier. Over the next few days, I enjoyed the need for me to focus on just one thing—the final preparations to enable me and my helicopter to reach the North Pole.

On Friday, 24 April, I left Yellowknife in conditions that were much better than during my second attempt the previous year. The temperature was now 0°C, compared to –15°C previously, and this time I had a small heater in the cockpit.

I flew north-east to Cambridge Bay, crossing the Arctic Circle and stopping at the Inuit village of Bay Chimo after spotting a group of people gathered outside. It was their sports day and I left them with a copy of *Australian Geographic* before continuing on. The next morning, bad weather forced me back to Cambridge Bay, but on Sunday, 26 April I battled snow squalls and poor visibility to reach Resolute, where Pip and the girls were waiting. I always love doing things with my family and the school holidays allowed us to be together for a part of this record attempt.

On Monday, 27 April, it was clear, sunny and –20°C. The forecast was excellent, so I took off for Ward Hunt Island, my last stepping stone on all my North Pole attempts. Along the way, I made a detour to deliver a stove to two French microlight pilots who were also aiming for the Pole.

At Ward Hunt Island, the weather was clear and the temperature only –28°C, a full 10 degrees warmer than the previous year. Pip had chartered a Twin Otter in Resolute, dropping off fuel and equipment then returning to Eureka, while I spent a nervous night trying to get some sleep.

The following morning, Tuesday, 28 April, I used a special heater to pre-warm *Delta India Kilo*'s engine before taking off for the Pole. Simultaneously, the Twin Otter, with Pip on board, left from Eureka with fuel for my return flight. The girls had been left building an igloo in Resolute.

The weather was perfect as I flew for hour after hour above the jumbled pressure ridges of the frozen Arctic Ocean. I continually scanned my instruments, steering by sun compass and omega while struggling to stay composed. After two attempts and so many hundreds of hours of preparation to reach this point, was it possible that I was about to succeed?

At 4.10 p.m., after four hours in the air, I gingerly lowered *Delta India Kilo* onto sea ice at the North Pole, a 2-metre crust above 4261 metres of ocean (as measured by the Russian *Mir* submersible). I'd flown more than 6500 kilometres from Vancouver and was shivering with excitement. I climbed out of the helicopter, planted my Australian flag in the snow and danced around it, singing 'Advance Australia Fair' and skipping through time changes and date lines with glee.

'I'm not an adventurous person by nature,' Pip later explained, 'but Dick's enthusiastic spirit is infectious. That's how I came to be sitting right behind pilot Allen McDonald and co-pilot Ron Kerr in the Twin Otter that was taking fuel to the North Pole for Dick's return flight.

'We were about 36 kilometres from the Pole and in radio contact with Dick, who was ahead of us, but we couldn't see him. Then I spotted him—a tiny dot on the horizon, flying low over the ice. Then I lost sight of him again.

'When we were still a mile or two from the Pole he radioed that he'd landed. When we flew over Dick's helicopter sitting on that vast expanse of ice, I think I was the most excited woman in the world. A few minutes later, when we landed not far away, I stepped out of the aircraft at the top of the world. It was a moment I'll never forget.'

As Pip stepped out of the Twin Otter, I hurried over to congratulate her on becoming the first Australian woman to reach the North Pole. We shared a few quiet minutes before it was time to refuel *Delta India Kilo*. We managed to get a radio contact back to the girls in Resolute, more than 1800 kilometres to our south, and within hours Hayley was fielding calls from the Australian media and doing radio interviews. Not bad for a fourteen year old.

The Twin Otter departed and I was there by myself, at one of the most isolated places on Earth. I had to be very careful with my navigation back to Ward Hunt Island. At the North Pole, every direction is south. One mistake and I could be heading for Russia! I carefully calculated the correct setting on my sun compass and took off, using the sun for direction.

On Wednesday, 6 May, I finally landed at Yellowknife, where Pip joined me. I planned to return in July to fly the helicopter to Anchorage, exploring Alaska's northern wilderness along the way, so we stored *Delta India Kilo* and caught a commercial flight home.

———

When Ike Bain had written to me in November 1986 to say he was interested in working with me again, I followed him up.

Remember my success secret—*surround yourself with capable people.*

'Why don't you come back and work with me at *Australian Geographic*,' I asked. Ike said that he didn't know a thing about publishing and I replied, 'Neither do I!' I offered him half the salary he was currently earning.

Ike already knew that, when working with me, taking a short-term loss for a long-term gain could well be worth it. And so it proved to be once again.

On his first day as *Australian Geographic*'s chief executive officer, I was still overseas on my North Pole adventure. But this didn't matter; we'd developed a strong, mutual trust over the years.

He spent the first few weeks observing, talking to people and finding out as much as he could about the business. Then, after a month, he sent me a memo outlining the goals we'd been discussing. These included raising the journal's subscriber number to 200,000 (we had about half that at the time), increasing our subscription renewal rate from 66 per cent to 75–80 per cent, producing the best maps possible and having the best staff.

At the very bottom of the page, Ike had written, 'After all this is done and you are happy, let's sell nature products by mail order, and possibly later through retail outlets, and do a DSE [Dick Smith Electronics] again.'

I wasn't surprised by the note. Ike had told me how impressed he'd been by a shop called The Nature Company he had seen in the USA. It was filled with nature-related products, wild-life-themed gifts and bushwalking gear. 'But I'm not motivated to build another retail business,' I cautioned him. 'I want to put something back into the country and do things that give me satisfaction—I have enough money!' I'm not sure he was listening.

One of the first things I asked Ike to do was look into the possibility of buying the rights to the *Australian Encyclopaedia*, which had first been published by George Robertson, founder of Angus & Robertson, in 1925. An American company, the Grolier Society, had bought it in the 1950s before it was sold to the New Zealand publisher David Bateman Ltd.

As we were getting *Australian Geographic* underway, I tried to buy a set of the *Australian Encyclopaedia* for our reference library and was astonished to find that the last edition had completely sold out—all 10,000 sets—and had been out of print for almost two years.

Then, by coincidence, David Bateman approached me, looking for sponsorship to produce a new edition. My first thought was, 'Wouldn't it be fantastic if we could bring it back to Australian ownership?' I asked Ike to look into it. He found that Grolier had struggled with costs, and no doubt David Bateman was in the same situation. Otherwise they wouldn't be looking for financial assistance.

Could we do better? I had no idea, but I felt strongly about bringing it back home. To my delight, Ike's discussions led to *Australian Geographic* buying the encyclopaedia. Once the deal was done, we had to decide whether to reprint immediately, to meet the demand of schools, libraries and the many individuals who were waiting, or take the longer course of a complete update.

In the end, we spent more than $1 million on research and major revisions, with some 80 per cent of the articles updated. The new edition also featured increased colour, as well as more maps and illustrations.

We printed 10,000 standard sets of the fifth edition and a limited edition of 500 numbered, beautifully bound sets. On 25 October 1988, my dad joined me in launching the new encyclopaedia from beside the historic Tank Stream, colonial Sydney's first water supply, hidden but still running beneath the streets of the city. This created a lot of publicity, which contributed to the encyclopaedia's outstanding success. Within a few months, we had sold 5000 sets at $595 each, all with a 50 per cent profit margin.

———

In October 1987, I had two big announcements for *Australian Geographic's* subscribers. The first was that we had set up our own cartography division. One of my first aims when I started the journal was to produce the finest, most authoritative maps in Australia.

At the time, I thought that maps produced by a company called Travelog Publications were very good, so I asked my secretary to find out who was doing the work and to invite them in for a meeting.

Travelog founder Will Pringle showed up for a meeting with Howard. Will had recently sold Travelog to Universal Publications, the company that produced UBD street directories, and had signed a three-year non-compete contract. Also, we were only looking for a part-time cartographer and Will needed full-time work.

By mid-year 1987, Howard and I weren't happy with the standard of the maps in our journal. We also knew that we would have more than enough work for a full-time cartographer, so I rang Will. He came in and we had a chat about the kind of maps I hoped we could produce. I then sent Will to meet Ike. The following day, we offered Will a job. Fortunately, UBD agreed to release him from his contract a year early.

Will later said that working at *Australian Geographic* was exactly what he had dreamed of—a business dedicated to producing quality, authoritative publications. He recalls that even before our first meeting, he told someone, 'One day I'll work for *Australian Geographic*.'

In our journal's ninth issue (Jan–Mar 1988), the credit line 'Australian Geographic Cartographic Division' first appeared under three maps: one of Heard Island, another being a crocodile distribution map and the third showing my route to the North Pole. Immediately it was clear that in Will we'd acquired an extraordinary talent.

Soon Will was producing poster maps to be inserted into the journal, ranging from the Birdsville Track to Shark Bay and the Canning Stock Route.

Third time lucky

But perhaps Will's greatest triumph was the incredible *Australia for Adventurers and Dreamers*. This giant poster map featured more than 350 captions about historical, adventurous and scenic places to visit. Icons showed sites for caving, rafting, ballooning, diving, skiing, climbing and more. On the back, it had climatic charts, national parks, roads and tracks.

Our researcher, Rosy Whelan, spent nearly a year finding the most useful and fascinating information and ended up writing the same number of words for the map as were found in a normal issue of the journal. The map became our most popular ever and has been reprinted many times since it was first released.

Will and his team continued to create dozens and dozens of the most incredible maps. I believe that the success of *Australian Geographic*, our travel books and many other products was due in no small part to the efforts of Will and our cartographic division. My aim had been to produce the finest maps in Australia, and we did.

Our second big announcement was that I had decided to form the Australian Geographic Society, a non-profit scientific and educational organisation to 'support scientific endeavour and spread geographical knowledge'. Its aims were to promote increased awareness about our country and to contribute to the world's knowledge of Australia and Australians.

Membership in the society was automatic when you subscribed to the journal and part of each subscription fee went towards financing the pursuits of many remarkable achievers.

The society published a quarterly newsletter that was sent out with each issue of the journal.

The response to the AG Society was overwhelming. From the start, I tried to encourage a sense that when you sub-scribed to *Australian Geographic*, you were becoming part of something, joining a community with the goal of promoting a positive look at Australia and encouraging the achievements of Australians. We even called our first subscribers Foundation Supporters.

The first eight issues of *Australian Geographic* carried the subhead, 'Dick Smith's Journal of Adventure and Discovery'. On issue nine, we changed this to 'The Journal of the Australian Geographic Society'. For me this was more than a symbolic gesture. It really felt like the journal was coming of age, that it was no longer 'my' journal, but was representing the more than 100,000 (and growing) membership of the society.

———

Ike had seen a large-format bird calendar produced by the Audubon Society and learned that it was a top-selling product among *National Geographic*'s readers. He was keen to see if we could do something similar. He worked out that if we hoped to make a reasonable profit on such a large format (500 × 433 millimetre) calendar, with fine art reproduction prints for every month, we'd have to charge $22.95 to obtain a 50 per cent margin.

'A lot of people I've spoken to have laughed, saying nobody would pay that much for a huge, heavy calendar,' Ike told me. 'They say they won't have enough space for it on the wall. My reply was that nobody in Australia has produced a calendar like this before, so we just don't know.'

For the *Australian Encyclopaedia*, we'd inserted a four-page, full-colour A3 brochure into Sunday newspapers. It was so successful that Ike decided to try the same with the calendar. The brochure focused on the paintings by brilliant wildlife artist Tony Oliver, and told the story about how much hard work Tony put into researching his subjects. The brochure included a reservation coupon that allowed people to order their calendar in advance.

Response to the brochure stunned everyone, including me. We quickly had mail orders for 10,000 calendars and went on to sell over twenty thousand. In fact, the calendars remained our best-selling Christmas gift for many years.

Ike didn't stop with the calendar. He quickly put together a list of adventure books, and added to this a list of videos covering everything from tall ships, Australian trains and the photography of Frank Hurley. He also came up with the idea of selling special collector's sets of the journal, gift cards, *Australian Geographic* t-shirts and sloppy-joes, and the *Australian Encyclopaedia*.

Thanks to Ike's hard work, our first *Australian Geographic Catalogue* was released in time for the Christmas 1988 gift-buying season and made more than $100,000 in sales. Just like the Dick Smith Electronics days, everything we sold had to have at least a 50 per cent margin.

———

From the earliest days of our journal, I was bothered by the wastage involved in distributing it through newsagents. It's hard to imagine, but it worked like this. The distributor (to whom we had to give a 40 per cent discount) would deliver a certain number of magazines to each newsagent, and at the end of the magazine's sale period, the newsagents would receive credit for the unsold copies by ripping the covers off and sending them back to the distributor, only paying for those that they'd sold. The unsold magazines would then be pulped.

The system had been in place for years, but I was horrified with the waste. In my *Publisher's Notes* in the October–December 1987 issue, I wrote: 'It seems impossible for the distributors to predict the exact number of journals each newsagent will sell over the three-month period and there are no facilities to move journals from one outlet to another. I feel it's a pity there has to be such waste.'

I soon decided that the best answer was to sell the journal by subscription only. By doing so, we'd know exactly how many copies we had to print, so there would be almost no wastage; no discount would have to be given; and they would be all paid for in advance. But we were selling up to 60,000 copies on the newsstands. What if those readers didn't take out subscriptions? That was the unknown.

Third time lucky

Fortunately, I didn't have a board to answer to and so our April–June 1988 issue was the first to be restricted to subscribers only. I soon challenged our members to sign up at least one new supporter each issue, with the goal of doubling our subscribers to more than two hundred thousand.

———

In October 1987, the share market crash affected people worldwide. Fortunately, *Australian Geographic* continued to boom. I kept the annual subscription price ($28) affordable, even during this downturn.

At the time, I began to question the almost universal belief that business had to be driven by constant growth. What if I capped subscriptions at 200,000, I thought, would the company just wither and die? During an interview on ABC Radio, I floated the idea of limiting the number of our subscribers and the listeners practically panicked. Our phones were jammed for nearly a week. In fact, callers knocked out the local telephone exchange. Our subscriptions eventually peaked at about two hundred and seven thousand.

In the same interview, I explained, 'I'm not running *Australian Geographic* for commercial reasons. I'm running it for the satisfaction I get out of it. I sold Dick Smith Electronics because I got fed up with just sitting in my office with five hundred people working for me, making lots of money but never being able to do all the wonderful things I wanted to do. I don't want to get into the same position.

'I'm against this mad drive to expand,' I said. 'One of the great things about Australia is our small population. Politicians are talking about growth all the time, everything's got to get bigger. In the United States, you can't even drive on the freeways, you can't breathe the air, you can't even go camping without a permit because there are so many people wanting to camp in the same area.' It was a theme I would come back to again and again in the coming years, yet it was happening within my own business.

With an ever-growing list of exclusive *Australian Geographic*-branded products, our mail order business grew from sales of several hundred thousand dollars in 1988 to just under three million in 1990. It wasn't long before Ike approached me about opening a shop. I wasn't that keen, but I knew from past experience that Ike was cautious about spending money and he had a real talent for retail sales. It was his passion.

He convinced me to put the question to a vote of our staff and he sent out a memo to all of them asking what they thought of the idea, putting the pros and cons case as even-handedly as he could. When the votes came in, there were only two who said 'No'—that was me and Pip.

The first Australian Geographic store opened a few months later. Despite the fact that we were opening the business in the teeth of a severe economic recession, the stores were an instant success and we would eventually go on to open twenty-five of them around the country. By the end of the first year, we were able to give away more than $5 million to charities and the society, far more than I had ever anticipated.

Fortunately, the public supported me, and the magazine and its associated businesses continued to thrive. But the challenge for me had always been in getting things from idea to reality, and soon enough I began thinking about new adventures. I knew I would be open to offers to sell the business, and given the profits we were making, they were sure to come.

What I didn't expect, however, was a call from Kerry Packer. Kerry could have bought me a dozen times over, or used his successful publishing arm to start a rival to *Australian Geographic*. Instead, he wanted to talk.

I wasn't all that keen on a meeting. In the few dealings I had had with him in the past, things hadn't gone particularly well, and I didn't think our subscribers would be too impressed if their fiercely independent magazine ended up in the hands of the biggest media proprietor in the country. Yet, I have to admit, I was intrigued to see up close how the mogul conducted business, and it wouldn't do me any harm to get an offer from him that might be useful in dealing with other potential suitors.

So Ike Bain and I went along to a meeting at the legendary Consolidated Press headquarters in Park Street, Sydney. We were met in the foyer by a very young James Packer, who escorted us up to his father's intimidating third-floor office.

It was clear from the beginning that Kerry thought I was keen to sell and would part with the business for a bargain price. I told him that in fact the business was making a fortune and there was no way I was selling for anything less than an equivalent asset. And no, that didn't mean shares in Kerry's company.

When Ike explained that our shops were returning annual sales of around $10,000 per square metre, almost unheard of levels, Kerry responded, 'I don't know a f***ing thing about retail, but that must be good, otherwise you wouldn't be f***ing telling me, would you? So how much do you want?'

I told him my private wealth was held in commercial property, so he needed to find a building worth at least $60 million if I was going to be interested. Kerry blustered; his increasingly colourful language now seemed to escalate to include the f-bomb in every sentence, if not every phrase. He growled to one of his offsiders, 'Do we own any f***ing property?' before he answered his own question quickly with the sudden realisation: 'F***, we own this f***ing building! How much is it f***ing worth?'

Nobody knew. So James was dispatched to find out. Always the deal maker, it seemed Kerry was prepared to do a deal then and there on a handshake if the valuation came close.

But, to everyone's surprise, James sheepishly returned a little later to say everybody was at lunch and no one could be found to give him a valuation. And so it was the sale that never happened.

I doubt that Kerry was really serious, unless he was convinced he was getting a bargain—his modus operandi was always to buy cheap and sell for top dollar. As for James, he did eventually move in and run things from Park Street after his father died. He ended up selling the building and leasing it back for a short while. And the price? Reportedly it sold for $50 million.

Third time lucky

As Australian Geographic grew, so too did the journal and the society's support for science and adventure. Our funding helped rebuild the Australian Inland Mission hospital in Innamincka and the childhood home of Sir Hubert Wilkins. As well, Australian adventurers were funded and this continues to this day.

Our 'Year in the Wilderness' project placed young couples into remote regions, first Michael and Susan Cusack in the Kimberley, then Damon and Deanne Howes in southwest Tasmania. They produced riveting journal stories and Michael and Susan's became a best-selling book.

But, after eleven years of operating *Australian Geographic*, the time was eventually right for me to move on. Once again, the business had become too big and I didn't know everyone working for me. When Fairfax came calling, I was receptive to an offer in the knowledge that Ike would stay on as chief executive to run it and keep up the high standards. I sold a business that I'd never expected to make any money from for $41 million.

I never did take an income from *Australian Geographic* and, after Pip and I sold it, we have since given all that money away.

CHAPTER 20

Off the edge of the world

My Scrawn. I hope this will be another wonderful and successful adventure for you. You have my full support as I know you are such a special person who needs a different challenge every now and then. I'm actually a little envious, as I will always remember how close we were during your first attempt on the North Pole. The girls and I will be tracking your every move on our map at home and our thoughts will always be with you. Have a great time, don't get too cold and if the weather is bad, stay on the ground. There is always tomorrow. Remember I will always love you. Pip xxoo

> The note Pip gave me before my attempt to
> fly around the world via the poles

Giles Kershaw, my co-pilot, and I finished our radio calls and taxied the De Havilland Twin Otter out onto the runway in Hobart. I took a deep breath. In the cabin behind us, twenty seats had been replaced with six auxiliary fuel tanks. Each one contained 150 US gallons, giving us the extra 900 gallons we would need to fly 3539 kilometres to Casey Station, in Antarctica.

It was nearly 5.30 p.m. on 5 November 1988 and the skies looked threatening at the start of our all-night flight. The plane's gross weight was a colossal 40 per cent above normal and Giles and I were well aware that the next two or three hours would be crucial.

If we lost just one of our two engines, we'd go down in the frigid Southern Ocean, unless we could dump enough fuel to keep us airborne. If we lived through the ditching, our special survival suits would allow us only a few minutes of consciousness to deploy a life raft and get inside it. It would be desperate.

With twin throttles pushed firmly forward, we began our take-off roll. The aircraft had never felt so heavy. This was going to be a risky flight.

———

In early April 1986, during an interview I did with a journalist from the *Calgary Herald* in Canada while on my first attempt to reach the North Pole by helicopter, I revealed a grander plan that I'd been keeping to myself. If I could successfully reach the North Pole, then I would endeavour to fly my helicopter from pole to pole.

'The Australian explorer said he isn't sure which route he will take when he heads south,' the journalist wrote. 'The plan is to stop in Fort Worth, Texas this summer before heading across Central America and the west coast of South America to Antarctica next fall and winter, when the weather is warmer.'

Of course, not all expeditions go according to plan. Less than a fortnight later, I was returning, defeated, from my attempt on the Pole. It was −38°C in my tiny, unheated cockpit and I was miserable. Just off my starboard side in the waning light, I saw the Twin Otter that Pip had chartered to ferry fuel onto the Arctic ice for me. I realised the advantages that a twin-engined and well-instrumented aircraft would provide. Most importantly, it could fly safely in cloud.

The Twin Otter was a versatile aircraft. It could take off and land in a short distance; it ran on turbine fuel that was available worldwide; and it wasn't pressurised, so I could open windows for photography and filming. Best of all, with extra tanks fitted, it could fly 4600 kilometres and still have fuel left in reserve.

Those thoughts stuck and, a year later, after finally reaching the North Pole on my third attempt, I decided to change my pole-to-pole aircraft from JetRanger to Twin Otter. I had decided that a pole-to-pole flight by helicopter was well beyond the boundaries of risk I had set for myself.

The idea of actually flying all the way around the world via each pole came later. In 1987, such a flight would have been impossible, because it meant flying across Siberia, and at that time the Soviet Union simply wouldn't allow that to happen.

In the meantime, I searched the world for a suitable Twin Otter. When I found one in Nairobi that had been doing geo-survey work, I contacted Stuart Weston, the chief pilot of Aeropelican Air Services, which regularly flew Twin Otters between Sydney and Newcastle; he agreed not only to come with me to pick up the plane in Africa, but also to teach me how to fly it.

From the moment I saw the magnificent, almost new aircraft, I loved it. We brought it back to Australia in December 1987; then I purchased extra fuel tanks, skis and navigation equipment.

A few years earlier, I'd become friends with Giles Kershaw, one of the world's leading polar pilots. When I rang to ask him if he'd like to join me on my pole flights, he said yes, but because he was now employed by Cathay Pacific, he wouldn't be able to fly the whole way. As he'd never flown in East Antarctica, he was particularly keen to do that leg. We also needed a full-time mechanic, a necessity when operating complex aircraft in remote locations. While on my North Pole flight, I'd met Rob Toma, a capable young man who helped me service my helicopter in sub-zero temperatures at Resolute. He was keen to join us.

While researching possible routes, I realised that no one had ever flown directly from Australia to the Australian Antarctic Territory. This was amazing, especially as the first person to fly in Antarctica was an Australian, Sir Hubert Wilkins. He'd taken off from Deception Island in November 1928 and flown south along the Antarctic Peninsula, trying to map it along the way. He was one of my heroes. In fact, I had registered and named the Twin Otter VH-SHW *Sir Hubert Wilkins* in his honour.

I didn't need approval to fly from Australia to Antarctica because, in essence, Antarctica is international territory. I would, however, need fuel in East Antarctica, which meant the cooperation of one or more government programs. It certainly wouldn't be the Americans. In the past, they had proven to be opposed to private expeditions.

I learned that, due to lack of funds, Australia's Antarctic Division had turned down a proposal from the De Havilland Aircraft Company of Canada to ferry two Twin Otters from Australia to Antarctica and operate them there. I immediately saw an opportunity. If I could help the division, it might be able to assist me.

I wrote to the division offering my Twin Otter for appraisal flights. First, to see whether a flight between Australia and Antarctica (and landing on a relatively unprepared ice runway) was feasible, and then to test the versatility of the Twin Otter for scientific work. After months of discussion, the division agreed to support the flights.

Undertaking the scientific program would require my aircraft to be modified for radio echo-sounding traverses of the Lambert Glacier in Mac. Robertson Land. I also mounted a video camera on the nose for ice surveys. Because of the scientific value of the venture, the Explorers Club of New York, of which I'm a member, awarded me one of its flags to carry on my flight.

My one concern continued to be fuel. Even though Adventure Network International (ANI) could cache a supply in the Patriot Hills on the South American side of the Pole,

I couldn't get there in one go from Casey Station. It meant that I'd have to ferry fuel up onto the polar plateau.

The simplest thing would be for the Americans to refuel us (at my expense) from their vast reserves at the South Pole. But not only did they refuse to do so; they said they wouldn't even supply me with weather information. They considered mine a private expedition, despite the work I would be doing for the Antarctic Division.

The problem was solved when the Soviets took up the offer and said they would tow fuel from their coastal base, Mirny Station, 1400 kilometres inland to Vostok Station. What an incredible response! It was the key to the success of the whole expedition.

The Antarctic Division agreed with my proposals and said they would transport Rob Toma, spares that had been lent to us and the aircraft skis on board their supply ship, *Icebird*. The skis couldn't travel with us due to their weight and our limited payload. If all went well, Rob and our equipment would be waiting for us when we reached Casey Station.

———

For twelve scary hours, most of them in darkness and cloud, Giles and I, after departing from Hobart, flew above one of the planet's most remote and dangerous oceans. We were beginning to think the worst was behind us, but that changed as we approached the Antarctic continent.

Off the edge of the world

'We're having problems with the Omega,' I said as I tapped the face of the navigation instrument. Flying at 8000 feet in pitch darkness, we were well past our 'point of no return' and so close to the South Magnetic Pole that our magnetic compass was useless. The Omega showed us that we were gradually turning and heading back the way we had come. If this was so, we would be heading for a ditching in the Southern Ocean as we ran out of fuel. This was a life-threatening situation. Giles switched on the landing lights and it was obvious we were flying in cloud.

'Let's try and get above the cloud and see if we can see the stars to confirm our heading,' I suggested and pulled back on the control column. A tense half an hour passed as we climbed to 18,000 feet, but we were still in the cloud. I felt sick inside and frightened. I thought we were going to die. We had no oxygen system, so we were suffering from hypoxia, making it hard for us to think clearly. We descended and, after what seemed an interminable time, eventually broke out of the cloud. I searched the night sky to try to find the Southern Cross. It wasn't there! I twisted my neck and put my face on the windscreen and eventually located the Southern Cross almost above us. Using my Scout training, I worked out where south was. This showed we were only about 15 degrees from our correct heading. We were going to live! We changed direction and a little later the sun appeared over the bottom of the world and we were able to confirm our exact heading from our sun compass.

About 110 kilometres from Casey Station, we picked up its radio directional beacon, and at 4.30 a.m. (7.30 a.m. Hobart time),

277

after fourteen hours in the air, we circled the 1100-metre runway on the icecap that station crew had prepared by dragging a steel beam behind a tractor.

We landed on wheels without a problem and were welcomed by about forty people, half the station's staff; many of them had been up all night listening in on our radio messages. But as we taxied off the runway, our tyres started to break through the surface. It was time for Rob to fit the skis he'd brought down on *Icebird*. Giles and I were dead tired, as it was more than twenty-four hours since we'd slept.

Over the next three weeks, we crammed in 136 flying hours, covering 33,000 kilometres for the Australian National Antarctic Research Expeditions (ANARE). Thanks to constant daylight and fantastic weather, we had no such thing as routine days and flew over more of the Australian territory than any aircraft before us.

Our first major internal flight was from Casey to Davis Station, 1400 kilometres to the west along the coast. On the way, the three of us—Rob was now on board—made an unscheduled stop at Mirny, which was the first permanent base the Russians had established in Antarctica. From the moment we landed, we were made to feel like long-lost friends. Station leader Nikolai Dimitryev invited us in to join their celebration of the anniversary of the Bolshevik Revolution. It included generous helpings of caviar and red salmon, but we had to decline the vodka toasts.

Next, after just over six hours of flying, we landed on sea ice in front of Davis Station. The next day, we were asked to fly out 300 kilometres to where *Icebird* was slowly making its way through thick pack ice. It was hoped that we might spot open leads in the ice, to help the supply ship progress more quickly, but we had no luck.

Then, as we attempted to land on a nearby ice floe, cracks began radiating out from the ice under the Twin Otter. Behind us I could hear Rob yelling, 'Put on the power! Put on the power!' Giles instantly pushed the throttles forward and the aircraft strained to take off. As it did so, there was a sudden 'Bang!' as we hit a bump. This bent the right-hand ski, but somehow Giles got us airborne. It was an incredibly risky undertaking.

After retreating to Davis and repairing the ski, we returned two days later to where the *Icebird* could move no closer to the station due to heavy pack ice. We landed 15 kilometres south of the ship, on an ice floe that had been carefully selected by ANARE staff after a helicopter recce flight. This time, we made several passes beforehand and touched our skis down gently for the length of the strip, getting those on the ice to check our tracks before finally landing.

Soon afterwards, *Icebird*'s three helicopters began ferrying expeditioners, mail and supplies from the ship to us, and we flew them to Davis, returning with staff from the previous winter, who were on their way home. Over the next two days, we shuttled for more than thirteen hours, carrying forty people and 4 tonnes of cargo. By the time we finished, I don't think anybody at Davis had doubts about the usefulness of fixed-wing aircraft in Antarctica.

Over the next five days, we carried the head of China's Antarctic program, Guo Kun, to nearby Larsemann Hills, where he hoped to choose a site for a station. We visited the Russian base Progress and the emperor penguin colony at Amanda Bay.

Our science support role began with an aerial ice-depth survey of the Lambert Glacier, which, at more than 400 kilometres long and an average of 40 kilometres wide, is the world's largest. It flows first into the Amery Ice Shelf, then another 300 kilometres to the ocean. The data collected would help scientists understand the relationship between the continent's snowfall and ice outflow. Glaciologist Ian Allison explained that any small changes in the polar icecap caused by global warming would be evident in how much ice flowed down the glacier. I was pleased that we could help with this important work.

On 22 November, we flew from Casey on a nine-hour flight over 3233-metre high Dome Charlie and landed on the sea ice close to the Greenpeace base at Cape Evans in McMurdo Sound at the foot of the Mt Erebus volcano.

Greenpeace had agreed to supply us with enough fuel to get to the South Pole and back as well as for our flight back to Casey. In return, we would take two members of their team along on this leg so they could inspect the American Amundsen-Scott Station located right at the South Pole.

The five of us took off the next morning and flew over the dirty sprawl of America's McMurdo Station. Over the next six hours, we traced Scott's footsteps 1400 kilometres across the Ross Ice Shelf, up the Beardmore Glacier and onto the polar plateau. It was incredibly emotional as we marked on our map the site of their One Ton Depot, near where Scott and his team perished.

The South Pole appeared on our radar from 150 kilometres away as a reflection from the aluminium geodesic dome that covered the buildings of the American base located there. We soon touched down on the massive 4260-metre snow runway and taxied up to the red-and-white barber's pole that was topped with a chrome sphere and surrounded by flags. It was 24 November 1988. After years of dreaming about it, I was at last at the South Pole. Whichever way I looked, the direction was north. Here we had landed on ice that was over 2800 metres thick, at an altitude higher than Mt Kosciuszko, so different to my landing on 2-metre thick ice at sea level at the North Pole.

Not far away was the entrance to a long, steel tunnel leading into the geodesic dome. Above the entrance was a sign that read, 'The United States welcomes you to the South Pole'—but it certainly wasn't the warmest of welcomes.

We were given a quick tour inside the base and, despite it being Thanksgiving, and the mouth-watering turkeys and ham cooling in their pans, which their chef proudly showed us, we were offered just a cup of coffee before it was hinted that we should be on our way. Rob Toma, our Canadian engineer, simply couldn't believe their inhospitality.

It wasn't until we were leaving that the Americans discovered that our companions, Keith Swenson and Wojtek Moskal, were from Greenpeace and had just made their first, if brief, inspection of the base. They became even more agitated when I unloaded a wooden box with our emergency supplies. I'd borrowed the box from Greenpeace and it still had its name stencilled on the outside.

As we flew back to Cape Evans, we were amazed to hear over the radio American officials discussing whether or not they should remove the box. Fortunately, cooler heads prevailed, but when Giles, Rob and I returned to the Pole a week later, we found that they had spray-painted over all the Greenpeace logos. We were bemused by their paranoia.

Back at Greenpeace's own station—their small, low-key World Park Base—we had an extremely pleasant stay, visiting nearby Scott's Hut and spending nearly a day hand-pumping eighteen drums of fuel into the Twin Otter.

Early on 26 November, we took off on our longest flight so far, along the eastern border of Australian Antarctica to the abandoned Russian base Leningradskaya, and then along the coast back to Casey Station, a distance of 3000 kilometres.

We flew over Mawson's Hut at Commonwealth Bay about midnight, continuing on to touch down in very low visibility on the sea ice in front of the French base Dumont d'Urville so we could deliver mail. When I jumped out, I was warned that the ice could break under us at any moment—so we were straight back into the air again.

On 29 November, we left Casey for our flight across the continent. For hour after hour, we droned above a featureless ice wilderness. Finally, about 75 kilometres from Vostok, we spied the tracks left by the tractor supply train that had rumbled along some 1400 kilometres from Mirny Station, hopefully with our fuel on board.

We landed easily on the frozen skiway at an elevation of 3489 metres and were greeted by Vostok's station leader, Arnold Budretsky. We'd arrived at the coldest place on Earth, where a temperature of −89.6°C had been recorded. Fortunately for our arrival, we enjoyed a relatively balmy −30°C temperature.

Once again, the Russians were very hospitable, giving us a tour of their base and telling us about their drilling program to recover deep ice cores. Some had been dated to 8000 years ago (and over the next decade the drill would reach 3623 metres, revealing climate information from 40,000 years ago).

I managed to catch a couple of hours' sleep on a divan in the station leader's office, but Rob wasn't so lucky. Every two hours, he had to go outside, put the battery back in and run up the Twin Otter's engines. Without these precautions, they might not start.

Thanks to Rob's efforts, they did, and we used up every bit of Vostok's skiway when departing. Full fuel tanks and the high elevation reduced our take-off performance so much that the aircraft's stall warning alarm sounded on take-off. This told us that at only a slightly lower airspeed, the lift from the wing would be lost, sending the plane crashing to the ice.

Over the next five and a half hours, 1278 kilometres of the polar plateau's vast icecap passed beneath us, until we landed for the second time at the South Pole.

We stayed just long enough to pick up our now 'unbranded' emergency supplies box and to wave the Australian flag, which seemed the most appropriate way I could mark the official start of my pole-to-pole flight.

Over the next four hours, and 1112 kilometres, we entered a different world as we looked down on the immense unspoiled natural beauty. The Thiel Mountains pierced the icecap ahead, followed by the Ellsworth Mountains and the Patriot Hills, on our flight to the ANI base camp alongside a wind-scoured, blue ice runway that was as hard as concrete. This was where wheeled aircraft from South America landed, and from here ski planes would fly adventurers to the start of South Pole treks and climbers to the 4892-metre high Mt Vinson, Antarctica's highest peak.

We topped up with ten drums of fuel, at US$3000 per drum. This was the first fuel we had had to pay for since leaving Hobart; it was expensive, but it had to be flown in 3000 kilometres from Punta Arenas. Rob set to work and removed the skis, replacing them with the wheels we had been carrying on board. We then spent a remarkably comfortable night in insulated fabric huts before continuing our flight.

The weather report for our next landing, at Teniente Rodolfo Marsh station on King George Island in the South Shetlands, was for visibility of 2 kilometres and a 75 kilometre per hour wind. It was nearly accurate. The station's air traffic controller tried to be helpful and kept telling us to go to an alternative landing site, but they all required skis and we'd left ours behind with ANI, as we would need wheels to land in South America.

With visibility less than a kilometre, thanks to blowing snow and a violent sea below, we made the approach into headwinds blasting straight down the gravel runway.

The runway appeared only moments before we touched down. What a relief it was to be on the ground and in the hands of the friendly Chileans.

After a day relaxing and exploring King George Island, we took off on our final Antarctic leg. Even though it was slightly out of our way, I wanted to fly over Deception Island. Sir Hubert Wilkins had begun his historic first Antarctic flight from the black sand beach of Whaler's Bay, inside the caldera of volcanic Deception Island, in November 1928. It made me proud to think that an Australian from a drought-stricken farming community in South Australia had had the drive and courage to take on such an incredible adventure.

After several circuits above the island, we turned north and flew across the notoriously stormy Drake Passage, but for us it was a perfectly sunny, calm day. We flew low past Cape Horn and up the Beagle Channel to Punta Arenas. As we arrived there and stepped out of the Twin Otter, I looked across the tarmac and saw a group of people preparing to board the ANI flight to Patriot Hills. Among them I recognised my friend Australian mountaineer Greg Mortimer.

'Greg,' I called out, 'what are you doing here?'

'I'm hoping to become the first Australian to climb Mt Vinson,' he replied.

'Wait a minute,' I said. 'I wanted to do that! How can a poor geologist like you afford such an expensive expedition?'

Greg gave me a cheeky grin. 'Because you're paying for it!' he said.

While I'd been away, Mike McDowell, an Australian pioneer of adventure travel and part owner of ANI, had offered Greg the chance to climb Mt Vinson with him if he could scrape up the airfare to and from South America. Greg put together a sponsorship proposal for *Australian Geographic* and it was approved. We both had a good laugh about it.

———

While still in Patagonia, I was already planning the next stage of my Twin Otter adventure. The friendliness of the Soviet Antarctic expeditioners I'd met had me dreaming about how wonderful it would be if I could continue the flight over the top of the world and down through Siberia, Mongolia and China to Sydney. If I could do this, it would be the first 'vertical' around-the-world flight landing at both poles.

Back in the warmth of a Sydney summer, I spent days writing letters and sending telexes seeking clearances for the flight through South America, the United States and Canada to the North Pole. I then grappled with the challenge of getting permission from the USSR and China to fly down through the closed areas.

I rang my friend Bill Hayden, who had recently stepped down as Australia's Minister for Foreign Affairs and was about to become governor-general. Interrupting his lawn-mowing to come to the phone, Bill said he would be happy to see what he could do through the USSR's minister for Foreign Affairs, Eduard Shevardnadze, whom he knew personally. I was secretly hoping that in this new era of glasnost and perestroika my request may get a positive answer.

Incredibly, within weeks I received approval to fly through Soviet territory and the Mongolian People's Republic. I was delighted when I was sent a copy of Mr Shevardnadze's letter to Bill, in which the Soviet minister wrote:

I would like to say that the energy and fearlessness of the famous Australian adventurer Dick Smith appealed to me from the purely human point of view. That is why I am glad to inform you that D. Smith has been granted permission to overfly the Soviet territory, and that the Soviet departments concerned are prepared to render him the necessary assistance. I hope that the success of the flight will become another mani-festation of the growing mutual interest and trust between our countries and peoples.

And so, on 5 February 1989, just two months after leaving the Twin Otter in Punta Arenas, I headed north. Pip and two of our friends, Frank and Leonie Young, joined me on this leisurely trip and we arrived on 15 February in Fort Worth, where I pushed VH-SHW into a hangar to await longer daylight in the far north.

I returned in April, with my friend Laurie McIver (yes, the Laurie who had sent me on my very first solo flight) as co-pilot and Pip as support crew. On 11 April, after a night in Wichita, Kansas, we flew to Winnipeg in Canada, and then to Churchill, 'Polar Bear Capital of the World'. I was now heading into familiar territory after my three attempts to reach the North Pole by helicopter. We continued north to Resolute, where we met Rob Toma once again and stayed with fellow adventurers at Bezal and Terry Jesudason's cosy guesthouse.

We then headed north again, this time to Lake Hazen, where Kenn Borek Air had graded the snow off the frozen lake to provide a smooth runway. We landed on wheels and then attached the skis that had been flown up from the Patriot Hills, Antarctica.

The following day, we flew north under clear blue skies, landing on the sea ice at the Geographic North Pole. We kept the engines running as we got out for photographs. It was Pip's and my second time here and just as thrilling to stand on moving pack ice.

The next day, it took us an hour to fly to north-western Greenland to visit the site of the American B-29 *Kee Bird*, which had run out of fuel and force landed on the icecap in February 1947 after a secret mission over Soviet territory. None of the crew were hurt and all were eventually rescued.

We landed the Twin Otter right next to *Kee Bird* and spent some time taking pictures and inspecting the historic plane. We were able to climb right into the cockpit, and the gun turrets on top still looked operable.

Ultimately, after a side trip to Spitsbergen, the Norwegian archipelago in the Arctic Ocean, we returned to Resolute and, after a rest at the Jesudason's guesthouse, I flew *Sir Hubert Wilkins* to Calgary for a service and to have the ANARE livery replaced with the *Australian Geographic* logo.

———

On 15 May 1989, we lifted off from Resolute with a 40 per cent overload. Giles and Rob were back on board and we were heading for the top of the world. Pip's place was now filled by Vladimir Gorinski, a navigator with Aeroflot who would be our interpreter and liaison with the authorities in the Soviet Union. A thirty-eight year old Muscovite, he proved to be good company.

This vital leg over the North Pole was to take us more than 2900 kilometres to the tiny island of Sredniy, a Soviet weather and scientific station. Unfortunately, Vladimir couldn't get a weather report for the island, either before or after we set off. After a radio conversation with an operator in Moscow, he laughed and said, 'She keeps telling me it is not her job to give it. You know what our country is like, Dick!'

He assured me that he hoped to get a reliable forecast before we reached our point of no return. So did I!

Six hours out of Resolute, we were at the North Pole again and then began to fly down the Sredniy side of the world—still without our forecast.

I was becoming more concerned as we continued; we now did not have enough fuel to return to where we had come from. Also, we'd just begun using charts stamped 'AIRCRAFT INFRINGING UPON NON-FREE FLYING TERRITORY MAY BE FIRED UPON WITHOUT WARNING'.

Finally, Vladimir overheard calls from a helicopter that was about to land in Sredniy. There the cloud ceiling was 700 feet, visibility was 2 kilometres in ice fog, with a temperature of −3°C. We came in on instruments, finding it hard to distinguish snow from cloud, and put down after twelve hours in the air.

On the ground, we were welcomed like heroes. Everyone was fantastically friendly and laughing. Never before had a foreign aircraft, let alone one privately owned, been in these parts. Nobody wanted to see our passports, and they wouldn't take any money for refuelling us. They said they'd never had to charge anybody before, and anyway the pump had no gauge. They added with a laugh, 'Next time you come through, we'll get a gauge!'

At 10.36 a.m. the next day, we left Sredniy and, after two hours, crossed the still-frozen Kara Sea. We flew over the Arctic port of Dikson at the head of the gulf leading to the mouth of the enormous Yenisey River. After just over four hours, we landed at bleak Norilsk, where, during Stalin's time, political prisoners were sent to mine the copper and nickel ores, and to build giant processing plants.

Awaiting us on the tarmac, the press contingent had difficulty grasping the fact that I personally owned the Twin Otter.

I gave them a brief version of how I started with $610 and built up a business worth millions.

'I'm a capitalist,' I explained, which raised delighted laughter.

'We may be able to do this for ourselves one day,' somebody called out, bringing more laughter.

On 17 May, we took off from Norilsk with a fierce cross-wind, blowing snow, only just able to see the runway light posts as we sped alongside them. We reached our cruising altitude with no visibility and some icing, but soon afterwards conditions improved. Beneath us tundra gave way to forests and great rivers, and after five hours and fifty-five minutes, we landed at Bratsk, a logging and ore-processing city of 150,000 people, surrounded by beautiful birch forests.

The following day, a short flight of one hour and forty minutes took us to Irkutsk and, after another warm welcome, we checked into a hotel, then were driven 60 kilometres south-east to the incredible Lake Baikal. At 635 kilometres long, it's the world's largest lake. In winter, it's so cold, trucks take short-cuts across its frozen surface. But for us, spring had arrived and everything looked magnificent.

I was amazed that since arriving in the Soviet Union, there had been no restrictions placed on us anywhere. It was so different to when I'd visited as a young tourist twenty-three years earlier, when people were afraid to open their mouths. A man in Irkutsk told me, 'Five years ago we never queried anything, because we thought everything we were doing was right. Now everybody queries everything.'

We flew across Lake Baikal the next morning on our leg to Ulaanbaatar, Mongolia's capital. Hugging the lake's southern shore was the famous Trans-Siberian Railway, the 9300-kilometre line from Moscow to Vladivostok, and beyond that, the snow-covered Khamar-daban Mountains, rising to 2300 metres—the first mountains we'd seen in Siberia.

I had wanted to visit Mongolia and the Gobi Desert ever since I had been a young schoolboy. For some reason, I expected the capital to be surrounded by desert, and to be quite backward. Instead, I found a modern city, its people well dressed and with living standards that appeared higher than those in the rest of the Soviet Union.

From Ulaanbaatar, we flew south in flawless weather. Near the Chinese border, we flew at low level over deserted airstrips with great concrete runways and fighter bays. A big Russian build-up had begun in 1966 but, with the easing of tensions between Moscow and Beijing, the Soviet Union was withdrawing its troops from the region.

In the Gobi desert, we photographed Mongol herdsmen with their distinctive yurts and camels, sheep and horses. Four hours out of Ulaanbaatar, the landscape changed from brown to vibrant green, and 110 kilometres north of Beijing, we descended for a closer look at the Great Wall of China.

Beijing's friendly air traffic controllers spoke perfect English as they directed us to the airport. Unbeknown to us, just a few hours earlier, martial law had been declared as students packed into Tiananmen Square calling for democracy, and freedom of the press and speech. Groups of them stopped our taxi on the way to the hotel—but were incredibly friendly. Giles and Robert later walked into the square and spent two hours among the crowds: they told me it was like a carnival night.

I had planned two more landings before leaving China, but in case the authorities decided to close the borders, we thought it wiser to fly direct to Hong Kong.

————

Although I was disappointed to cut short our visit, it was with some relief that we made our approach over Hong Kong's harbour and into the famous Kai Tak Airport at Kowloon. I was especially looking forward to seeing Pip again; she was joining us for the final leg of our flight to Sydney. It was time for Giles to get back to work for Cathay Pacific, so he bade us goodbye, with his place being taken by Stuart Weston, who, of course, had first taught me how to fly Twin Otters.

We left Hong Kong and were now on the home stretch, enjoying the continuation of the planet's surprising contrasts over the next few days. Three days later, as we took off from Alice Springs, air traffic control warned us not to fly over the Pine Gap restricted area. It was the only warning I received on the entire trip! Pine Gap is a US–Australian Joint Defence Space Research Facility, controlled by the US Central Intelligence Agency as an electronic espionage satellite ground station. Its main job is to collect intelligence on nuclear weapons and missiles.

Later that day, we landed on a small airstrip at Innamincka, between the beautiful Sturt Stony Desert and Cooper Creek, then in flood. We walked along the banks of the Cooper, where we had the first *Australian Geographic* expedition, one of my favourite places on Earth.

I slipped out late that night to admire the dazzling night sky, the first time since our flight into Casey that I could truly see the stars. In Antarctica and the Arctic, there was no night, and everywhere else there was either too much pollution or city glare, so that the stars were hidden or faded.

On 28 May, as the Twin Otter ate up the final 1279 kilometres to Sydney, I was thankful for Australia's vast open spaces and the good fortune that we aren't being crowded in. As we flew above the Sydney basin, helicopters from the TV stations arrived to escort us to Bankstown Aerodrome, where our adventure had begun seven months before. As we touched down and taxied to the crowd of friends and media, I felt overwhelmed by just what a fantastic planet it is that we live on. While we shut down the engines, I vowed to myself that somehow I must get this message out, so everybody can understand how important it is to conserve as much of it as we can.

When I look back on my five flights around the world and my flights to the North Pole, I have never put a mark on an aircraft, been delayed, had an injury or had to call out the rescue services. Yes, I have indeed been fortunate, but my good fortune has gone hand-in-hand with what I call 'responsible risk-taking'—not attempting an adventure if I judge that the risk is too great.

My dream of going on adventures for work had become a reality.

CHAPTER 21

Never-ending adventure

My vertical trip, circling Earth via the two poles, was by no means the last of my adventures.

Pip often tells people that she's 'not an adventurous person', but I disagree. From the earliest times that we went out together, she was always willing to give it a go, whether it was abseiling into Claustral Canyon, rock climbing in the Blue Mountains or sleeping in swags as we explored the outback.

When I flew solo around the world in my helicopter in 1982–83, Pip mostly stayed home to look after Hayley and Jenny, but she came to meet me along the way whenever she could. She provided crucial ground support on my three attempts to fly solo to the North Pole, accompanied me on some of the legs of my Twin Otter circumnavigation via the poles and shared local adventures as we waited for our daughters to grow up and make lives of their own.

My search for the *Kookaburra* in 1977–78 had inspired me to solve more homegrown historical mysteries. While researching an *Australian Geographic* article about the Woomera rocket range in South Australia, I learned that the only satellite Australia has ever successfully launched blasted off from there on 29 November 1967. This was Sparta, a three-stage rocket that used an American Redstone rocket as its first stage. After blast-off, Sparta and its payload speared in a northerly direction for two minutes ten seconds before its first stage—Redstone, a massive white cylinder the size of a semi-trailer—flamed out 70 kilometres above the Simpson Desert and simply disappeared.

'What happened to it?' I wondered. I contacted Bruce Henderson, the safety officer at Woomera, who used radar tracking records to plot its probable impact site. Then, while flying my helicopter across Australia in August 1988, I altered course to have a search for it, but with no luck. I asked Bruce to refine his estimate, allowing for wind drift and atmospheric drag, and he responded with an impact area covering 85 square kilometres.

On 6 October 1989, I set out again in the helicopter, this time with Pip, Jenny and her friend Guy. We flew from Terrey Hills to Dalhousie Springs, then followed the French Line, a surveyor's track across the Simpson to Poeppel Corner, the intersection of the NT, SA and Queensland borders. After refuelling from drums left for us by Birdsville policeman Bob Goad, and navigating by dead reckoning alone, we skimmed at 500 feet above the red dunes and into the desert's untracked heart. Arriving at the target area, we began a search pattern, and it wasn't long before Pip's excited cry of 'There it is!' announced the Redstone's discovery.

Almost hidden in the desert scrub, it was broken in two. Its white paint and kangaroo emblem had been blistered off by the desert sun to reveal its true colours—military green. It was the first time it had been seen in twenty-two years. We landed and got an accurate position fix. It was so exciting, and I'm delighted that it has since been recovered and returned to Woomera.

———

Ultimately, Jenny finished high school and headed for the outback to work as a jillaroo; Hayley, after moving to Cairns and becoming a scuba diving instructor, later worked on expedition cruise ships all over the world. The girls were on their own life journeys, so Pip had more time to join me on my adventures.

One of our most memorable was an amazing flight over Mt Everest. In 1990, I had purchased a Citation business jet. Most of the time it was boring to fly, because to get a reasonable range you had to fly above 20,000 feet—so different to my helicopters, which I mostly tried to fly at 500 feet above ground level for the best views. But there was one situation where the

Citation could excel—flying over the 29,029-foot (8850-metre) Mt Everest. Being right on the border between Nepal and China, it was well known to aviators as a no-go area. Fortunately, when I was chairman of the CAA, I had met Nepal's director of Civil Aviation and he kindly arranged approval for my proposed flight.

On 15 October 1991, Pip and I, with our friends Frank and Leonie Young, took off at first light from Kathmandu and climbed to 29,000 feet. For thirty minutes we watched as foothills gave way to the great Himalayas, where snaking rivers carved gorges and the timber line was left behind. It was magical as we circled Everest, or Chomolungma, Mother Goddess of the Earth. The weather was so clear we could pick out footprints left by some Spanish mountaineers who had summited the previous day. Looking down on the north face, I traced the dramatic new line established by the Australian team that had put Tim Macartney-Snape and Greg Mortimer on top. It looked impossible!

In 1993, I became involved in an aviation adventure of a different sort when balloonist John Wallington and I attempted the first balloon crossing of Australia. There had been seven previous attempts, including one by UK balloonist Julian Nott, who got as far as Broken Hill from the west coast. The plan was to launch the balloon and hopefully climb to the winds of the jet stream that lies high over Australia during winter. I had no idea where such a journey would end and, even if we succeeded, I knew we might land anywhere between Tasmania and Cape York. Although we hoped to be the first across, I was equally inspired by the idea of simply drifting in silence as our magnificent continent passed below.

In the months leading up to this attempt, I gained my balloon licence and *Australian Geographic* sent special 'study kits' to eleven thousand schools, encouraging students to set up weather stations and to study conditions that would allow them to predict the best flight pattern and cruising height for us. The school in each state and territory that came closest to predicting our final landing spot would win a set of the *Australian Encyclopaedia.*

John and I departed from Carnarvon, in Western Australia, at 10.52 p.m. on 17 June 1993 in perfect, calm weather. There had been a tremendous send-off by our ground crew and hundreds of well-wishers. As we lifted off, strains of 'Advance Australia Fair', played by the town's school band, drifted up to us.

But after initially climbing at 400 feet per minute, our rate of ascent began to slow. Instead of reaching the strong westerlies that would carry our *Australian Geographic Flyer* across the country, the wind was pushing us in the opposite direction— over the Indian Ocean towards Africa. It was pitch dark, we were packed into our tiny gondola and the pilot lights that lit our propane burners that kept us aloft wouldn't stay alight.

As we struggled to stay airborne, I thought of the dark waters below and the massive shark feeding frenzy I'd seen there just days ago. We solved the pilot light problem by keeping the main propane valve partly shut.

Fortunately, after half an hour, our spirits lifted as we passed 10,000 feet. As we donned oxygen masks, our global positioning system showed us tracking south-east, back across land and heading for the east coast on a journey we expected would cover 4500 kilometres and take up to six days.

After seven hours of flying, I climbed outside our enclosed gondola to watch dawn breaking from a small 1-metre square verandah-like platform that I called the Sun Deck. I had built the Sun Deck because I didn't like the idea of being cooped up for the entire trip. It afforded the most magnificent vista of our amazing outback. To the north was the Canning Stock Route and the endless sandhills of the Gibson Desert. Beside me, a 16,000-foot drop commanded views of magnificent salt lakes filled with water from recent rains.

By nightfall, we were over the ocean again, the winds had taken us to the Great Australian Bight. I asked John what he thought of the flight so far. 'Daunting,' he answered. We took turns attempting to sleep and flying the balloon—that is, firing the burner to stay at the optimum altitude for the best wind direction and speed.

On our second day, flying at 21,900 feet and 160 kilometres per hour (our greatest altitude and speed), we realised that we might reach the coast before nightfall. Our goal was now within our grasp! Sitting out on the platform on my deckchair, I got a radio call from Pip, who was flying past in the

Citation taking photographs. 'Put your safety harness on,' she ordered. Fortunately, I don't have a fear of heights, but I did as Pip asked.

As the hours passed, John's and my stress levels increased. We both knew that landing without injury would only be possible if ground level winds were below 20 kilometres per hour.

Then, at about 4 p.m., as we approached Tenterfield, in northern New South Wales and just west of the Great Dividing Range, we reluctantly agreed that it would be safest to land short of the mountains, as darkness was approaching. It would mean failing in our mission, but at least we would be alive. We continued to wrestle with our decision, however, and decided to take the risk. It was a decision neither of us would regret.

At 4.15 p.m., Brisbane air traffic control phoned our mission control with the official news: the *Australian Geographic Flyer* had crossed the Great Dividing Range. We were still at 20,000 feet, but, with no previous experience of landing a combination hot air and helium balloon, neither of us knew how quickly we could bring it down.

John took control of the descent. He pulled the gas valve line to vent helium from the top of the balloon and slowly we began to descend. I was sure we hadn't released nearly enough gas and persuaded him to open the valve for another 45 seconds. But this was far too long and moments later we were descending at an alarming 1000 feet per minute. We emptied a bag of sand to check our descent, only to have it blow back in our faces as we overtook it.

After checking that no one was below, we dumped our heavy generator as an emergency measure and slowed the descent to 100 feet per minute. Now low enough to assess ground conditions, I said in amazement, 'John, there's absolutely no surface wind!'

Suddenly we realised that the flight was going to end as it had begun. It was unbelievable. We'd taken off with no wind, then flown across Australia at speeds of up to 160 kilometres per hour, and were now landing in dead calm. Our flight had lasted forty hours and twenty minutes, covering just over 3867 kilometres.

————

Just before my balloon flight across Australia, I'd bought an amazing helicopter, a Sikorsky S-76, previously owned by the King of Jordan. With its twin jet turbine engines, and when fitted with auxiliary fuel tanks, the Sikorsky had the power and range to make another of my dreams possible—to fly around the world in the opposite direction to my solo circumnavigation flight, accompanied by Pip.

We weren't out to break any speed records; we just wanted to share an adventure and have a good look at the countries that passed beneath us. During the flight, I concentrated on flying, navigating and putting the helicopter in the best position for photographs. Pip was the expedition photographer and videographer, responsible for both shooting and using the newly invented GPS to log the location of each shot. Our plan was to produce a database that sometime in the future could be used to show how much our planet is changing.

I named the Sikorsky *World Explorer* and had painted on its fuselage the image of a soaring albatross, an incredible seabird renowned for its ability to fly around the world.

We divided this long journey into stages. The seasons usually dictated the dates of each stage—for instance, it would be too dangerous to cross the North Atlantic in winter. We took off on our first leg—from Sydney to Nepal—from our front lawn in Terrey Hills in February 1994. We left the helicopter in Kathmandu and returned home for a break. Our second stage was from Nepal to Dubai; the next stage was from there to Egypt; then we flew to Greece and Germany. This was followed by Denmark then across the Atlantic via Greenland to the USA; and finally via Alaska and Russia and back home to Australia, where we landed back on our front lawn. Each leg had its own highlights and challenges.

We had one very frightening time during the flight. We had left Manila on the last leg and found ourselves flying through the edge of a typhoon. We were low over the ocean in heavy rain and terrible visibility when suddenly the helicopter started rolling uncontrollably. At the same time, the emergency annunciator panel lit up with numerous warning messages. I thought we were going to crash.

Pip started to send an SOS via the Inmarsat unit while I gained some control of the helicopter. We eventually found the coastline of Panay Island and managed to get the helicopter down safely by landing in a schoolyard. The fault had been caused by water getting into the stability systems inverter box, so we asked the school principal if we could use her kitchen oven to dry the box out. She readily agreed and also offered us lunch. After two hours on the ground and a great meal, we were on our away again. Such are the advantages of a helicopter.

Ultimately, Pip and I covered 73,352 kilometres on our flight. It was the first time anyone had flown a helicopter around the world from east to west. Pip catalogued 10,725 transparencies, which featured along with her writings in our book *Above the World*, published by *Australian Geographic* in 1996.

——

In 1995, I replaced our Sikorsky helicopter with a Cessna 208 Caravan. The Sikorsky was a wonderful machine, but could only fly relatively short distances compared to a fixed-wing aircraft. I chose the Caravan for its reliability and, when fitted with long-range fuel tanks, its ability to make some of the world's longer ocean crossings. I even had special windows put in so Pip could photograph from them.

Between 1999 and 2003, I flew the Caravan twice around the world. The first section was from Alaska, through the Caribbean and South America, and down to Antarctica, one of my favourite places on Earth. I then crossed the Atlantic via Ascension Island, flying down Africa's west coast to South Africa, and then across the Indian Ocean via the Maldives to Australia and back to the United States via Hawaii.

I was keen to see places I'd previously missed, but the final leg was inspired by my curiosity. As a child, sometimes when I was naughty, my parents would threaten me with, 'We're going to send you to Timbuktu'! How could I resist seeing this legendary place for myself? We crossed the Atlantic via the Azores, then flew south to what was once the hub of Arab–African trade, Timbuktu, in Mali. Nicknamed the 'City of Gold', Timbuktu was a town of fascinating mosques and camel-leading Bedouins, but sadly it was losing its battle against the sands of the Sahara.

Another dream was to visit the Rwenzori Mountains, or 'Mountains of the Moon'. But, thanks to political unrest in Uganda, I couldn't persuade anyone to go there with me. So I decided to go alone, rediscovering the joy of flying solo. On an unusually clear day, I looked down on completely untouched rainforest that gave way to glaciers flowing from the 5100 metre Mt Stanley, birthplace of the Nile River. It was the most exciting day of the trip.

I finished my fifth circumnavigation via India, Indonesia and Australia, before heading back to Alaska. Since my first circumnavigation, two amazing technologies, GPS and the satellite telephone, had significantly reduced the risks. The former by indicating ground speed and fuel consumption as you cross vast oceans, and the latter by giving you access to weather information virtually anywhere in the world. But one thing hasn't changed: the adrenaline rush that comes from setting off on an adventure of which, despite the best-laid plans and technology, the outcome is uncertain. I love it.

———

Keen for another ballooning adventure, I floated the idea with John Wallington of attempting the first balloon flight across the Tasman, from Australia to New Zealand. To have a bit of fun, I got John Singleton to bet me $100,000 I couldn't go the other way—'against the wind', from New Zealand to Australia. The money would go to charity.

At first I thought it would be impossible, but then I rang the Bureau of Meteorology and they took a close look at weather patterns and found that, under special circumstances, it just might be possible. If there's a stationary high pressure system sitting between Tasmania and New Zealand that's blocked by another system in the Great Australian Bight, and if a balloon flies at a low altitude, the anti-clockwise winds might just carry it from east to west. But this would only be possible if the high pressure system remained in place for three to four days. If it moved more quickly, the balloon would end up being carried south to Antarctica.

That was how John and I came to be on a rugby field in Kaitaia, on the northern tip of New Zealand, on a cold night in February 2000. Pip was there as well, as the official photographer for *Australian Geographic*.

Never-ending adventure

We'd hoped to launch around midnight; according to the Bureau of Meteorology in Australia, we could anticipate flying north for 6–12 hours before reaching the winds that would hopefully carry us westward over the Tasman Sea. But it was not until 5.55 a.m. that conditions became favourable for what we had in mind and we finally lifted into the sky.

By that afternoon, we were well over the Tasman and making a speed of 36 kilometres per hour. By the following morning, the advice from our mission control in Sydney was: 'You need to stay high and keep tracking northward throughout most of today. The latest trajectory is right on target for the southern Queensland–northern NSW area.'

John and I had always imagined the perfect end to our flight would be to surf the gondola onto a beach—and that was exactly what we did. We landed just north of Iluka on the New South Wales north coast. After 55 hours and 17 minutes in the air, we were greeted by well-wishers on the beach and, in the air, half a dozen helicopters, some light aircraft and a Tiger Moth performing acrobatics. Pip managed to get herself to the beach in our friend Peter Pigott's helicopter and photographed us as we landed.

———

Having been lucky enough to complete five flights around the world, seeing the most wonderful sights from the air, I decided to drive around the world. Pip said she would come as long as there was a toilet and a shower on board.

In 2006, I found a versatile vehicle called an Earthroamer, in Denver, USA. It was a big Ford F550 pick-up truck, as they're known in America, with a purpose-built fibreglass campervan on the back. The vehicle had a powerful diesel engine and was four-wheel drive.

Our Earthroamer trip took us from Anchorage in Alaska via the Alaskan Highway to New York, through the most beautiful American national parks including Yellowstone, Grand Teton and the spectacular sandstone arches and towers of Monument Valley. From New York, we shipped the vehicle to the UK and drove from Land's End to John o' Groats, then travelled on the ferry to Norway and on to Sweden, where friends told us we would be robbed in Russia.

But it was quite the opposite—we were treated with utter friendliness and always felt safe. We would normally pull off the road into a small town and look for a house that had kids' play-things in the front yard. We would park outside and I would walk up to the door, knock on it and hand over a sheet of paper that, translated in Russian, said, 'We are Australians driving around the world, can we park our vehicle here tonight?'

The gruff Russian faces would transform into immediate smiles and, from then on, they would do everything they could to help—including inviting us to come into their homes for a sauna, or knocking on our door and offering us dried fish or some beautiful hand-picked berries.

In Mongolia, the vehicle broke down about a quarter of the way across the Gobi Desert. Fortunately, we managed to get a coal truck to tow us 122 kilometres to the nearest town, across a 1500-metre mountain pass with snow blowing across the road. We left the vehicle there and managed to get back to Australia. We then rang Ford in Detroit and asked for warranty roadside service. Believe it or not, Ford contacted their dealer in Ulaanbaatar, who sent a mechanic out across the Gobi Desert and managed to repair the vehicle. We then continued through Siberia and on to Vladivosktok, where a short ferry crossing took us to Japan.

We shipped the Earthroamer from Japan to Perth and revelled in the wildflowers on the way to Shark Bay, before heading to Meekatharra and east on the corrugated Gunbarrel Highway to Alice Springs. Skirting the Simpson Desert, we dropped in to the Birdsville Pub, crossed Cooper Creek to Quilpie and on to Byron Bay, having traversed Australia from its most western to most eastern point. From there, it was a quick hop down the coast to our home in Terrey Hills. The last leg came after we shipped Earthroamer to Los Angeles and drove to our starting point in Denver.

What a fantastic trip it was, experiencing the world from ground level. In all, we visited fifteen countries and covered a distance of more than 45,000 kilometres. Everywhere we went, we found that, as long as we had a smile on our faces, people would be helpful and friendly.

CHAPTER 22

Marching to a different drum

I wonder would the apathy of wealthy men endure
Were all their windows level with the faces of the Poor?

Henry Lawson, 'Faces in the Street'

After I sold *Australian Geographic* to Fairfax, that didn't end up being my last start-up business.

When I was no longer involved with aviation reform, I was looking for something else to do and someone mentioned that Vegemite was owned by the Americans. I couldn't believe it. I thought Vegemite was as Australian as Skippy, kookaburras and koalas. I grew up spreading it on my toast and loved the taste.

In fact, Vegemite had been sold to the American multinational Kraft as far back as 1935, and in 1988 it had been bought by the tobacco company Philip Morris. When I learned this,

I was shocked. Was it possible that such an Australian icon could be owned by the same company that was pushing an addictive drug to our schoolchildren?

From then on, I took more notice of who actually owned 'Australian' food brands. Cottee's was part of the Swiss company, Schweppes; Arnott's biscuits was owned by America's Campbell Soup Company, Rosella tomato sauce by the British–Dutch Unilever, and even Aeroplane Jelly, another childhood favourite, by McCormick & Co—again American.

I always understood that with globalisation, countries would do what they are good at. Asia made the best electronics, Switzerland the best watches, and Australia the finest food. I learned that, while we did grow lots of our food, most of the famous brands were now foreign owned.

For a bit of fun, I decided to produce Dickhead matches. The famous Redhead matches, which were originally Australian owned, had been taken over by a Swedish company. On the reverse side of our boxes of Dickheads, it said: 'We would have to be complete dickheads to let most of our famous Australian brands be taken over by foreign companies. Brands such as Vegemite, Aeroplane Jelly, Arnott's, Speedo and Redhead Matches are in overseas hands. This means the profit and wealth created goes overseas and robs our children and grandchildren of a future.' Yes, it was a bit of fun, but the message was serious.

On 8 July 1999, I announced the launch of Dick Smith Foods with a full-page advertisement in the *Australian Financial Review* newspaper. I said that I wanted to set up a food company which used only Australian food that was processed in Australia, creating jobs for Australians and keeping profits in Australia, and paying full tax in Australia.

About this time, I noticed Paul Newman's Own salad dressing in our pantry. The label said '100% of profits go to charity'. I thought, 'Well, I've done pretty well, and I don't really need to make any more money, so why not do the same?'

My plan was to start with an Aussie version of Vegemite, which I decided to call OzEmite, then move on to other products where I could support Australian manufacturers and growers.

In fact, OzEmite took many years to perfect. It was so difficult to get the taste similar to Vegemite. In fact, I wanted it to taste like the Vegemite that I knew as a kid, as Kraft had changed the formula several times without telling anyone.

While working on the OzEmite formula, I decided to go ahead with other products, the first one being peanut butter. Australia's bestseller, Kraft peanut butter, was owned by Kraft in the USA and every cent of the wealth creation headed off to the northern hemisphere.

Hayley came and worked for me in getting Dick Smith Foods going. It was great to have her ideas, and I really enjoyed working with her.

I managed to get a small Aussie company called Green's Foods to make a special peanut butter for Dick Smith Foods. It used Australian-grown peanuts from Kingaroy and was produced by Aussie workers in the Green's factory in the Western Suburbs of Sydney. I really enjoyed going to the factory with Hayley to watch the peanut butter being produced and then flying to Kingaroy to talk to the farmers who grew the peanuts. It gave me immense satisfaction.

Within two years, we had quite a range of products, from peanut butter to cordial, canola oil, cheese, Helicopter Jelly, biscuits, tomato and barbecue sauce, jam and even ice cream, all under the Dick Smith Foods' name.

I was proud to be supporting Australian farmers and giving jobs to Australians. I thought that if we could get just 5 per cent of Australians to buy our locally made and locally owned foods, it would make a huge difference. We could employ tens of thousands of Australians and fight back against global food companies that were sending their profits overseas.

———

Dick Smith Foods was able to give Australian farmers and producers business at a retail level of nearly $500 million. Most importantly, we were able to donate over $11 million to charity—including the Country Women's Association, the Salvation Army, St Vincent de Paul and Mission Australia.

In the end, I was forced to close down Dick Smith Foods because we simply couldn't compete with foreign-owned companies like Aldi and Costco. These companies are incredibly shrewd, but I don't understand their greed.

For example, Aldi is owned by two super-secretive German billionaires who are worth more than $40 billion. Why would they want any more money? I am sure they haven't come to Australia for charitable reasons. But here they are in Australia with an incredibly successful German formula. Basically, they employ half as many staff as traditional Australian food retailers. Whereas the Australian-owned Woolworths and Coles supermarkets spend about 8 per cent of their turnover in paying Aussie wages, with Aldi it is about 4 per cent. In effect, if Woolworths and Coles want to compete on price, they will have to sack half of their staff—that's over 150,000 Australians losing their jobs.

Our peanut butter, produced in Australia from Aussie peanuts, was selling for over a dollar more than Aldi's peanut butter. Why were they so cheap? They were really astute; I call it 'extreme capitalism'. Aldi grew their peanuts in Argentina and made its peanut butter there too—as farm and factory workers receive very low wages.

I couldn't believe that even some of my wealthy friends loved and supported Aldi. In fact, Aldi was voted as the most trusted brand in Australia, even ahead of Qantas, while being at the same time the most profitable supermarket as well as the cheapest. There is no doubt in my mind that they are the smartest and most ruthless retailers in the world. But with the advantage of the cheaper prices globalisation offers, you also get the disadvantage that our wonderful Aussie owned and made products, and the jobs they create, will disappear.

To keep our products on the shelves, the supermarkets said we had to have at least a 3 per cent market share. But when Aldi started selling everything cheaper, we didn't even have that, and the writing was on the wall for us.

I do wonder how the Aussie owned companies will ever compete in the long term. At least Woolworths and Coles are on the stock exchange, so Australians can share in their wealth creation. You can't do that with Aldi.

In 2017, there was a ray of sunshine when Bega Cheese bought Vegemite from Kraft, bringing the iconic brand back home. I was delighted when I heard the news. After all, Kraft's ownership of Vegemite had triggered my move to start Dick Smith Foods. I hoped that my publicising the fact that Vegemite was foreign owned played a part in bringing it back to Australia. I felt as if things had come full circle.

Finally, in July 2018, I announced that I would be closing down Dick Smith Foods. I held a press conference to announce the closure and found it impossible to hold back the tears. 'Well, it's terrible on a personal level,' I said, 'because even though I'm glad to have done nineteen years of business, I failed. I said I would keep your jobs. I couldn't. It's beyond me.'

Two years later, as the Covid pandemic swept around the globe, the importance of retaking control of Australia's food security was clear. Hopefully, new, energetic entrepreneurs will take on the challenge and bring food production back home.

———

Despite Dick Smith Foods closing down, or maybe because of it, I found myself getting more and more concerned about the wealth disparity in Australia. I wasn't alone. In April 2017, Bernie Fraser, the former governor of the Reserve Bank, had said, 'Australia is approaching a "danger point" where the gap between rich and poor becomes so vast it could have "awful" far-reaching consequences at every level in Australian society.'

Oxfam released a report saying that Australia's wealthiest 1 per cent owned more than the seventeen million Aussies (70 per cent) who were the least wealthy. Almost five million of the poorest were living from pay cheque to pay cheque, without any savings at all. I found this very worrying. I'd been brought up believing that Australia was the country of the fair go—not just for the wealthy, but for everyone. Though I'd started out with little, I was now one of the wealthiest 1 per cent: that didn't make me feel good.

In 2018, I set up the Dick Smith Fair Go Group. The aim was simple, to work towards 'an economy that benefits everyone— not just the 1%—enabling more young Aussies to have a full-time career, and so older Aussies can afford to keep warm in winter'. Despite a major television and radio campaign, which encouraged 62,000 people to join us, we had little effect on the political parties. One of my failed ideas was that the wealthiest 1 per cent should pay 15 per cent more tax, which would be used to assist the less well off. Not one politician dared show any support for my idea.

I believe that we have to do something about the impossibility of endless economic growth. It won't be easy, because all public companies are under pressure from their investors to grow exponentially. In fact, it was this very pressure that eventually destroyed Dick Smith Electronics (or DSE, as I refer to it below).

After I sold DSE to Woolworths, they ran it for over twenty-nine years, making good profits and ultimately generating an annual turnover of $1.6 billion and employing thousands of Aussies. DSE's original success was based on selling high-margin but low cost products to electronic enthusiasts. Given our population, I always thought it had the potential to open a maximum of 100 shops in Australia. But, because the Woolworths Board was under continuous pressure to grow the business, they eventually opened 350 stores and started selling low-margin products, like TV sets, in so-called 'Dick Smith Powerhouse' superstores. But, ultimately, the business no longer generated a never-ending growth in profits.

In 2012, DSE was sold to Anchorage Capital, a private equity firm, for $115 million, but it appears that Anchorage only ever stumped up $10 million in cash, in what the media called 'the greatest equity heist of all time'. Anchorage floated the company two years later, at a market value of $520 million. It soon became unprofitable and, after two years, the public company went into liquidation, shedding 2460 workers and owing creditors $260 million.

So sad and so unnecessary, I thought. On the positive side, I know it employed and trained many thousands of Australians—some still stop me in the street and tell me it was the start of their successful career. That makes me feel good.

When I was young, Sir Edward Hallstrom was always in the news. He was a public benefactor and ran a company making Silent Knight refrigerators.

He was called a philanthropist. My mother told me years later that one day I said to her, 'What's a *philanthropit?*' (not being able to say it correctly because of my speech defect). She said, 'Oh that's a person who has done well and gives money away to important causes.' She said that I replied, 'If ever I do well, I'm going to become one of those.'

I made my first donation when I was at the Dick Smith building at Gore Hill. I had received a letter from a Dr Tony Kidman, who was across the road at the place where I'd trained for my electronics certificate the year after I left school. He was doing research into muscular dystrophy, and I think I gave about $10,000 towards it. Tony's letter, seeking support, inspired me and I was pleased to help over the coming years. Looking back, I'm certain my Scout training had ingrained in me the importance of helping others when you can.

Pip and I have gained much happiness through sharing our good fortune with others. But, in truth, my philanthropy has always been for quite selfish reasons. That is, it is self-satisfying— it makes me feel good and allows me not to feel too guilty about the wealth I have, compared to many people. We have a family foundation that gives money away—at least $1 million a year to important charities like the Muscular Dystrophy Association of New South Wales, the Salvation Army and Life Education. It's quite separate from the Dick Smith Foods donations.

While I look on the charitable donations as fulfilling an obligation, I'm not opposed to having fun while raising money for a worthwhile cause. One of the best money-raising ideas I have ever had was the Bourke to Burketown Bash car trial.

When I was young and living in Roseville Chase, the Redex Trials went through Roseville. I remember going with my cousin Bob to watch the cars screaming through along the Pacific Highway. I thought, 'One day I am going to go on the Redex Trial.' By the time I got my driving licence, the Redex Trials were no more, so I came up with the idea of starting a type of Redex Trial, but with a fun twist—cheating, lying and conniving would be allowed and encouraged.

To stop my wealthy friends from showing off with the latest in expensive four-wheel drives, I said that all vehicles must be of low value and at least twenty years old, and any entrants who were judged (by me) to be taking the trial too seriously would have points deducted. Points would also be deducted for cheating; however, the entrant judged the greatest cheat at the finish would be given extra points!

As with my Antarctic flights, I decided that the trial should raise money for charity and chose Variety Australia, which helps underprivileged children.

The first Bourke to Burketown Bash started from the Sydney Opera House on 1 June 1985. It included a BBC film crew and famous people like John Newcombe, John Singleton and his wife, ex-Miss World Belinda Green, as drivers. We had a total of fifty-two cars altogether.

I was the chief judge, scrutineer and mischief maker. Anyone could bribe me to come first on a particular section, as long as the cheque was written out to Variety.

On that first Bash, we raised over two hundred thousand dollars. Tony Hasham, the Chief Barker at Variety at the time, took on the idea and organised that the Bash would continue.

There have now been over thirty Bashes and they have raised over $200 million for this important children's charity.

I'm surprised that, with some honourable exceptions, many wealthy Australians are reluctant to be involved in charitable work. From what I can see, wealthy Australians lack the tradition of many successful Americans, who feel an obligation to openly give back to society. I have attempted to get the publishers of the rich lists to show the record on charitable-giving for each entry. They have refused, claiming it will offend too many people.

Epilogue

I've flown five times round the world at low altitude, taking in the view from pole to pole and over some of its remotest corners. And I have driven once around, for good measure. I doubt that many others have ever had such a unique perspective of this small and beautiful planet we call home.

The lasting impression I have is that, seen from above at just a few hundred metres, it is clear just what a major impact we humans have made on it. Nature is in retreat everywhere, as populations continue to grow, extract more resources, turn forests into concrete and wilderness into high rise.

In just my lifetime, the population of Earth has more than tripled, from a little over two billion when I was born, to more than 7.6 billion as I write this. My grandkids will likely share the world with ten billion inhabitants, and I truly worry about what that means for both the planet and the population. Just about every problem we have in the world today will be harder to fix with more people.

On my first flight, I remember the view over India, where tens of millions of people were packed together along the river-banks. The smoke from their wood-burning stoves filled the air, so thick that I could barely fly through it, and a blood red sun set way above the horizon. I worried then how vulnerable they would be if the yearly monsoon failed.

Even the most remote regions clearly show the impact humans are having on the world. I remember being shocked way back in 1983 as I looked down on the coastal beaches along the Aleutian Island chain that arcs nearly 2000 kilometres from Alaska to Russia. The beaches in this remote wilderness were choked with flotsam and rubbish, piles of nets and plastic, and other waste.

What is also clear from a bird's eye view of Earth is just how unevenly distributed are all the riches of the planet. From above, you can see enclaves of extreme wealth, with high walls separating the rich from their impoverished neighbours. But like all the walls built in history, and all the unfair borders drawn on the maps, I wonder how long they will hold back the tide? The world's poor will rightly demand an equal share, and I doubt that there will be enough resources left to give everyone an acceptable standard of living. As we've seen with the terrible coronavirus, we kid ourselves if we think that on this small planet, which even my little helicopter could hop across, we are not all in this together.

History tells us that the greatest civilisations of the past ultimately collapsed. I have looked down on the Inca ruins and the fallen temples of Cambodia, Egypt and the Roman Empire. I believe it's clear that our world too could collapse one day if we don't make major changes now.

For many years I have been expressing my fears about our present world economic system which requires endless growth in population and in the use of energy and resources. Currently we are consuming resources at the rate of 1.5 times the planet's ability to renew them. This is not sustainable in a finite world and it's obvious that one day we will have to live in balance.

Most importantly, the problems that are being caused by climate change will be harder to solve if we continue on the perpetual growth trajectory. The biggest challenge is that this is a crisis that unfolds in slow motion. Will we be able to change direction by choice, or will we be forced to once it becomes clear that our system cannot be sustained?

As a nation, we have no plan. No political party dares tackle this issue for fear of being attacked in the pro-growth media. No doubt our politicians believe they would be quickly out of a job if they questioned the idea of an endlessly growing economy. Our obsession with growth, and our failure to seriously contemplate alternatives, is our greatest weakness.

I always thought that our small population and our beautiful environment are our greatest advantage. But, for too long, it's been considered a weakness; influential people in the media and business have tried to convince us that bigger is better. I have personally benefited from growth and it would be easier for me to say nothing, but I'm concerned for future generations.

I never planned to turn Dick Smith Electronics into a huge corporation. When I started out, I was just trying to create a small business. I loved it when I knew everyone there, which was about a hundred employees. But I was constantly being urged by advisers to keep expanding, to take the business overseas and move into new ventures.

Of course, I've welcomed the freedom that wealth brings. It's allowed me to indulge in my passion for aviation and adventure, as well as to speak out on important issues. But, in recent years, I've been getting rid of most of my toys—the big boat with the helipad on board, the corporate jet and the ocean-front holiday house. I have found a simpler life more fulfilling. I also believe that as a society we have found the sweet spot to be elusive—material wealth no longer brings any real benefits for many.

I have been charmed, by good fortune, to be born in Australia in the 1940s and to have grown up a free-range kid. I have lived through a time of great prosperity, and every day I am reminded of my good luck. Pip, the girl I married when she was just nineteen, has been my best friend and partner through life, even though she had no idea what she was getting into. Fifty years later, we are still happy and in love, and we have had the joy of seeing our girls grow up and make successful, independent lives for themselves. They never acted like rich kids and just got on with doing things, and I like to think that some of that came from us always sitting down together for dinner as a family to discuss what was going on in the world, just as my parents had done with me. The family has both forgiven and encouraged what I call my 'responsible risk-taking', knowing I'd be impossible to live with if I hadn't gone out there and done all this.

I was addicted to excitement, and, like all addictions, you can never get enough of it. I found even after I'd completed my world flights that I'd be flying up the New South Wales coast in my helicopter and I'd be thinking, well, gee, what would it be like to try and fly to New Zealand by helicopter? And I had this urge to almost turn right and fly over the ocean, just to see if I could get away with it.

When I was flying across the Atlantic, and got into terribly bad weather between Greenland and Iceland, I thought, 'If I get out of this alive, I will put the helicopter on a ship, go home and make up some excuse, because it's just far too risky.' And many times during the flight, I told myself, 'This is complete madness. I shouldn't be here.' But the amazing thing was that, when I landed, I'd have a cup of coffee and, after a while, I'd convince myself that it wasn't too bad: 'Maybe I should just go on to the next leg.' And that is really what my whole journey through life has been like.

My favourite photograph shows Pip, Hayley and Jenny standing with me at Darling Harbour in Sydney as I'm leaving on the third stage of my round-the-world helicopter flight, which included that mid-ocean shipboard landing. As I look at that photo, I think how mad I was—how my addiction to adrenaline-pumping excitement would make me leave this wonderful young family behind. Yet my drug was sending me off on what was a very dangerous trip, unnecessary to everyone but me. I look at it now and I think how could I have been so foolish to do that?

But not only did I do it, I had the support of Pip, Hayley and Jenny as well. I just looked on it as this great adventure. It was utter self-interest, and my only excuse today is that it has given me some insight into what drives humanity.

Despite a few close calls, I have returned safely from all my adventures. As I am not a religious person and don't have a God to thank for my safe return, I can only give thanks to my family for putting up with me. Given I don't expect any rewards in an afterlife, I feel my responsibility is to this world and the people we share it with. So the years ahead for me will be about giving back.

Life itself is the greatest adventure of all, of course, and I have always tried to make the most of mine. It certainly hasn't been boring.

Acknowledgements

I would like to thank everyone who assisted me in producing this book. In particular, writers Carl Ruhen, Simon Nasht and, most importantly, Howard Whelan. Also editor Rebecca Kaiser and commissioning publisher Richard Walsh. Without Richard's enthusiasm and direction, the book would not have existed. I would also like to thank my wife Pip for supporting me in so many ways, and also those who worked for me at Dick Smith Electronics, Australian Geographic and Dick Smith Foods. I am still in contact with many of you today. It was certainly a great adventure that we had together. My success has only come from surrounding myself with capable people, so thanks.

Index

Index

Index

Index

Index

Woolworths
  Anchorage Capital, sale of DSE to 320
  sale of DSE to 116, 118, 150–1, 158,
    197–8
Woomera 298, 299
World War II
  impact on family 4–5

World Wildlife Fund 218
Worrall, John 143, 144–7
Wran, Neville 147, 185

Yamamoto, Rocky 112
Young, Frank 287, 300
Young, Leonie 287, 300